ISRAEL
AND THE POST-ZIONISTS
A Nation at Risk

ISRAEL

AND THE POST-ZIONISTS

A Nation at Risk

Edited by

Shlomo Sharan

sussex
ACADEMIC
PRESS
Brighton • Portland • Toronto

2 4 6 8 10 9 7 5 3

First published 2003, reprinted 2012, in Great Britain by
SUSSEX ACADEMIC PRESS
PO Box 139
Eastbourne BN24 9BP

SUSSEX ACADEMIC PRESS
PO Box 139
Eastbourne BN24 9BP

and in the United States of America by
SUSSEX ACADEMIC PRESS
920 NE 58th Ave   Suite 300
Portland, Oregon 97213-3786

and in Canada by
SUSSEX ACADEMIC PRESS (CANADA)
8000 Bathurst Street, Unit 1, PO Box 30010, Vaughan, Ontario L4J 0C6

British Library Cataloguing in Publication Data
A CIP catalogue record for this book is available from the British Library.

Library of Congress Cataloging-in-Publication Data
Israel and the Post-Zionists : a nation at risk / edited by Shlomo Sharan.
p. cm.
Includes bibliographical references and index.
ISBN 978-1-903900-52-9 (paperback)
1. Post-Zionism—Philosophy. 2. Post-Zionism—History.
3. Zionism—Philosophy. 4. Israel—Social condition—20th century.
I. Sharan, Shlomo, 1932–
DS113.4.I87 2003
320.54'095694—dc21
                                                                    2003001562

MIX
Paper from
responsible sources
FSC
www.fsc.org   FSC® C013056

Typeset and designed by G&G Editorial, Brighton.
Printed by TJ International, Padstow, Cornwall.
This book is printed on acid-free paper.

Contents

Acknowledgments   xii

Introduction   1
Shlomo Sharan

1   Redefining the Israeli Ethos: Transforming Israeli Society   13
Yoav Gelber

2   Zionism, the Post-Zionists and Myth   26
Shlomo Sharan

3   Israeli Intellectuals and Israeli Politics   56
Edward Alexander

4   The Frankfurt School and Post-Zionist Thought   71
Hanan A. Alexander

5   The Leftist Media and the al-Aqsa Uprising   87
David Bukay

6   Post-Zionism and Democracy   114
Raya Epstein

7   The Future of the Ideological Civil War Within the West   136
John Fonte

8   The West and Yasser Arafat   155
Norman Doidge

9   Israeli Anti-Semitism   163
Arieh Stav

❖ v ❖

Contents

10 Post-Zionism and Anti-Zionism in Israeli Literature   188
Yosef Oren

11 The Messianic Theme in the Works of A. B. Yehoshua
and Amos Oz   204
Hillel Weiss

12 Pluralism, the Post-Zionists, and Israel as a Jewish Nation   227
Shlomo Sharan

The Contributors   249

Name Index   251

Subject Index   255

Acknowledgments

I wish to acknowledge with gratitude the advice, support and encouragement of Arieh Stav, Director of the Ariel Center for Policy Research, in the publication of this book. Arieh, and the staff at the Center, especially Leah Kochanowitz, have assisted in numerous ways to make sure that the publishing process has been smooth and essentially problem free. I am also grateful to Anthony Grahame, Editorial Director at Sussex Academic Press, for the close liaison with the Center, which has greatly assisted my duties as Editor.

The deepest inspiration for me to assume and perform this small editorial task ultimately derives from the lives and experiences of all those people whose existence nourished, sustained and guided me as a Jew throughout my lifetime. Though many of these colleagues and friends have passed away, the image of what they stood for will always shape my experience and fill my memories. In particular I would like to mention Rabbi Chaim Yehezkel Worona and Professor Yehezkel Kaufmann, of blessed memory. I pray that Professor Milton Arfa may continue for many years to perform more deeds of lovingkindness for so many people as he has done throughout his life.

It is my fervent hope that my children, David Amichai and Naomi Rachel, have accepted this great legacy and that they and their descendants will form new links in the historic chain of the nation of Israel.

Od nimshechet ha-shalshelet.

SHLOMO SHARAN

Introduction

SHLOMO SHARAN

> If I forget you, O Jerusalem
> let my right hand wither;
> let my tongue stick to my palate
> if I cease to think of you,
> if I do not keep Jerusalem in memory
> even at my happiest hour.
>
> Psalm 137: 5–6

Jews have recited these verses from the Book of Psalms for two millennia. These verses are recited during holidays, at weddings, and on many other occasions in everyday life. The verses are recited by Jews wherever they live in the world, in many different languages, and in diverse living conditions. No set of ideas, claims, arguments, rationalizations or political positions of any kind can change that fact. Jewry's historic attachment to the Land of Israel never was, is not now, and can never be, anything less than that.

What Problems are Addressed in this Book?

Eighteen hundred years of statelessness created distinct patterns of social and mental orientation among Jews toward their own political and social situation. In each generation there are those who sought freedom for the Jewish People from the yoke of foreign rule, from its exile in foreign lands, and for the rejuvenation of its national and religious integrity. The majority of Jews from all walks of life apparently remained uninvolved in these efforts. Some even opposed them. Yet, even though the flow of Jews to Palestine from the Diaspora waned now and then, it never ceased. The

Land of Israel was permanently and indelibly inscribed on the hearts and minds and yearnings of the Jewish People.

Zionism as an organized movement for the political renewal of the Jewish People is the embodiment of Jewry's historical continuity and striving for national redemption. Zionism achieved several of its more important goals: An independent political entity and the concentration in Israel of a fairly large number of members of the Jewish People. Zionism is Jewish national identity and independence embodied in the nation of Israel. Nevertheless, some Jews and non-Jews have opposed Zionism for a variety of reasons that change in part as events unfold.

Numerous publications of Israeli authors from a variety of disciplines, known collectively as post-Zionists, have mounted an ideological onslaught on Zionism and on the nation of Israel. These authors assert that the justification for Zionism, and for the Jewish state itself, once recognized as axiomatic, is now passé. For most of the post-Zionists, albeit probably not for all of them, the Arab version of modern history is morally justified, while the Jewish-Zionist view is a "misleading myth." From the point of view of Zionism, the post-Zionists' proclamation is a rejection of the Jewish state per se. If someone would announce that he or she is a post-Frenchist or a post-Belgianist, in effect they would be trying to deny the right of France or Belgium to exist as a nation. Of course that notion is so absurd that no sane person does that. It is not always clear that the post-Zionists fully comprehend the implications of their proclamations. The only condition under which post-Zionism could exist in reality, and not only in words, is if and when, God forbid, Israel would be destroyed or eliminated. Only that state of affairs constitutes what Israeli objectors to Zionism call post-Zionism. Post-Zionists who know of what they speak are truly a threat to the nation of Israel. The "mythologization" of Zionism turns Jewry's right to the Land of Israel into a historical farce, or, if you will, back into a dream about supernatural intervention in history (Aharonson, 1997; **chapters 2 and 11**).

The chapters in this book present a concerted critique of the post-Zionists' works and a rebuttal of their claims, ideas and reasoning. Because post-Zionist writers did not emerge from a specific discipline, thus far no one person has written a systemic rejoinder to their views. Except for the two authors who deal with contemporary Hebrew literature **(chapters 10 and 11)**, the chapters in this book do not overlap to any remarkable degree in terms of their references to post-Zionist publications, in part because each author writes from a different disciplinary perspective. Ironically, it is hoped that this volume, whose aim is explicitly to combat the essential concepts of post-Zionist authors, will also clarify their views.

Directly and indirectly, the chapters presented here also try to provide clues for understanding the problem of why the post-Zionists take the positions they do. How do Jews, many born and bred in Israel, come to oppose their own national existence, the collective existence of their own People **(chapter 12)**? Is it not patently clear to them that their ideas express the desire to undermine the foundations of Jewish identity and history?

It may be helpful to conceive of the chapters in this book as a series of replies to several basic questions about Zionism and post-Zionism. One version of these questions follows:

- What are the salient ideas and claims found in post-Zionist publications compared to Zionism, and what do their authors expect to accomplish in these works? **(chapters 1–4)**.
- How do Israel's news media affect the Jewish public with respect to Zionism and the post-Zionist ideology? **(chapter 5)**.
- What perspectives emerge in post-Zionist positions regarding the basic principles of Democracy? **(chapters 6, 7 and 8)**.
- What do post-Zionists, including some of Israel's better-known novelists and short-story writers, say about Jews and the Jewish historical heritage in Israel? **(chapters 9, 10 and 11)**.
- Why have post-Zionists adopted ideas opposed to Zionism? What can account for their attitudes toward Israel, the Jewish People, and Zionism? **(chapter 12)**.

Israel: Geography, Demography and Political Reality

Readers of this book in English, who do not reside in Israel, can place the ideas expressed herein in their proper context if they keep in mind the geographical and demographic facts of the nation of Israel. Apropos the need for a realistic context necessary to comprehend Israel's situation, I am reminded of an incident that occurred in the latter part of the 1980s when serving as a visiting professor at a university in the western United States. At a social gathering I asked the chairperson of the university senate if he had information about the size of the population of Israel. He said, "It's smaller than Italy, I think about 30 million or so." Then I asked about what he thought was the size of the country, and he replied: "Oh, I think it's about the size of Arizona . . . not very big . . ."

The conflict over the proper perspective on Israel's existence and identity between Zionism and the post-Zionists takes place in a relatively "new" country (or in the "Old New Land" as Herzl called it) recognized internationally in 1948. It now has a population of 5 million Jews and a million Arabs (not counting the Arabs in Judea, Samaria and Gaza). Israel consists of a total of 10,614 square miles, including the Golan Heights, Judea and Samaria. Without the latter three areas, Israel is 7,992 square miles. Arizona, it should be pointed out, is 10 to 14 times the size of Israel (depending upon what areas are included) with some 114,000 square miles, although the population of Arizona (among the more sparsely populated states) is not much over 5 million people. Also, Israel is about 250 miles long and 7 miles wide in its narrow part (between the Mediterranean Sea at Netanya on the west, and the "Green Line" of the ceasefire border on the east) and about 65 miles wide in its widest part between the southern town of Rafiah on the Israel–Egyptian border near the Mediterranean Sea and Israel's eastern border with Jordan south of the Dead Sea. More similar to Israel is the state of Maryland that has 12,400 square miles, with a population of about 5.3 million people. The constant flow of reports about Israel by some worldwide news networks creates the impression in the minds of many citizens in the United States and elsewhere, that Israel must be at least the size of Russia, as one person on the street in New York told me.

In my experience as someone who was born and grew up in the United States, it is very unusual and difficult for Americans, the vast majority of whom have not traveled to small countries outside the US, to conceive of what it means to live in a country like Israel in terms of its physical size and population. Given the fact that the United States has the world's great oceans on its Eastern and Western borders, and friendly (and militarily weak) neighbors to the north and south, Americans can hardly know from experience what it means to have sworn enemies on all its borders (except the Mediterranean Sea to Israel's west).

In order to obtain an overview of Israel's political condition, these geographical facts must be considered in combination with Israel's minis-cule demographic make-up, and with living under conditions of prolonged economic, political and military siege. In 1948, when Israel became a nation, the Jewish population numbered about 640,000. The population has increased almost eight fold over the 54 years of Israel's existence, in large part due to immigration. A majority of the population has lived in Israel for two generations or less. Twenty percent of Israel's population arrived during the past 20 years (as of the year 2003). The country needs time to have its population stabilize and coalesce to a greater degree than it has had time to do thus far. Perhaps then the kind of ideological and political controversies raging now will be less threat-ening to Israel's social integrity.

It is important for readers to recall as well that Israel adopted Hebrew as its official language. Hebrew is Jewry's ancient language that was used by Jews throughout the ages in written form for many different purposes (including business, poetry, law, prayer, and so forth) except, perhaps, for speaking to one another face to face. Hebrew underwent an intensive period of rejuvenation in Europe particularly during the late eighteenth through the early twentieth centuries. Jews returning to their historic homeland also returned to their original language that carries Jewry's historical images and culture. Hebrew thus contributes significantly to the social integration of the Jews into Israel society. There are still many Jews here who have only rudimentary knowledge of the language, much like the large waves of immigrants to the United States at the end of the nineteenth and beginning of the twentieth centuries who learned English in the extensive Americanization programs of the time. Yet, not they but their children's generation became literate in English, and the same is to be expected of immigrant populations anywhere, however strong might be their motivation to learn the language of their new country. Social and linguistic integration at a far more advanced and desirable level remain among the major social processes and goals of Israel, as they would in every immigrant society.

On the more positive side of the ledger one can point to the statistic about Israel's striking productivity: Per capita earnings in Israel today, considered to be not the best of times, (after two years of sustained terrorists attacks on Israel), is identical with that of the United Kingdom: $20,000 per annum. If the number of people in Israel's armed services is not taken into consideration, the per capita productivity is $18,500 per annum. That, too, is remarkable.

Israel's economy, industry, hi-tech and technological advances, as well as the development of its military capacities despite limitations in numbers of personnel, contributed to the depiction of Israel by Arab and European propagandists as a huge and powerful Goliath overshadowing the young shepherd, David, standing alone in the field with his sling, ready to fight the giant. Israeli post-Zionists have repeated this stereotype, even though, in reality, the reverse is the truth. The Arab nations bordering on Israel (except for Jordan) have huge populations and hundreds of thousands of square miles of territory. The number of men in Arab armies is also extremely high by comparison to almost all other countries in the world (Huntington, 1996: 258, table 10.3), while the number of personnel in Israel's armed forces is relatively very small. The Palestinian Authority alone has sixty thousand men under arms (compared to the fifteen thousand police they were to have as per the agreement with Israel). Those troops were armed by Egypt and are indubitably a branch of the Egyptian army, the peace treaty with Israel notwithstanding. The Egyptian and Syrian standing armies combined number one million men, or more than six times the 180,000 troops in Israel's standing army (not counting reserves in any of the countries). These figures exclude the armed forces of all the other Arab or Muslim countries of the Middle East who call for Israel's destruction, including Iran, Saudi Arabia, Sudan, Iraq and Libya, three of which have programs for developing weapons of mass destruction.

In the environment just described, a serious ideological conflict touching upon the very foundations of the Jewish nation takes on a far more decisive and threatening character than would a similar conflict in most European countries (with the possible exception of the smaller ones) or in the United States. For example, a serious conflict may be brewing in the United States over the issues surrounding the concept of transnationalism discussed in this book by the historian of US culture, John Fonte **(chapter 7)**. The doctrines of transnationalism could potentially entail major political changes, and perhaps some social disruption, in the United States, even though that eventuality might seem to some people as relatively remote. More to the point for our purposes, a conflict over transnationalism in the US or Europe does not evoke the image of a potentially catastrophic social cataclysm for the large populations in those countries.

What Dangers Do Post-Zionists Pose for Israel?

The conflict within Israel's Jewish population over Zionism and post-Zionism has been given direct and palpable expression in the highest political echelons as well as in Israel's news media. Fortunately, despite the media, thus far daily life does not appear to reflect specific consequences of these ideological struggles. Nevertheless, there is good reason to be concerned about the possibility that this conflict could set groups of citizens against each other in a political and cultural battle that spreads pervasive bitterness and animosity. Intellectual and social neutrality are not the defining characteristics of the ideological and cultural tension within the Israeli public, and the fabric of social life in this country is not immune to what could become irreparable damage. Tiny Israel cannot absorb the kind of deep cleavages that appear to be endemic to many multi-ethnic societies, even to the United States of America, and still survive. The cleavages that exist in Israel's highly variegated Jewish population who came here from "seventy nations" place this country's social unity under considerable stress, in addition to the prolonged and relentless attacks on the lives of the Jewish citizens of Israel by Arab nations and terrorists over the past eighty years. Still, no one can really predict that the dissension within the Jewish public will produce a visible social rupture. The fundamental cohesion of Israel's Jewish society, based on Jewry's 3,000-year history and its religious background, however much modernism has eroded them, seems to be maintaining itself quite remarkably. Deep cleavages prevail in the societies of other countries of the Middle East (Ye'or, 2002) but their non-democratic governments and the dominant culture of Islam do not allow those phenomena to gain public expression.

There is a pressing need to provide some counterbalance to the post-Zionists' assertions, claims and arguments. Israel's population itself must be supported against the flood of Jewish self-denunciation and distortion emanating from anti-Zionist circles of academics and some artists (Alexander, 1993). Perhaps this book can make some contribution to that effort, as well as to the information and views it provides to the English-language readership outside of Israel. Public opinion in different countries antagonistic to Israel, and negatively affected by some networks of the news media, exerts extremely destructive effects on Jews everywhere as well as on Israel's Jewish population. Post-Zionist voices and publications feed the anti-Israel pronouncements of Europe and the Arabs. Leftists and post-Zionists have even been known to join public protests against Israel organized by Arab/Muslim groups both in and outside of Israel.

The specter of European anti-Semitism, thinly disguised as anti-Israelism, is already casting its shadow. It is distressing to watch how distinctly that shadow of hatred inhibits Israel's ability to defend its citizens from terrorism and other forms of warfare in a manner similar to what most if not all nations would never hesitate to do under similar circumstances. The consequences of this inhibition to act against terrorism as demanded by any kind of rational defense strategy have been nightmarish and could become even more tragic than they have been, if the past is any precedent for the future. It is equally sad to observe how some Jews in Israel protest the government's operations against the nation's enemies. The same people almost never express a word condemning the murder of their fellow Jews.

Barbara Tuchman describes an event from the American Revolutionary War with England that is reminiscent of Israel's present behavior regarding Arab Palestinian terrorism. In May of 1778, Lord George Germain, Secretary for the Colonies in the British government, ordered general Sir Henry Clinton to send 8,000 (out of a total of 14,000) troops under his command in Philadelphia to the West Indies to strengthen the forces there against France. Regarding this move, Tuchman observed: "It was not the last case of the peculiar foolishness of withdrawing forces while trying to make an enemy come to terms . . ." (1984: 223). Israel's repeated withdrawals from Arab centers of terrorism against Israel (located just a few miles from Israel's major urban centers) have become routine, and routinely they lead to precisely the same consequences as elsewhere in the world. The withdrawals, at the cost of many civilian lives lost to Arab suicide bombers, drive-by shootings from automatic weapons, and the like (more than 700 during 2001–2002) are carried out repeatedly, as in the case of the British in the American colonies in the eighteenth century, because Israel fears the reaction of the European Union (EU) or the United States. Within hours or days after Israel withdraws from terrorist centers in Judea, Samaria and Gaza, hostile activities are resumed at the same spot. Israel's Leftists and post-Zionists consistently demonstrate in favor of these withdrawals (which they euphemistically call a "return to ourselves") and hail them as victories for their "sane" policy that will allegedly contribute to peace with the Arab Palestinians. The post-Zionists and other Leftists persist in their view that the post-Zionists may have erred in the past in some details, but it was the nationalist Zionists in Israel who allegedly made the egregious mistake of "occupying" Arab centers in Judea and Samaria. For the Left and the post-Zionists, only withdrawal from the Arab-Palestinian Authority will lead to peace (*Ma'ariv*, January 10, 2003). No precedent of unabated terror and outright rejection of peace offers are sufficient to prove or disprove anything.

The EU, Post-Zionists and Israel

The malevolent influence of the European countries, and even of some irresponsible groups in the United States, has been clearly identified by some observers in Israel as acting through the agency of a few radical post-Zionists, although the pro-Leftist media refrain from mentioning it. This influence is expressed, first and foremost, through the EU's financial support of post-Zionist extra-parliamentary factions (Non-Governmental Organizations or NGOs, as they are known in the US) and their political activities in Israel, thereby circumventing the nation's democratic institutions. The EU also maintains official representation in Israel that issues statements of a distinctly political nature, occasionally under the guise of "humanitarian" concerns for the Arabs (but not, of course, for the Jews), adding its weight to Arab propaganda circulated through Israel's news media.

The most direct threat that post-Zionists pose to the integrity of Israel's society is their public support for the goals of the PLO and the Arab Palestinians that have been adopted hook, line and sinker by the EU and by many of the non-European countries of the UN. The Arab/Muslim countries demand that Israel and the UN agree to set up still another Arab country on the territory of Judea, Samaria and Gaza, in addition to Jordan carved by England in 1922 out of the League of Nations' Mandate for Palestine. The Post-Zionist and other Leftists Jews in Israel who publicly adhere to the Arab position, contrary to all formal positions taken by both Labor and Likud-led governments in Israel, receive the moral, political and financial backing of Europe.

The role of the EU's support of factions within non-EU countries like Israel can be understood even more clearly against the background of the EU's recent activities in Serbia and Macedonia. The EU's financial and moral support of the post-Zionists is accompanied by even greater diplomatic pressure and gross interference with Israel's internal political affairs than the pressure exerted by the EU on Serbia and on Macedonia to capitulate to the demands of the Muslim Albanians in those countries. The EU, and the UN in general, follow a consistent pro-Muslim policy. The aim is to prevent any rupture between Europe and the Muslim nations of the Middle East, especially since millions of Middle Eastern Muslims now reside in European countries and pressure those countries to be more outspoken in their pro-Muslim, anti-Israel and anti-American policies. Post-Zionists and some Leftists in Israel accept support from the EU because they agree with the EU's pro-Muslim policy despite the fact that this policy unequivocally supports and favors Israel's enemies

The post-Zionist Jews are a minority within their own country. The majority of Jews rejects Arab demands that, apart from their extremely destructive consequences for the entire region, are blatantly nothing more than another step in its well-publicized multi-stage effort to dismantle Israel entirely and eliminate the Jewish state. But, the vocal minority of the post-anti-Zionists joins with Israel's enemies to try to convince the majority of the political elites and the electorate in Israel to agree to Arab demands. The illusion of peace is powerful, and, as various authors in this book demonstrate, the illusion that somehow peace can be achieved by setting up a new Arab country next to Israel is supported by Europe and even by a friend of Israel, the United States.

Nothing in human history, and surely not in the events of the past century, offers even the most meager basis for this glaring "march of folly" that is so contrary to the interests and survival of the Jewish People. The projected Palestinian Arab state in Judea, Samaria and Gaza is of a far greater threat than any Trojan horse ever was, and the machinery of the Leftist media **(chapter 5)** relentlessly silences the voice of any Laocoön or Cassandra who is sufficiently indiscriminate and tactless to tell the truth in public. The post-Zionists of today are akin to the Trojans who rejoiced upon receiving into their midst the giant hollow horse crammed with enemy soldiers that was shrewdly built by the Greeks. They had waged war against Troy for ten years and could not conquer the well-defended city-state. The hollow horse was actually a last desperate act on the part of the Greeks on the eve of abandoning the battlefield (Tuchman, 1984).

The threat to Israel and Jewish society here stems not from the post-Zionists themselves but from their alignment with Israel's enemies, namely, with the European countries and the Arabs whom the Europeans support almost blindly, often in the face of, or because of, US policy. As such, the threat of the post-Zionists to Zionism and Israel is one of an elitist minority that uses many different strategies to impose its will on the majority through the agency of pressure exerted by external forces. At best, it is a situation in which a decisive step by the Israel government to abandon its opposition to a terrorist Arab nation on the soil of Judea, Samaria and Gaza, could be taken when at least half, if not more, of the population disagrees with it. In most democratic countries no decision of that kind would ever be raised anywhere, and the constitutions of democratic countries have no provision for such an eventuality because it would never occur to anyone that such a step would be possible. No country would ever consider having its government debate whether 25 percent of its national territory should be relinquished to some other country, friend or foe. Certainly no debate of that kind could ever occur in a nation whose enemy on its border is publicly committed to the gradual but nonetheless total elimination of the nation and its population! Why should Israel express acceptance of an irredentist political entity such as a new Arab-Palestinian nation located on Israel's vulnerable eastern border that will enjoy legal international recognition and sovereignty? That agenda of "Peace Now," if realized, will quickly become "War Forever" in far more violent terms than it has been for the past few years. How many votes would be needed in the US Congress to "return" Alaska to Russia or Texas to Mexico? What would have to be done in the British Parliament to pass a motion to "give back" the Falkland Islands to Argentina? The foreign policy of democratic nations, like Europe and the United States, does not take into consideration the decisions made by other democratic governments, especially by very small nations, who represent their citizens, if that decision is considered to be at odds with their own best interests. Israel's best interests, even interests that clearly impinge on its survival, are not sufficiently important for the super-powers to compromise their status in the eyes of the Arabs, even after 9/11.

The post-Zionists claim that they want to save Israel from itself. Self righteousness knows no greater danger on the level of national existence than the claim that a very special and limited group of self-declared clair-voyants preach the nation's doom unless it conforms to their ideological view, when that view is the very same one tirelessly proclaimed by the nation's sworn enemies. In large nations like Germany (over 85 million), France and Italy (both with populations over 50 million) an internal threat of that kind can be disregarded with mild irritation. Not so in the tiny nation of Israel. Here, even small numbers of people who have a reputation for being post-Zionist or Leftists and are respected academics have frequent access to the media **(chapter 5)** and their voices are heard by large sections of the population. They also provide Israel's enemies with convenient evidence that Israeli Jews themselves support their position against Israel's government. "What more convincing evidence of the need to dismantle the Jewish state than ferocious vituperation emanating from its own disenchanted intellectuals" (R. and E. Isaacs, 1993: 133).

The Arabs in the Middle East have exposed their virulent and violent hatred toward Israel, and toward the United States as well, in no uncertain terms. They actually despise Western culture as a whole (Huntington, 1996) as well as Jewry and Judaism, but they are not so foolish as to cut off the nose on their face by emphasizing their animosity toward the Christian nations of Europe. Yet, hardly anyone speaks of the gruesome persecution of eastern Christians in Muslim countries in the twentieth century, not to speak of earlier centuries (Groiss, 2003; Ye'or, 2002).

In addition to all of their commercial, technological and political connections with Middle Eastern countries, most European nations have allowed millions of Muslim immigrants from the Middle East to settle permanently in their territory to escape from poverty and dictatorship. These Arab populations now exert enormous political pressure on European nations in favor of the Arab world. Moreover, Europe provides extensive financial support, in the form of a constant flow of millions of dollars every month, to the terrorists known as the PLO and the Palestinian Authority **(chapter 8)**. The EU issues automatic denials whenever someone states in public, in complete disregard for what is politically correct, that the EU's money finances the killing of Jews and supports Arab terrorism. The EU also supports and politically protects many Muslim nations, including Iran, Syria, Pakistan, Saudi Arabia, and other rogue nations who openly aid and abet terrorism, harbor weapons of mass destruction, and engage in international ruthlessness. But that does not prevent spokesmen for the post-Zionist viewpoint to accept financial and other assistance from the EU.

The struggle for the heart and mind of the Jewish nation will continue, probably for an unforeseeably long time. Nevertheless, Jews from the Diaspora continue to flow to Israel and to settle here permanently, whether out of insecurity or fear in their present environment, or out of love for their own People, nation and culture. That process will go on for generations to come until a large majority of the Jewish People will have returned to its historic home in Israel to rebuild its civilization. That is the apex of Zionism, the supreme mission of Israel and the foundation of its astonishing success.

References

Aharonson, Shlomo (1997) "Zionism and post-Zionism: The historical-ideological context." In Y. Weitz (ed.), *From Vision to Revision: A hundred years of historiography in Zionism.* Jerusalem: The Zalman Shazar Center, pp. 291–309 (Hebrew).

Alexander, Edward (Ed.) (1993) *With Friends Like These: The Jewish critics of Israel.* New York: SPI Books/Shapolsky Publishers.

Groiss, Arnon (2003) *The West, Christians and Jews in Saudi Arabian Textbooks.* New York: Center for Monitoring the Impact of Peace – The American-Jewish Committee.

Huntington, Samuel (1996) *The Clash of Civilizations and the Remaking of the World Order.* New York: Touchstone/Simon and Schuster.

Isaacs, Rael Jean and Eric (1993) "Israelis against themselves." In E. Alexander (ed.), *With Friends like These.* New York: SPI Books/Shapolsky Publishers, pp. 133–41.

Ma'ariv (supplement), January 10, 2003, p. 14 ff.

Tuchman, Barbara (1984) *The March of Folly.* New York: Ballantine.

Ye'or, Bat (2002) *Islam and Dhimmitude.* Teaneck, NJ: Farleigh Dickinson University Press.

1

Redefining the Israeli Ethos

Transforming Israeli Society

YOAV GELBER

An ethos is a system of beliefs, standards, values and guiding principles that characterize a group, community, nation or an ideological movement. It is the spirit that activates the ideas, conduct and habits of people in a given era. An ethos draws its power, among other things, from myths.

Originally, myths were legends invented by our ancestors to explain phenomena which they could not comprehend or for which they had no explanation, like the creation. Later, the essence of this term expanded. Modern myths embrace stories concocted for polemic purposes, to substantiate claims in continuous political or religious controversies. They are also invented for spreading educational and moral lessons or for strengthening the people's spirit in harsh times. The events treated in historical myths are usually fiascos, since successes speak for themselves and do not need myths to amplify them.

We, Israeli and sometimes other historians, who have studied the emergence of the Zionist–Israeli ethos and criticized its old myths, have witnessed in the recent years the emergence of a new Israeli ethos and the invention of new myths to validate it.

The continuous debate in Israel about its identity has sharpened, turning into a dispute over the state's source of authority and the society's ethos: who compose it; what are its properties, values, contents and symbols; and who are the elite who will lead it in the new century that has just begun. Newspapers and TV sketch these controversies as ideological and historical arguments between representatives of an old anachronistic generation of "Zionists" and a group of younger academics and journalists defining themselves as "post-Zionists." However, the main essence of post-Zionism is not ideological, if it has a distinct ideology at all, but the post-Zionist practices shared by wider circles of society.

Political elections, including Netanyahu's rise to power in the summer of 1996, and Barak's electoral victory three years later, have not resolved and probably are incapable of deciding the issues that have persisted under different political regimes. In an allegedly non-ideological era, ideological differences still separate political adversaries and divide all political groups in Israel from within. Post-Zionist practices, by contrast, are common to many on both sides of the political barricade.

The current so-called post-Zionism is no more than a new label for an old narrative. The story's onetime title, from the late nineteenth century until the aftermath of the Holocaust and the attainment of Jewish statehood, was anti-Zionism. It was deeply rooted in the European Diaspora, and derived from three different sources:

1 *Religious ultra-orthodoxy.* The national-secular essence that Zionism introduced into Judaism exacerbated the reaction of ultra-religious (*Haredim*) Jews. They objected to what they conceived as the Zionists' ambition to facilitate the coming of the Messiah and opposed it as a collective assimilationism. They also opposed some Zionists' explicit goal of secularizing Jewish culture.

2 *Socialism and peoples' fraternity.* The Jewish socialists, except for the Zionist Labor Movement, believed that the solution to the "Jewish question" would be a by-product of the new and better general world order of which they dreamt, the so called "world of tomorrow." Therefore, they objected to the Zionist stress on the Jews' uniqueness or particularism, and to Zionism's promotion of Jewish national consciousness.

3 *Assimilationism.* The assimilationists opposed any Jewish distinctiveness or exclusiveness as an obstacle to the Jews' integration into their social environment.

Contemporary post-Zionism is blue and white, an Israeli product. Its spokesmen of all of the three versions just mentioned are Israeli-born, frequently Israeli educated (though not a few received higher degrees abroad) who strive to modify the essence of Israeli identity from a Zionist one to something else. What are the burning issues in this domestic struggle over the identity of the Jewish state? Different groups within Israel society pose different problems that they view as important. Even in the domain of what are Israel's society's critical problems there is no consensus. Hence, the problems mentioned here do not reflect the view of any particular sector of Israeli society.

(1) The state's source of authority. Should it be the people, through its elected representatives? Should it be God who "speaks" through the Rabbis, or a constitutional document (that still remains to be adopted) that rules through its interpreters (such as the Supreme Court's judges)? While the first two divide secular and religious Jews, the third one represents an attempt by a decaying elite to perpetuate its dominant position by securing for its members the role of interpreting the source of authority.

(2) What is the role of public opinion in deciding military, political, economic and other issues? Who is entitled to speak for the public: its elected delegates? Journalists? Opinion polls' manipulators?

(3) What weight should be assigned to international public opinion and international law when they obviously conflict with Israel's national interest? (Note the Arab-dominated UN's deprecation of Zionism as racism). How moral is a violation of the state's sovereignty and interests by a minority group within Israel that calls for international pressure and intervention when its position has been rejected by the majority of Jews in Israel?

(4) What should be the status of religion in Israel and what should be the state's jurisdiction in religious matters?

(5) Israeli society's composition and the definition of its membership. Should it be Jewish by origin and consciousness? Should Arabs, non-Jewish immigrants from the former Soviet Union and others assimilate into it; should it be a pluralist society, equally open to all citizens regardless of their national origins, including Arabs and hundreds of thousands of foreign laborers who have flocked recently to Israel? The term pluralism in and of itself means very little. Would it be a pluralism of individuals directly affiliated to society, or would it be a pluralism of ethnic and religious communities mediating between the individual and society?

These issues emanate from a more profound question about the essence of society: Is it only an aggregate of individuals and groups, or does it have an independent entity that goes beyond the arithmetical sum of its members? Who should come first, society or the individual? Can a nation survive whose individuals have no affiliation to a collective framework?

(6) Other questions concern the character of this society. Should it have a distinct ethos or will it be "a generation of claimants" in the manner of the slogan "An Entire Generation Demands Peace" (Israelis have forgotten to "ask," they just "demand," "deserve," "claim" or "insist"). Will Israeli society become no more than a conglomerate of interest groups who insist on getting what they think they deserve, a collection of pressure groups competing for power and privileges in a kind of "catch as you can" match? Will these groups have anything in common in addition to a formal governmental structure to regulate their competitive activities?

(7) What ethical views will this society cherish? Will they be determined by the old scale stretching from capital to labor, or along a scale ranging from solidarity to unscrupulous competition? Can these two extremes be properly balanced? What will be the place of values such as equality, service, mission, simplicity, humility, loyalty, sharing, initiative, self-fulfillment, personal example, success, excellence or power on the scale of the Israel society's ethical values?

(8) What contents should this society cultivate: Traditional Jewish? secular Israeli? American? If, as is quite likely, they may be a mixture of some or all of these, in what proportions?

(9) What symbols – such as flag, anthem, ceremonies, holidays and memorial days – should this society should have: distinctly Jewish, symbols common to all its components, or should there be separate sets of symbols for each of the component groups?

Who will constitute the cultural–political elites who will lead Israel in the twenty-firstst century and what will be their function? Will they serve the people or exploit it? Will an elitist be he who gives more or he who succeeds in squeezing more?

Some of these questions are as old as Jewish statehood and so far have not been resolved. Others have emerged only recently. They emanate from events and processes that the Jewish state and Israeli society have undergone in the last generation. They also result from the confrontation between Zionism and "post-Zionism" and from the increasing contact with the outside world, the so-called "global village," which is American actually and not global at all.

Zionism shaped its ethos in accordance with collective existential experiences, primarily national survival and revival. Its myths sanctified the individual's enlistment in the service of the nation, the society and the country. They emphasized the sense of mission, service and duty. Not long ago, the meaning of self-fulfillment was doing what was necessary for the people's benefit, not what is good primarily for the self. Selfishness was deemed a vice. Theoretically at least, agreement about this demanding ethos was driven by external dangers that menaced the Jewish community in Palestine/Israel since the Arab revolt in 1936 until the Six Day War in 1967. The external perils threatened all members of the Jewish community without distinction as to ideological creed or socio-economic status, as had always been the case in every country where Jews lived throughout Jewish history. These threats forced all elements of the heterogeneous, largely voluntary and relatively newly-formed Jewish society in the Land of Israel to adopt a minimum ideological consensus about their goals and the means for achieving them. This acceptance also implied agreed-upon procedures for political behavior. Those who opposed this joint platform, or the authority of the national institutions that embodied it, were excluded from society and labeled "dissidents," whether they were ultra-religious, communists or revisionists.

Consciousness of an existential external threat has diminished since the Six Day War. This weakening of the apparent external threat gradually cracked the consensus around the Zionist ethos and ultimately eroded it. Consequently, some of the more articulate elements in Israeli society, such as parts of the upper middle class and the kibbutzim, have broken or abandoned the Zionist ethos' values and myths. Simultaneously, the same circles have formed a new ethos based on new myths. Contrary to the old collective ethos, the new one has focused on individual self-fulfillment and prerogatives, namely on the right to self-centerdness.

The flagship of the new ethos has been privatization. This concept belongs to economic life, where it has advantages and shortcomings. However, privatization has been lagging behind, particularly in Israel's economy, while post-Zionism has penetrated under various guises into other spheres of life, disrupting the few remnants of social solidarity. The few examples detailed below are deliberately taken from different spheres of life to underscore the comprehensiveness and intensity of the transformation:

(1) The partisans of the non-Zionist or even post-Zionist ethos have privatized the concept "security." Traditionally, the term security concerned the collective existence, freedom and sovereignty of Israel as a nation and society. Today, many Israelis grasp "security" in terms of safeguarding their personal well-being. Such an atomized security is unrealistic even in larger and more tranquil countries than Israel - the United States, for example. Futile attempts to accomplish such a state of affairs have been made at the expense of collective security. The latter is imperative for thwarting the real threats that menace Israel's national existence, interests and sovereignty.

Consequently, the new ethos has also "privatized" the domain of patriotism and bereavement, unfortunately all too well known in Israel in the wake of Islamic terrorism. Exploiting parenthood, particularly motherhood, for political ends is not new: It has precedents in the activities of Zionist left-wing parties during World War II and in the War of Independence. Recently, however, it has become far more extensive. Groups of women, preferably mothers of soldiers, have rallied around pet political causes, demonstrating and waving their motherhood, such as the group called Mothers in Black that exerted enormous pressure on the government to withdraw Israel's troops from Lebanon, and Women in Green who protest against terrorism, although the two are certainly not comparable in terms of their goals. At one time, parenthood, sacrifice and bereavement were outside the bounds of ideological and political dispute since they were perceived as shared by everyone. In the era of individualism they cease to be factors supporting solidarity and have become sources of social friction.

(2) Adoption of children was a symbol of society's responsibility for homeless or parentless children. The child's well-being was the cornerstone of the judicial and administrative handling of adoption cases. This concept has recently been neglected in favor of the right to parenthood (legally and biologically) as the guiding principle. Subsequently, the state's monopoly of adoption is being abolished and private agencies enter this field to meet the growing demand for parenthood. The clients of these agencies are the would-be parents, not the adopted children, and it is easy to imagine whose interests they serve.

(3) Israel's public education is quietly undergoing a slow but persistent process of privatization with the slogan of "self-fulfillment." This has been done at the urging of certain groups of professors at the expense of traditional principles, such as equality of opportunity, bridging social and cultural gaps, absorbing immigration and social solidarity in general. The present trend leads to increasing segregation of students by social-economic criteria. Of concern here is the rapid transformation of public schooling in Israel to a non-Zionist process aimed exclusively at individual economic advancement at the expense of values related to Jewry's collective historical future.

(4) Even commemorating the Holocaust has been individualized. The Shoah was a national tragedy of the Jewish people. In recent years, its commemoration has increasingly underscored the individual by means of the slogan "Every person had a name," rather than the collective loss. Once it was primarily the Holocaust of the victims. Nowadays, the survivors and their testimonies, or the claimant heirs of stolen Jewish property, stand at the crux of the public interest in the Holocaust.

Nonetheless, the ethos of the individual has not yet taken over completely. It is still struggling for legitimacy and like its predecessor, endeavors to achieve it by cultivating its own new myths.

"Peace" has become the central myth of the individualistic post-Zionist ethos. Its foolhardy propagandists imagine that this non-existent peace will abolish the need for the social solidarity cultivated by Zionism for the past 100 years. Limiting the social and economic gap between various sub-groups in Israel will soon be a forgotton value once the post-Zionist era is firmly established. The post-Zionist dream, as opposed to the political reality of Jewry in Palestine/Israel over the past 80 years at least, is that there will be no restrictions on individual freedoms required today by reason of national security. Demands made on Israel's citizens to devote time, resources and, sometimes, even their lives for the protection of their country will no longer be necessary. It is ironic to note that post-Zionist Hebrew writers accuse Zionism of perpetrating the unrealistic dream of a peaceful transition from Jewry's status as a community during the period of the British mandate, to the status of a politically sovereign entity. Are they aware that the tables have turned on them?

The concept "peace on earth," as distinct from "peace in heaven," has undergone mystification. It has been transferred from the sphere (also a mystical term) of political relations between nations and states into the sphere of the individual's dreams and visions. It has become the magic wand for resolving all problems of survival and self-fulfillment in the virtual "new Middle East." This disposition is reminiscent of the communists' efforts to undermine and brainwash the West during the Cold War by means of "peace" propaganda. They camouflaged themselves as "Peace Camps" and initiated "Leagues for Peace" to conceal their true identity behind the natural and self-evident human aspiration for tranquility.

Extracting peace from reality and turning it into a vision, transforming it from a means for achieving ends into a supreme value, endangers the freedom of every democracy and its citizens. The world to which Israel wants to belong has not achieved its present status by worshipping the idols of peace. It has accomplished this state of affairs by means of its readiness to sacrifice tranquility for liberty, independence and survival. Readiness to fight and sacrifice if and when necessary, not appeasement *à la* Chamberlain and not an implacable pugnacity, is Israel's only chance of ever achieving peace.

"Democracy" is another myth of the new ethos. Of course, Democracy has many advantages and critical features. It is also full of contradictions, deficiencies, shortcomings, dangers and distortions. Once democracy ruled in the name of "the people," then in the name of "majority's rule" and now in the name of "individual rights." Democracy has been a tool in the hands of demagogues, selfish politicians, pressure groups, unscrupulous journalists and even dictators. In comparison with the accumulated historical experience of other regimes, democracy is still the least of all evils but hardly the best of all possibilities, a view once clearly articlated by Winston Churchill. But it possesses neither sanctity nor purity.

There are several variants of democracy, each trying to find a harmony between its internal discrepancies, to adapt the political order to changing circumstances and to new social realities as well as to national requirements. French and British democracy differ from one another and from the American model. Their diversity stems from different historical developments and from the dissimilar patterns of the societies they serve. Of all the democratic variants, those who hold democracy as the *summum bonum* more important for Israel than Jewry's Zionist values, frequently cite the American model of government and democratic process as an example, although they do not emulate it in practice. They also portray the government of Israel as the enemy of the citizens and their rights. The Jews waited 2,000 years for national sovereignty. A mere 50 years after achieving it, some Israelis view their nation and their elected government as a despotic monarchy, repressing liberties and infringing on the lives of individuals. At times it appears that some Israelis concieve of their government as a copy of Czarist rule in Russia, although – again ironically – the post-Zionists were strongly influenced by Marxist-Leninist doctrines imported from Russia by radical Leftist Jews and infiltrated several Zionist political parties (Dotan, 1996; Shiloah, 1991; Yariv [Ben-Gurion], 1953).

Israeli democracy is in need of many fundamental reforms to strengthen its ability to ensure the survival of the nation and to guarantee accountability to its electorate. Nevertheless, the very endurance of Israeli democracy in a society whose members came primarily from a patriarchal, monarchical, theocratic or bolshevik background, is close to miraculous. On the one hand, perseverance of this precarious situation has been possible due to the sensitivity and tolerance displayed by the democratic majority toward other traditions. On the other hand, Israel's external threats forced non-democratic elements to comply with the rules formed by the democratic majority. Preserving the principles of tolerance and balance, in speech and practice, is an essential prerequisite for the continuing existence of Israeli democracy. Provocations aimed at putting these principles to radical tests, ostensibly in the name of democracy and the rights of the individual, only threaten democracy's survival, they do not support it. They can easily get out of control and bring about chaos and anarchy.

Tolerance and open-mindedness are basic democratic virtues, but in the process of turning democracy into a myth, its radical sanctifiers have declared it a supreme value. They are attempting to make Israeli democracy uniform ("liberal-secular" leftist, anti-religious) intolerant, inconsiderate, infallible, and therefore undemocratic. This is nothing but veiled fascism on the part of the radical Left using the sacred name of democracy.

A third myth of the new ethos is "the rule of law," replacing the "rule by law." The weakness of Israel's political leadership and system since the 1973 war, and the decay of agreed values, has created a vacuum. A school of lawyers, believing in the omnipotence of the law, exploited the opportunity to fill this emptiness. According to this school, the judiciary is capable of tackling any problem and of solving it by legal means, thereby by-passing the electorate. The legal elites arrogate the power of judgment to themselves, displaying contempt for the public. Furthermore, they assert that not only the action within the procedures of the law, but also the public and professional discretion of politicians, officials, officers, physicians, engineers, professors etc., are subject to judicial scrutiny. In their view, judges, lawyers and legal advisers to the executive should be the competent authority for examining their acceptability. This strategy is an extreme deviation from principles that had been accepted by the judiciary itself until a few years ago. It is morally deficient, violating the rule of "judge as you would be judged." This judiciary school usurps authority without being accountable for the consequences of its decisions. All this is done with supreme confidence in the unassailable justice of their post-Zionist, cosmopolitan, Leftist-"liberal" value system that frequently does not coincide with obvious and pressing needs of the Jewish nation's struggle to protect itself.

With all due respect for the law and its servants, and for their honorable role in every civilized society, they are inappropriate for, and incapable of, providing satisfactory answers to every controversial issue. Religious, ideological, historical, military-operational, medical and even political problems usually do not have, cannot have and should not have judicial answers. An unrestricted judicial imperialism is a boomerang. It is likely to cut off the branch of the tree of law on which it rests. Attempts to judicate non-judicial matters will erode the judiciary's authority, prestige, and the public's respect for the judges. Ultimately, the status of the judiciary will deteriorate, thereby damaging its legitimacy in matters in which a judicial decision has no substitute. This may hinder the real, not mythical, jurisdiction of the law, an authority without which no civilized society can be dispensed.

In recent years, a serious deterioration of observing and enforcing the law has become conspicuous in Israel. I submit that this could be expected as an unavoidable outcome of the courts' "overkill," i.e., inappropriately invoking the Rule of Law, instead of political, moral, military, religious, historical or scientific considerations, for example. A totalitarian "rule of law" is also morally degrading especially when it consistently represents a transparently leftist political perspective. When legalism becomes an absolute criterion, other values vanish, and Israel is clearly hyper-legalized. Under this regime, a person can hold any government or academic office as long as he is not convicted. An ethically decent society should insist on its leaders, office-holders, public opinion makers and other elites being more than just "criminals who have not been convicted."

The weaknesses of the Israeli political system on the one hand, coupled with the current judicial imperialism on the other hand, have disturbed the equilibrium between the various pillars of government. We have recently witnessed struggles between lawmakers (many of whom are entangled themselves, to varying degrees, with violating this or another law), officers of the law, its interpreters, attorneys and enforcers. If this tendency persists, the day is not far off when journalists and not judges will decide the verdicts. Journalists already shape the atmosphere and the background in which an investigation and legal proceedings take place and the overwhelming majority of journalists belong to the same Leftist portion of the political spectrum. They criticize the judges and their judgments. They deliver judicial information to the public based on gossip as well as on their personal opinions and inclinations, not on the basis of proper training, which they lack, or on the basis of the complete evidence, to which they do not have access. Trial by media is too similar for health to a lynching party.

The fourth myth that has come to supplant Israel's pioneering spirit of the past is careerism, and the worship of so-called "excellence," material success or advancement in the organization by being politically correct. Of course discussion of this complex phenomenon is relevant to many societies and takes us too far afield from the immediate focus of this chapter.

In this context it must be pointed out that the myth of "excellence" illustrates not only the ideological transformation of Israeli society but also the current struggle between the old and new elites. The Zionist ethos was formerly carried by a pioneering elite devoted to serving Jewry's collective goals in Palestine/Israel: settlers, warriors, people concerned with the welfare and adjustment of new immigrants, intellectuals, teachers, rejuvenators of the Hebrew language and culture, and founders of various economic and technological fields. The elite that carries the new ethos consists of financiers and merchants, businessmen and industrialists, lawyers and accountants, media people and entertainers. Unscrupulous careerism parading slogans of excellence, success, contribution and efficiency has replaced "service" and a sense of historical mission as the elites' main virtue.

The tension between decaying and emerging values has propelled Israeli society into a spin. It has lost the balance between authority and accountability; reward and punishment; rights and obligations; service and parasitism; wealth and poverty; labor and capital; solidarity and competition. If, under the enormous strains exerted on him, the pilot of this aircraft will fail to pull the national carrier out of the spin, the aircraft is doomed to crash no matter what happens around it.

Let us look at "the peace process," which gave a decisive impetus to these ideological and social transformations. Has it justified the change or was it only self-deception?

For a long time, Israel sought to be accepted by its surroundings and to establish a *modus vivendi* with its neighbors. The majority of Israelis realized that to accomplish this end they would have to make concessions and compromises. Domestic arguments focused on the extent of the concessions and compromise, but it seems that the majority conceded the principle of compromise. On the other hand, the Palestinians' goal has been neither coexistence nor compromise but their view of justice. The ultimate settlement with Israel should remedy the wrongs that had allegedly been done to them in the past. Justice, however, is absolute and recognizes no compromises.

The so-called Israeli–Palestinian dialogue has been taking place on two different levels that can hardly converge. What Israelis regard as indispensable concessions for the sake of reconciliation, the Palestinians consider their own by right, not something freely conceded by their partners or deserving of reciprocity. As long as Israel's concessions corresponded to the Palestinians' concept of Justice, the "peace process" moved forward. The moment Israel stopped conceding and insisted on retaining its position, the Palestinians reverted to violence. This reaction has highlighted their unwillingness to surrender anything they regard as theirs. It also revived the Israelis' suspicions of the Palestinians' sincerity.

Events in Israel since the signing of the Oslo agreements have had a devastating effect. Expectations for peace have dropped dramatically accompanied by a sharp upturn in apprehension. If the rapprochement seemingly initiated with the Oslo agreements had been genuine, the very opposite should have happened. The forces that activate and perpetuate the profound conflict between the Arabs in Judea, Samaria and Gaza and the Jews of Israel are far more recalcitrant to change than the virtual reality seen on TV newscasts or heard in the diplomats' reports made in public. They are even stronger than the political and economic interests of significant sectors on both sides.

Contrary to many Israelis' expectations, or illusions, history did not change course in the summer of 1993. Arab reluctance to accept a strong and prosperous Israel did not show signs of having been altered: if anything, it deepened and intensified. The social, economic and political conditions of the Arabs in Judea, Samaria and Gaza were not improved, despite the great flow of funds from European and Arab sources. The huge sums of money never trickled down to the level where they could make some palpable contribution to people's lives in the territory of the Palestinian Authority. The Palestinian Arabs unleashed a violent struggle against Zionism that escalated from civil disobedience to terrorism. Terrorist assaults were actually facilitated by the options granted to the terrorists under the Oslo pact and subsequent agreements. The naïve belief, amazingly accepted by Yitzhak Rabin and Shimon Peres, that the Palestinian security services and police would serve as Israel's proxies in fighting terrorism, was shattered at a very high cost in lives. Whatever hopes and expectations of future peace prevailed at the time of the Oslo agreement proved to be a fateful fiasco. Some die-hard Israeli leftists, along with their European Arabo-philic and a-moral materialists or anti-Semites, ignore or reject that conclusion even today.

All these conclusions were evident *before* Rabin was assassinated: They were not its consequences. Like many other historical fiascos, the Oslo agreement between Israel and the PLO turned out to be a gruesome myth with Rabin as its hero. The people who promote this myth only throw salt on the wounds of Israelis who were shocked morally and emotionally by the assassination. Yet, a myth can only substitute a fantasy for reality, it cannot change the facts. The basic reasons that hindered peace before Rabin's assassination remain unchanged; nor has there been a change in the distance between the Mediterranean Sea and the Jordan River. The territory of Israel, including Judea, Samaria and Gaza, remains the same. No new sources of fresh water have been discovered suddenly, and no positive changes in the Arabs' attitudes toward the Jews are evident anywhere. There has been noteworthy deterioration in the political atmosphere in the Middle East and in the world following the terrorist bombing of the twin towers in New York, with a distinct increase in animosity between many Islamic groups and countries and Western nations such as the United States and Israel. Europe is still trying hard to retain its balance on the high wire that leads across the "great divide" between the Judeo-Christian West and the Islamic Middle East (including Pakistan), while it tries to jettison the "Judeo" element as much as possible.

The transformations in Israeli society during the last generation conceal a profound illusion. One hundred years ago, Zionism offered a collective-national solution to the problem of Jewry's existence in face of European society that had repudiated it. Europe made Jewish assimilation and integration ever more difficult, and ultimately annihilated the Jews of Europe almost totally. Zionism's success in solving the Jewish question has been legion but incomplete. The emergence of Israel transferred the problem of Jewish survival from Europe to the Middle East and elevated it from the individual and communal levels to the national and international where it became the object of relentless national conflict. The Arab nations surrounding Israel, and even those further away that do not border on Israel (such as Iran, Pakistan, Sudan, Libya and so forth) refuse to be reconciled with a sovereign Jewish nation in the Middle East, just as Europe always opposed any collective form of Jewish existence and the perpetuation of its historical culture. Quite evident is Europe's alignment with the Arabs in repudiating Jewry's present national status.

Meanwhile, it appears that Jews as individuals have found a successful alternative answer to the question of their survival the pluralistic society of the United States. The Jewish collectivity in the United States is confronting many serious impediments to its survival, first and foremost an unprecedented rate of intermarriage and close-to-total cultural assimilation except for a minority of observant Jews. Ostensibly, what could be simpler than imitating the American prototype in the Middle East? In other words, what is more natural than eliminating the problem of Jewish collective survival by giving up the idea of a Jewish nation-state and replacing it with a non-Jewishly-identified pluralistic nation?

This is precisely the post-Zionist illusion. Israel remains in the Middle East, not in the Middle-West of the United States. The Middle East, and for that matter much of the known world outside the United States, Canada and Australia, does not recognize the concept of "pluralism" in the sense of a multi-national nation whose historical-ethnic-cultural identity is not largely determined by a dominant group. There may be room for reexamining, refreshing and updating some of the original concepts of the Zionist ethos, and to relinquish some of its anachronistic myths. Yet, adoption of an American pluralistic ethos is a radical negation of Zionism's essence that, from the perspective of Jewish history, can lead only to national self-destruction.

References

Dotan, Shmuel (1996) *Reds in Palestine*. Kfar Sava: Shavna Hasofer (Hebrew).
Shiloah, Zvi (1991) *Leftism in Israel*. Beit-El: Yaron Golan.
Yariv, S. S. (1953) (pen-name for David Ben-Gurion) *On the Communism and Zionism of Hashomer Hatsair*. Tel Aviv: The Israel Labor Party (MAPAI).

2

Zionism, the
Post-Zionists and Myth

SHLOMO SHARAN

Post-Zionist writers over the past decade or more have asserted that the fundamental postulates and principles of Zionism and the Zionist movement are anchored in myths. Some authors go so far as to claim that these myths were fabricated to serve the purposes of Zionism's political goals. It is instructive to examine closely these notions of the post-Zionists and their implications for Jewry, Israel and the Zionist enterprise[1]. First and foremost, it is necessary to consider the meaning of the term myth as used by thinkers, scholars and the post-Zionists (PZ).

The Meanings of Myth

At least two diametrically opposed meanings of the term myth are in use today. One is a colloquial and derogatory meaning alluding to falsehood or deception. In this sense myth is attributed to the way in which an individual, group or institution presents a false version of a person's life or of past events. The myth, while often based on a set of events that actually occurred, is expanded and edited to the point where it is no longer historically credible and has lost its original meaning. PZ writers assert that, on occasion, Zionist "myths" were composed with the explicit intention of presenting a distorted view of matters for purposes of political or religious gain. Contemporary critique of these myths, say PZ writers, seeks to expose these myths to the public in the hope it will elicit a negative reaction (Almog, 1997; Ben-Yehuda, 1995; Zerubavel, 1995).

A different approach to understanding myth appears in the works of scholars and thinkers. The philosopher of human culture, Ernst Cassirer (1925/1955) contends that the central message of myth can be grasped by understanding its symbolism, i.e. the ideas and/or feelings for which it stands, without recourse to the historical or psychological circumstances of its origin (called "the genetic fallacy"). Myth constitutes a cultural phenomenon in its own right, with its own unique features and meaning. Myth symbolizes a perspective on human consciousness of both nature and the human spirit, which is to say it refers simultaneously to both the external and internal manifestations of existence. Each myth has its special spiritual meaning. Myth is an inextricable component of the symbolic systems serving civilization's needs for expressing values, goals, feelings and ideas.

In this sense myth is an idea or a story that expresses people's inner-most response to the natural, social and personal world. Since time immemorial, myths have been generated by individuals and by groups, and are a universal cultural phenomenon. Moreover, they can reflect many different levels of human development, from the extremely primitive to the most sophisticated and spiritually edifying. Myths can contain elements of both a very limited local kind and of a broad universal kind. They may undergo many alterations in form and substance as they migrate from one culture to another and evolve over the course of time. In short, myths are a basic manifestation of human symbolic culture.

Like all forms of literature, myths are expressed through the medium of symbols, not through logical or formal exposition. The myth consists of the story or narrative, the ideas and feelings conveyed. Symbols are its means of expression. The ideas or stories that comprise a myth symbolize a range and depth of feeling and meaning . Often myths must be deciphered and interpreted, although the feelings and meaning expressed in some myths can be transparent. Myths can reveal the inner life and outlook of nations and people everywhere. One prominent example of a formal "mythical" symbol is the use of objects or verbal pronouncements during national, religious or secular public ceremonies. Language, lighted candles, flags, a cross, music, painting, body movements, and so forth almost ad infinitum, are all examples of symbols that stand for ideas, strivings or feelings.

On specific occasions, these symbols represent or propel an uplifting of men's spirits. This spiritual power is not "located" in the object or in the words. An object or words are symbols only when people understand that they represent or express ideas or feelings not present in the object or words themselves. Undeniably, millions of people from all faiths, cultural spheres and nations, cling to the belief that the symbols' power or sanctity inheres in the object itself, rather than in the ideas or feelings for which it stands.

Some myths designated as political myths were discussed by Henry Tudor (1972) who cites the definition of Georges Sorel regarding the meaning of myth. Sorel asserts that myth "provides a vision of the future . . . It gives men a fixed point by reference to which they can express their feelings and explain their experience . . . without stultifying their will to act . . . Myths . . . depict the future . . . not description of things, but expressions of a determination to act . . . No doubt, many religious ideas are to be found in myths . . . but it is not the case that all myths contain religious ideas or that we have any good reason to regard myth as a kind of religion" (Tudor, 1972, 15–16).

The goal of a particular myth and its meaning are completely dependent on the context in which it is presented and the intentions of those who present it. The original or ancient meaning of a myth does not necessarily survive in the meaning attributed to it by people in a later era. Its original meaning is discarded like any other notion that has outworn its usefulness. While they may contain religious elements, they are not to be confused with religion, as Cassirer (1955, 97–142) warned, even though their followers "believe" the myth. Myths are historical phenomena like all others. To deny their historical meaning by dismissing them as falsehood is to fail completely to understand them.

Theories that predict social events or situations are myths and not history if they exist only in the thoughts of the person or people who predicted them and do not find expression in people's behavior. Some myths become translated into reality because they directed people's overt behavior. Once they become reality, they are, of course, no longer only myths. Undoubtedly, some myths turn out to be sorely misleading, and their followers are left with bitter disappointment. That may or may not deter them from their faith in the myth.

Myth is not to be equated with history despite their similarities, and despite the fact that the two are frequently interwoven. Tudor noted that the historian's methods of evidence differ significantly from those of mythmakers. Historical statements are believed to be true by citing official documents, eyewitness reports, archaeological finds and so forth. The view of the world in myths is always a practical view. Its aim is either to advocate a certain course of action or to justify acceptance of an existing state of affairs. Myths are believed to be true, not because the historical evidence is compelling, but because they make sense of men's present experience.

> Events are selected for inclusion in a myth partly because they coincide with what men think ought to have happened, and partly because they are consis-

tent with the drama as a whole . . . it is a fact that, in their practice, men often view themselves as acting in the light of eternally valid principles. They wish their deeds to be possessed of a significance that is more than merely temporal, and they plunge themselves into practical affairs in the hope of finding some way to overcome the destructiveness of time. (Tudor, 1972)

The future is always of primary importance for myth and is invariably the subject of much speculation. Myths provide a kind of compass to assist people, as groups or as individuals, to set out their path into the future.

The theory of social change formulated by Karl Marx, for example, is a classic example of a "political" myth. What Marxian theory predicted as the desired consequences of the proletarian revolution, namely the establishment of a classless society, did not become reality, and thereby disappointed its devotees. The dream became a nightmare. Myths become nightmares when they no longer hold out hope to their devotees.

The Rift between the Post-Zionists and the Jewish People

During the past two centuries Jewry has seen the emergence of several major cleavages between Jewish groups of varying persuasions. On occasion we encounter publications that shed some light on a rupture within the Jewish People that hitherto was relatively ignored or largely unknown. While anti-Zionist groups have been outspoken in their opposition to Zionism ever since the latter emerged in history, their Post-Zionist derivative is less recognized. Post-Zionist publications and activities testify to a profound rift between them and the entire Zionist enterprise since its inception in *Hibbat Zion* in the last half of the nineteenth century. That includes a rift with the countless numbers of Jews, in the past and present, some of who shared in Zionism's realization in Palestine/Israel. Indeed, it is fair to say that the rift is between the Post-Zionists and the Jewish People itself, very few of who take exception to Zionism in the manner evident in Post-Zionist writings.

Most post-Zionists were born and raised in Zionist Palestine/Israel. It was in Israel that they developed their apathy toward, and alienation from, and in some, a burning hatred for, Zionism. Books by post-Zionists are often suffused with a searing animus toward Zionism and Jews. This aspect of the Post-Zionist writings is rarely mentioned in public, in or outside of Israel. Why and how this phenomenon developed, of Israel-born Jews who live in or outside of Israel, who make a career of defaming and denouncing their own People, are questions that are discussed later in this book **(chapter 12)**.

The Zionist Myths According to the Post-Zionists

Almost all of the ideas associated with Zionism, whether drawn from the world of Jewish history, religious tradition, and literature, or from Zionist thought in the modern era, have received the imprimatur of "myth." The post-Zionists did not adopt the term myth in its universal symbolic sense of expressing people's innermost view of the world. Rather, they employ the term myth in its pejorative meaning of fraud and deception. Just what are the basic ideas of Zionism that were given the honorific title of "myth?" It is to those concepts that we must now turn. Note that the concepts of Zionism discussed here are not all on the same phenomenological level. Some are abstract theories or hopes for the future, while others refer to manifest behavior.

The (Hebrew) term "*aliyah*" can serve as an example. In English, *aliyah* literally means "going up" or "ascending." But in common Hebrew parlance it refers to "immigration" to Israel. Judaism and Zionism always referred to a Jew who comes from some country in the Diaspora and settles in Israel as "going up" to the Land of Israel. Since the period of the Second Temple, Jewish tradition considered the act of settling in Israel as possessing an added spiritual dimension and not just a physical act of immigration from one country to another. This dimension of significance added by Jewry long ago to the idea of immigration to the Holy Land is what labels this concept a mythological idea in the eyes of the PZs. The huge chasm separating them from the majority of Jews who do not share their point of view is expressed quite pointedly in the totally different way in which this concept is used by the PZs. In their view, attributing a "mystical" notion of spiritual ascent to the act of immigrating to Israel is senseless, superstitious and misleading. Hence it is a mythical idea. For Jews who retain a historical Jewish and/or Zionist identification, this concept symbolizes an entire world of positive spiritual and social–cultural meaning whose manifestations are embodied in the political and social reality of the Jewish People in Israel. The term "myth" clearly seeks to empty the concept of "*aliyah*" of its historical–traditional–symbolic meaning, and reduce it to the level of the ordinary event of immigration (Almog, 1997). That is the rationale and implication of placing the stamp of "myth" on one of the basic concepts of Judaism and Zionism.

The list of Zionist myths according to the Post-Zionists, include the following:

Historical Determinism. Jewish life follows a path largely set out for it in the past, in ancient Jewish history. The alleged relationship between modern times and the period of the Bible is akin to a "blood pact" between the Land and the Jews. This pact "between Biblical mythology and Israeli life in the present" served for Zionism as proof of the legitimacy for the conquest by Jews in recent times of the Land of Israel. All of this was done to create a link between "the mythological past of the Jewish nation to the present days of the [Zionist] pioneers" (Almog, 1972, 50–72).

"Going up" and "ascending" (to the Land of Israel). Zionism believed that it was elevating the Jews to a higher plane of existence. Each new project to create Jewish communities in Palestine/Israel expressed an "ascent on a moral and spiritual scale": ascent to the Land, ascent to Jerusalem, ascent to the mountains, and so forth. The PZ's view is that the repeated use of the term "ascent" (*aliyah*) is "mythological semantics" inherited from Jewish religious tradition. The fact that the term was borrowed from religion confirms that it is sheer prevarication and lacks basic morality. Jews who came from other countries to reside in Palestine/Israel were simply immigrants whose presence here was, and is, "a random collection of individuals" (Almog, 1997, 45). Any other description is religio-mythology, according to Oz Almog.

Delivers Us from the Hands of Our Enemies. The myth of "the redemption of Israel" is fundamental in Judaism and Zionism. It states that "the Jewish People rises from the dust to be delivered at the last moment" by the God of Israel the Redeemer. Jewish folklore on many holidays – such as Passover, Purim, Lag B'Omer, and Chanukah – repeats the refrain: "More than one tyrant rose up to annihilate us." Children in kindergartens and schools are "brainwashed" with these ideas (Almog, 1997, 67–8).

The Few Against Many. "The quality, uniqueness and superiority of the Jewish People . . . comprise one of the important myths of Judaism and Zionism." This myth "is salient in the war stories so obviously influenced by Hollywood's Western movies that were very popular during the 1940s and 1950s." The Israeli public perceived the Sinai Campaign as a miracle whose only explanation was this myth. The Sinai Campaign "endowed the myth of 'the few against the many' with enormous power in the eyes of the Israeli public. Once again, the small and weak Jewish People – said public sentiment – overcame powerful opponents who outnumbered us" (Almog, 1997, 69–72).

The Binding of Isaac: Abraham the Pioneer (Halutz), and Isaac the Sabra. For purposes of consumption by the public, the young soldiers who fell in the battles (particularly in the battles of the War of Independence in 1948) were depicted as sacrificial lambs on the altar of the nation and of the homeland. This interpretation of the Biblical story of the Binding of Isaac in the book of Genesis appeared with unusually high frequency in the Hebrew literature of the day. The Zionist interpretation of the topic of "sacrifice" removes it from its objective context, says Almog. In the "objective" PZ and postmodern context, a soldier who falls in battle is someone "whose luck ran out and who lost his life." The Zionists transferred this "objective view" to a mythological plane by asserting that the soldier consciously sacrificed his life as an act of benevolent free will for the sake of the nation, as an act of exalted patriotism. The mythological component in the public's collective memory attributes to the soldiers who were killed the motive of self-sacrifice for the sake of saving the nation. Jews in Palestine of the 1948 generation, and their heirs, thought that the soldiers were a link in the chain of historical continuity with the Jews of past generations who died "for the sanctification of the Name." That tradition has been a leitmotif in Jewish history since the days of the Bar Kochba rebellion against Rome (135 CE) and the ten martyrs, through the Middle Ages, World War II and Israel's wars with the Arabs, as if the tradition of self-sacrifice links the war dead of our day with their ancestors of previous generations.

The Israeli public "internalized" the myth of the "Binding of Isaac" as if they made peace with the fact that their loved ones who died in battle offered themselves as sacrifices on the alter of the homeland.

It is worth noting here that the meaning of the Biblical story of the Binding of Isaac carries the distinct message that God does not want Isaac to be sacrificed, but only to test Abraham. His preparedness to comply with God's command in all of the ten trials to which he was subjected proved that he was worthy of being the father of his nation. His reward is God's promise that his descendants would gain immortality as a nation (not as individuals). Modern writers of Hebrew literature frequently employed Biblical stories in the opposite sense of the original text.

The Redemption of Israel (the Jewish People). "Jewish history aims from its very inception toward the goal of realizing the Zionist dream in the Land of Israel." "The Law of Redemption" is a fundamental component of Zionist ideology (Almog, 76).

In the words of David Ben-Gurion:

> Whatever is new in our generation . . . cannot be understood without seeing that the vision of The Messianic Redemption is planted in the heart of the Jewish People . . . This is true not only after the destruction of the Second Temple, but ever since the days of the first literary prophets . . . this vision has filled the annals of Jewish history . . . with the certainty of the laws of Nature. (quoted by Almog from Becker, 1958, 28)

This conception prevailed among most of Israel's leaders who believed wholeheartedly in this myth. The schools' curriculum and textbooks present the establishment of the State of Israel as "a victory for the relentless striving for Zion" by the Jewish People throughout the ages. In a widely disseminated history book of that time, Dr. Ephraim Shmueli (1950) summarized how Kabbalists viewed the subject of Exile and Redemption. Shmueli wrote:

> Wherever Israel was in Exile, the *Sh'chinah* [God's Presence] went into exile with them to protect them . . . On the great day, at the end of time, the Land of Israel will return to serve as the center of supreme holiness and the complete unification of God with Israel [the Jewish People]. The masses of Israel will assemble in the Land of Israel. (quoted by Almog from Shmueli, 1950, 71–81)

The proximity in time of the Holocaust to the defeat of the Nazis and the establishment of the State of Israel reinforced in the mind of the Jewish public the relationship of Zionism to the "realization of prophecy" according to "the mythological scenario" (Almog, 77).

Jewry's Right to the Land of Israel. Zionism justified the settlement of Jews in Palestine by claiming that it was historical justice. According to Almog (1997) use of the name "The Land of Israel" expresses the Zionist belief in the right of the Jewish People to reclaim the territory over which, they believed, Jewry possessed ownership. Many practical and moral explanations were offered as to Jewry's rights to the Land of Israel, but "mythological" reasons of a meta-physical character were invoked as well alongside the rational explanations. The main explanation cited the belief in God's promise to give this land to the Israelites. This myth convinced the native-born Jews (*sabras*) that it was justified for the Jews to take possession of land abandoned by the Arabs during the War of Independence (in Israel this war was commonly known as the War of Liberation).

If the territory they liberated was ancestral soil, the *sabra*-warriors were not just second generation immigrants from Europe, but were carrying on the tradition of Biblical youth. The myth implanted the sense of being natives, of ownership, in the *sabras* who were actually immigrants or the offspring of immigrants.

The Post-Zionists' Goal Is To Vilify Zionism, Not To Reveal The Truth

Readers of PZ books, and among them the book by Almog (1997), will quickly discern that the primary purpose of these authors is to negate

Zionism as completely as possible. First and foremost PZs seek to show that religious ideas, national patriotism and a host of other condemnable features contaminate Zionism.

Instead, PZ authors write the kind of political propaganda that they accuse Zionism of using. They insist on identifying Israel Jewry's efforts at transmitting Jewish historical tradition to schoolchildren as an act of brainwashing. That claim had been made explicitly in several books on education written by the well-known Israeli novelist and short-story writer Yizhar Smilansky, who summarily denigrates the transmission of all historical–cultural values as indoctrination.

What Yizhar Smilansky, Tom Segev, Oz Almog and other post-Zionists fail to mention is that all nations, cultural and political groups, religions, families and ideological groups (including radical left-wing groups of all kinds), not just the Jews, consider it to be their moral and existential responsibility to transmit their heritage to the next generation. No group willingly commits historical and social suicide by creating a cultural vacuum for its children, which is precisely what the Smilanskys, Almogs and their nihilist ideological associates, advocate. We shall return to this topic later.

PZ publications are aimed primarily at vilifying Zionism, not necessarily at telling the truth about recent Jewish history, as they would have us believe. They do not assert, as they might have, that Zionism declined because its social–historical or cultural tasks are no longer relevant, and that during the course of its 100-year existence, new tasks and goals emerged that have replaced the older Zionist cause. The title "Post-Zionism" might suggest to some people that it was modeled on the postmodern school of thought. But postmodern thinkers did not become embroiled in the morass of trying to demolish, defame, delegitimize or ridicule all of the thinkers or ideas that flourished during the "Modern" period to which the "post-Modernists" were allegedly the heirs. Post-Zionists sought to create the impression that they were advancing intellectually along with the postmodernists of the Western world in terms of their interpretation of history and society. Their proclamation of the "decline of Zionism" was intended to sound like the harbinger of a new era that historically was replacing Zionism, as if the PZs were saying that Zionism had outlived its purpose.

What the post-Zionists said in fact is very different. To their mind, Zionism was always a criminal enterprise founded on lies and distortions. The PZs are bitter enemies of Zionism. No other characterization befits a group of people whose animosity toward Zionism drives them to make statements in print such as: "the pioneer ideology insinuated itself into the most miniscule capillaries of society's blood stream until it became an all-encompassing religious way of life" (Almog, 81). This statement and many others of similar import have no legitimate place in an historical or sociological study of any kind and deserve unequivocal rejection by investigators regardless of their personal political orientation. These statements should arouse serious questions in the minds of readers regarding the nature of the feelings and thoughts of those who employ such grotesque metaphors. "Post-Zionism" sounds like a respectable academic title, but it clearly serves to conceal a great deal of hostility much like the way Arab and Christian anti-Semites have used that word ever since its appearance on the stage of history (Ye'or, 2002).

Turning to a critical evaluation of the myths presented earlier, our main purpose is to identify the major motifs and assumptions of the post-Zionists' outlook concerning some of these "myths."

Commissioned Agents of Zionism

On numerous occasions the assertion was repeated that the Zionist movement commissioned many agents to compose and disseminate its ideology (Almog, 1997). Yet, no evidence was offered by any post-Zionist writer to substantiate that view. No one ever tried to document who engaged the writers to act as "agents" for the Zionist movement, how they were engaged, or what they were promised in return. More important, how can anyone explain the life-long and systematic work published by a given historian or poet that expresses a consistent view of Zionism, of Jewry, of the world? How could that – and not just some specific product – result from a "commission" offered by a public institution, unless the author was accepting payment to produce what he or she would have done in any case? One would be hard pressed to believe that the foremost intellectuals, writers, poets, etc. of that era would agree to produce scholarly or literary works that were commissioned by a non-literary or non-academic, political institution to produce their work. Those who knew these writers or those acquainted with their works know just how inconceivable it is that they would produce their literary or scholarly work for the explicit purpose of disseminating ideas in which they, the authors, were not in full agreement.

Yitschak Lamdan was one of the truly pure souls of Hebrew letters, poet extraordinaire and editor of one of the finest Hebrew literary journals ever to appear in Israel (*Gilyonot*), who almost never owned more than two suits of clothing. No one can seriously entertain the notion that he was a paid agent hired by some political functionary or institution. Lamdan's landmark poem "Masada" (1927) is cited frequently by post-

Zionists as a literary work responsible for popularizing one of Zionism's major myths. PZ writers certainly understand that Lamdan's poem used Masada (or *M'tsada*, meaning "fortress") exclusively as a symbol, and that he was not referring to the historical events that took place there, or even to Masada's geographical location.

Another of the many classic works produced during this period is the extraordinary two-volume study by Yehezkel Kaufmann (*Golah V'neichar – Exile and Alienation*) devoted to the historical sociology of the Jewish People. This work of 1,150 pages was published during the period of 1930–2, after Kaufmann settled in Palestine. No group, political organization or institution ever commissioned Kaufmann to produce any of his great works, and certainly not this gigantic opus, which is, by far and away, one of the truly monumental socio-historical works of the twentieth century in the Hebrew language. In that work Kaufmann deals with the enigma of Jewish survival within the framework of contemporary scholarship and systematic historical investigation. This work provides powerful support for the soundness of Zionism's grasp of Jewish history and of the problems confronting Jewish national and cultural survival in the modern world. That is the kind of work that Zionism typically should have commissioned.

Ironically, many of the writers cited by Almog and others as Zionist propaganda agents actually were rather sharp critics of the Zionist Organization, albeit not at all in the manner common among the post-Zionists. Very few of the intellectuals allegedly commissioned by the Zionist establishment to carry out its propaganda effort identified with Socialism in any way. From the beginning of the 1930s, and thereafter, Kaufmann (1936) chastized the Labor Party repeatedly for adopting Socialism as an important component of Zionist ideology and unceasingly warned the Zionist leadership that their socialist orientation would wreak disastrous effects on Jewry's national aspirations in Palestine from both an economic and a territorial point of view. Insisting on a platform of social and economic reform would distract the Zionist enterprise from its primary and overarching goal of reclaiming the territory of Palestine for the Jewish People. The results could be catastrophic, warned Kaufmann in the mid-1930s. Those were the days when the Communist star shone brightly in the firmament of Western intellectuals, including secular Zionist Jews in Europe and Palestine, over whom it held a powerful fascination and attraction. The Union of Hebrew Workers in Palestine (the *Histadrut*) at the time, which controlled a large portion of the funds available for "cultural" activities in the country, clung zealously to the Marxist notion of the unity of the Workers' International and the struggle for a classless society, albeit not by means of a bloody revolution. The Zionist-

Hebrew writers in Palestine and Europe were, for the most part, demonstrably anti-communist. Lamdan, Kaufmann, Alterman, Vilnai, Greenberg, Hazaz, Shenhar, Agnon, Yitschak Baer, and many other great luminaries of Jewish literature and scholarship in Palestine/Israel during the decades discussed here clearly saw the darker side of Communism and wrote that it left little room for Mankind to surpass the level of animals. It is hardly reasonable to argue that a Zionist Organization dominated by Socialists would commission such spokesmen as agents to disseminate its views.

Since the writers referred to by the post-Zionists identified personally and profoundly with Zionism, they would have written works with a distinctly Zionist orientation without being encouraged by any official suggestion or invitation. Constant repetition of the claim that these writers and scholars were commissioned as Zionist agents testifies to the post-Zionists' willingness to capitalize on any sensationalist claim they can drum up regardless of its merits. These men number among the great intellectual architects of Zionist thought and modern Hebrew literary–historical culture. Their works enriched Jewry and Zionism, not the other way around!

The Few Against Many

The Arab armies outnumbered the Jewish soldiers during all the wars between Israel and the Arabs. The Jews were always at a dangerous numerical disadvantage. For the PZ writer Oz Almog, this fact is a "myth" that was "reinforced by reality" because the Jews in fact were outnumbered in every war with the Arab nations. This confusion between what is fact or fiction discloses a serious structural flaw in the entire argument of the post-Zionist position. If the numerical superiority of the Arab armies over the Jewish army is a fact, then why is it consistently called a myth, and especially a myth with the explicit meaning of a lie? A myth is never just a simple fact, although facts can be part of myths. A myth is always a much broader phenomenon than a fact, providing a wider canvas of ideas, hopes and observations about the world and about life than a mere recitation of facts.

If facts and myths are indistinguishable, then, theoretically at least, where do we locate the objective world? What happens to the experiential distinction between fact and fantasy, between history and hopes for the future, between reality and dreams? Does history not leave behind any fingerprints of people, groups or nations who lived their lives in the three-dimensional world, or do they too belong to the realm of "deceptive myths"? PZ writings include many instances of identifying historical reality as myth in an attempt to reduce the meaning of Jewry's national, political, cultural and social existence to disembodied ideology. The battles in which relatively few Jewish soldiers held out against, and often defeated, large numbers of Arab soldiers is one of the instances in which PZ social scientists and historians fail to distinguish between myth and reality because they would prefer that the reality be nothing more than what they call myth!

No doubt the history of the Jews challenges the accepted definitions of nation, religion, People, homeland, and other concepts. The confusion stems from the fact that the Jews were a nation in exile for 2,000 years who, beyond all reason, returned to their ancestral country and reestablished sovereignty there, as well as replanting their religion, language and other cultural features. These facts are unparalleled in world history, and hence defy understanding by analogy or comparison to similar phenomena that occurred among other nations.

Moreover, many concepts of Jewish historical–religious tradition appeared to be totally abstract and disconnected from territorial reality, i.e. "myths," unlike other nations whose connection to their land meant they enjoyed permanent residence in their geographical home, even if they were conquered for short or long periods of time by other nations. Jewry only lately had the opportunity to embody many of its seemingly spiritual notions in concrete form. Places named in prayers assumed physical shape, Jewish laws discussed in the Talmud were relevant to social situations for the first time in more than a millennium, legendary figures of the Bible had walked the roadways and towns where ordinary Jews today plough the soil or drive their cars. Many Jews still seem to be unable, or unwilling, to make the transition from the world of verbal symbols easily manipulated in writing or in speech (or speeches), to that of a political–social reality that impinges on unmediated experience.

PZ writers ignored the concept and reality of *The Ingathering of the Exiles* that has assumed physical–social reality during the past decades. Instead, these writers preferred to engage in their relentless denunciation of Judaic–Zionist "myths" as a mechanism for delegitimizing Zionist ideology. For the majority of Jewry, attempts to diminish the validity, accuracy and even the morality of concepts or legends from the Judaic–Zionist cultural heritage will not discredit the reality created by Zionism in the State of Israel, although that is precisely the goal of the post-anti-Zionists. The genuine embodiment of all of these ideas inscribed on the flag of the Zionist enterprise is the idea of the Ingathering of the Exiles as it is being realized in Israel to this very day. Obviously, it is an idea of enormous vitality that sustains the hope for Jewry's future in Israel, as individuals and as a collectivity. The subject of *The Ingathering of the Exiles* as a basic concept of Zionism is discussed later in this essay.

"Myth" as Fraud and Deception

Several of Israel's distinguished historians have observed that "the popular use of the term 'myth' in its connotation of referring to . . . an erroneous idea that can be refuted by logical analysis . . . has frequently been adopted in a naïve way by the revisionist historians . . . " (Ohana and Wistrich, 1996, 13). But one may ask if, indeed, they are naïve, or are the PZs propelled by a logic which inexorably leads them to the conclusion that Zionism is founded on fraud and deception in the form of "myth"? If so, just what is it that coerces them to adopt that position?

We have suggested that the PZs derived direction from the postmodern school of social thought. Postmodernism has a fundamentally deconstructionist orientation. This view claims that the links historians make between prior and later events that create the sense of an unfolding of events, of a connection between events and ideas current in different times and places, are the product of interpretation and imagination. Continuity in human history exists only in the mind. It is not part of objective reality and cannot withstand criticism based on an empirical examination of the events and of people's lives.

From a strictly empirical perspective, says Deconstructionism, each and every event constitutes a separate independent unit that has no necessary link to other such units. In that sense, historians and theoreticians of the "Idea of History," such as R. G. Collingwood and his followers, are hopelessly lost. They claim that history is a reconstruction of the thoughts entertained by people in a given period. By reconstructing these thoughts, the historian can comprehend the relationship between the behavior of different people (or groups, or nations) who preceded or followed them in the course of time, or who flourished at the same time in different places. Collingwood's theory of the historian's task is built on the notion of the interrelatedness of historical periods, of groups and individuals, in an attempt to attribute meaning to human experience that, in its entirety, is called "history." Such meaning, say postmodern writers, emerges from the creative imagination of the historian but it is not inherent in any way in the events themselves.

To assist their radical negation of the meaning that Zionism attached to a series of ideas and events, the PZs adopted a view of history that involves an atomization of human experience itself. Elimination of inter-personal, inter-group, inter-period continuity, of the relationship between events and ideas and so forth, leaves in its wake a bare skeleton of discon-nected elements. There is no longer any "living history" but only "the corpse of history" known as "a chronicle of events." That is the corpse that remains after the living organism has relinquished its soul, as Collingwood put it (Collingwood, 1946/1993, 218–19). The death of living history was caused by the reinterpretation of human existence as a random collection of events and bits of behavior displayed by a motley crowd of people who lack an "identity." An interpretation of history of this kind allows PZs to think that they have virtually dismantled Zionist ideology since it is contingent upon a view of Jewish history as the mean-ingful continuity of the Jewish People.

In sum, post-Zionism based its approach to Zionism on several assump-tions regarding the nature of human history, its study and presentation by its "practitioners." These assumptions explain how it is possible for acad-emically based scholars to suggest that the Jews who came to Palestine/Israel were a random group of immigrants not members of a People seeking to return to their historic homeland. The entire list of Zionist myths can be explained away by the same deconstructionist ratio-nale.

"The Ingathering of Exiles" and the List of Zionist Myths

The vision of the "Ingathering of Exiles" from the countries of their dispersion is an ancient component of Judaism. It certainly qualifies as a "myth" in terms defined by Cassirer, Tudor and others. Amazingly, this concept was omitted from the PZs' list of Zionist myths. How could such a central idea of Zionist ideology, and of Judaic tradition through the centuries, be overlooked by the myth-seekers among the post-Zionists? "The Ingathering of the Exiles" is such an essential component of the Jewish ethos that a prayer for its realization has been recited three times a day for the past 1,500 years by all Jews who pray:

> Give a loud blast on the shofar to announce our freedom, perform a miracle to gather us from our countries of exile, and bring us together from the four corners of the earth. Blessed are Thou Lord who gathers in the dispersed ones of His People Israel.

Of course this vision was enunciated earlier (eighth century BCE and after) by the Biblical prophets (Jeremiah 31: 9–11; 32: 38–40; Ezekiel 36: 25–27; Isaiah 11: 12; Amos 9: 14–15), as well as in other ancient sources such as in the book of Ben-Sirah (Ecclesiasticus, written between 250 and

245 BCE). See chapter 36, verse 10: "Collect all the tribes of Jacob and let them settle [in the Land] as in earlier times." The Ingathering of the Exiles echoes throughout the entire length of Judaic literature in Hebrew and other languages in all eras and in all countries where Jews resided. Herzl's political Zionism placed this vision at its very foundation in full consciousness of its being Jewry's modern expression of its ancient Messianic dream. By virtue of its Messianic vision, Zionism earned its honored place among the basic ideas and strivings of many Jews until it finally, albeit barely, reached its most central goal of a Jewish national entity, Israel.

No one can disregard the fact that, almost since its inception, Zionism was opposed by a variety of Jewish groups, such as: ultra-Orthodox groups in Eastern Europe (after they heard that the Zionist congress would deal with "cultural" matters and not only with political ones) and later in the United States (followers of the Satmer rebbe); the American Council for Judaism (Rabbi Berger); many, but not all, Reform rabbis and theologians in Germany (before World War II) and the United States; Communist and Socialist Jews (such as the *Bund*) in Europe before World War II as well as in Palestine/Israel. In more recent times, Zionism has been opposed by some, but not all, of the ultra-Orthodox groups in Brooklyn and Jerusalem (such as the *Neturei Karta* or Guardians of the City); by many Leftists and some well-known academics in the United States, such as Noam Chomsky and his followers; by some journalists such as Anthony Lewis of the *New York Times*, for example; and, last but not least, by the PZs of today, inside and outside of Israel. These groups can be viewed as trying to derail the collective will of the great majority of the Jewish People, even if one thinks that the idea of a "collective will" is a myth. It is a myth in the same sense that all groups who express some form of social idealism have formulated a vision by which they live. Most important, as noted previously, the collective will of the Jewish People has assumed a distinct material, cultural and political form. Hence, it is a myth that has become history. The result is that PZs are trying to undo their own People's history, in all its manifestations.

In modern times, the vision of the Ingathering of Exiles caused stormy arguments among Jews, especially when Britain offered Uganda as a solution to the "Jewish problem." Many Jews thought that Palestine was too small and barren to accommodate all the Jews of Europe who, they thought, would move to a Jewish country (Kaufmann, 1932). It was deemed imperative to settle many Jews in another territory in addition to Palestine. The conflict within the Zionist movement over the Uganda offer must be understood against the background of the principle of The Ingathering of Exiles that was so fundamental in Jewish thinking about the future of the Jewish People, and, hence, in Zionism as well. In December 1952, in Jerusalem, in the course of a conversation, Professor Yehezkel Kaufmann rather unexpectedly said that a few hours earlier he had been visiting David Ben-Gurion who told him that "there was room for two million Jews in the Negev." Kaufmann expressed relief at Ben-Gurion's statement because he, Kaufmann, was among those who were skeptical about the possibility of finding space and sustenance in the miniscule country of Israel for all of the Jews (even after the Holocaust). Hence for a short time he had supported the suggestion of settling Jews in another territory in addition to Palestine. That anecdote illustrates to what extent The Ingathering of the Exiles dominated the thinking of modern Zionist thinkers and political figures.

Why then was "The Ingathering of the Exiles" omitted from the PZs' list of Zionist myths? Clearly, the subject of The Ingathering of Exiles poses a difficult intellectual–theoretical challenge for the PZs. That "myth" cannot be explained as another example of Zionist fraud and deception. Even Arab antisemitic and anti-Zionist propagandists have not succeeded in treating this subject in any way, however hard they try to de-Judaize the Bible and the history of the Middle East (Ye'or, 2002). During the centuries of exile the Ingathering of Exiles warranted the title of a myth that Jews clung to. In Herzl's day, at the end of the nineteenth and the beginning of the twentieth century, that idea still occupied the status of a myth as explained by Cassirer and like-minded scholars. However, that status underwent significant change by the 1930s as its effect on the behavior of tens of thousands of Jews who undertook practical, non-dreamlike settlement in Palestine and transformed the myth into social–historical reality. In a decade or two from the time these lines are written, the Jews of Israel will constitute the majority of the Jewish People in the world for the first time since the destruction of the Second Temple in 70 CE.

In order to deal satisfactorily with the concept of The Ingathering of the Exiles, the PZs, anti-Zionists in Europe, and the Arabs, would have to admit that Zionism is far from being merely a series of myths, and is now a social, political and cultural reality born from a social vision. If, despite all that, PZs persist in dubbing Zionism a myth, then logically the same label should be applied to any national-social movement that bears the distinctive signs of being a dream whose followers are devoted to turning it into a reality. Such was the rebellion of the American colonies against Britain at the end of the eighteenth century, or the dismantling of apartheid in South Africa under the pressure of the black political organizations there in the 1990s. They too were founded on myths not dissimilar to the Zionist myth except for the one, unparalleled and unprecedented fact that the Jews were not located geographically on the soil of their national home and had to exit from the many countries of their dispersion to occupy the Land of Israel once again. Clearly the title "myth" is a glaring misnomer when applied to Zionism, just as it would be if applied to the United States, or to the recent termination of apartheid in South Africa, as if it has not happened yet! PZ theory confuses its ideological objections to Zionism with social reality.

Undoubtedly, many idealists became disaffected over Zionism's failure to solve all of the major problems confronting Jewry's return to the Land of Israel, and over the continuous stream of anti-Semitic venom, in words and deeds, directed at Israel and the Jews. However, The Ingathering of the Exiles continues to be a high level priority in Zionism, and great strides have been made thus far to transform this great historical–moral vision of the Jewish People since Biblical antiquity into social–political reality.

Post-Zionism and Nihilism

The deconstructionist approach to the understanding of human history is nihilistic in the extreme. PZs are no less nihilistic in their approach to Jewish history, to Judaism in general and to Zionism. Can readers of the PZ's writings actually be taken in by the mendacious claim that millions of Jews from all over the world came to Palestine/Israel randomly, whether out of Zionist convictions or because circumstances forced them to leave their country of birth? How can anyone give credence to the idea that chance factors can explain the remarkable phenomenon of the rebirth of the Jewish nation in Israel? At the beginning of the twentieth century there was less than 1 percent of the total number of Jews in the world living in Palestine.

Now, a century later, there are over five million who comprise almost 40 percent of world Jewry. From the point of view of statistical probability alone, without any reference to ideas of any kind, those numbers contradict any notion of randomness. Social scientists with only an elementary knowledge of statistics should know better than to make such a claim, whatever their ideological orientation *vis-à-vis* Zionism. Furthermore, no random collection of individuals with a self-perception of being disconnected socially and historically from the other immigrants, regardless of their number, would ever be able to accomplish the rebuilding of Jewish society in Israel. The economic and cultural accomplishments of Israel demand a relatively high level of social cohesiveness. Post-Zionist historians and sociologists who overlook these facts display the depth of their antagonism toward their own People. That antagosim leads to identifying with the claims of Jewry's enemies that nothing the Jews have dome in Israel can have any legitimacy.

Zionism appeared as the greatest historical hope that the Jewish People has known for the past 300 years or more. That hope was the *raison d'être* and foundation of Israel's cultural, social, and economic development. The Zionist "myth" propelled itself into reality to a degree far beyond anyone's expectations, including those of its first Prime Minister, David Ben-Gurion, who foresaw an Israel of three million Jews as the realistic limits of his fondest dreams for the country (there were 650,000 Jews in Palestine in 1948 when Israel gained independence). With all its limitations, Zionism is the single most successful movement of social and national idealism in the Western world since the French Revolution (before Robespierre).

The Messianic Core of Zionism

Another dimension of the Ingathering of the Exiles is the messianic vision eloquently expressed by the Biblical Prophets. That core concept of the Judeo-Zionist vision was totally missed by post-Zionist writers. As such it also missed the dubious honor of being dubbed a "Zionist myth." The single most powerful and significant message to Jewry of the Judeo–Zionist ethos is the messianic vision. In more colloquial but no less expressive terms, the significance of Zionism derives from the Prophetic worldview that orients Jewry toward the future. The messianic message holds out the promise of redemption from exile and suffering and offers hope for a redeemed world. Authentic Biblical Messianism (as distinct from the messianism of many social utopians) in its very essence transforms all present time into preparation for the future: "It places the tension of the future at the heart of the present."

From Biblical times to today, Judaism never ignored the past in its orientation toward the future. The legacy of the patriarchs, the Exodus from Egypt, the "glory" of David's kingdom, the Destruction of the Temple, and so forth, were never neglected. Nevertheless, the prophetic vision of the future is not just a paean to the glories of the past and a hope that it will be restored. Jerusalem and the Land of Israel are the location of Jewry's restoration, but the social order, the nature of Israel's life in the future, the condition of the nations of the world in the future, are not mere repetition of the past. It is *not* a case of "what was is what will be." The prophetic vision is unlike other nations' hopes to restore the former glory of Athens, Rome, Byzantium or any other sacred or semi-sacred place on earth that nations wished to have rebuilt after its destruction. It is certainly not the Paradise of Islam, the Heavenly Jerusalem of Christianity or Valhalla of the Germanic tribes. It remains located uncompromisingly in this world. It is also not a utopia where everyone will be equal materially and in social status, although it distinctly anticipates an end to international warfare in the "end of days."

The future orientation of the prophets was thoroughly absorbed into the fabric of all authentic Jewish thought including that of the foremost Zionist thinkers and leaders. It was, and is, the source of hope and optimism for survival and for the recreation of Jewish civilization radiated by Judaism and Zionism throughout Jewry's exile, in the face of horrendous and unrelenting destruction, slaughter, enslavement, dispersion, forced conversion, repeated expulsions, homelessness, communal incarceration in ghettoes, starvation, and on and on. We will not speak of the horrors of Jewish life between the two world wars or during World War II.

The assertion by PZ writers that the myths of heroism that Zionism sought to propagate ignored the tragic end of the historical events related in the myths is a pathological mockery of Jewish history and memory. Jewry never failed to commemorate the tragic events that the nation experienced throughout history.

In their zeal to delegitimize Zionism, the PZs fall into the trap of making contradictory demands or claims about Zionism. On the one hand, the "myths" developed and circulated by Zionism are misleading and not historically accurate or complete. The story of Masada disseminated among Jewish youth in Israel and elsewhere should have focused on the defenders' decision not to allow themselves to be enslaved and on their ultimate suicide, rather than on their resistance against the Roman army that surrounded them in the years 70–72 CE. On the other hand, the Masada story deserves to be called a myth because it intends to commemorate the bravery of Ben-Yair and his followers who held the hilltop fortress at Masada but fails to mention that the defenders of Masada died without even trying to fight off the Romans (Zerubavel, 1995). The underlying and unarticulated assumption is that myth has no legitimate function of its own if it is not purely historical. To the extent that it departs from historical facts, myth is deception and falsehood.

We have already seen how that position is utterly untenable and bears no relation to any objective examination of the symbolic nature of myth and its social-historical function, for Jewry or for any other group or nation. As an instructive analogy, one could point to the innumerable "myths" circulated in American history books about the great achievement of Abraham Lincoln of saving the Union (of the US) and preventing the secession of the southern States. Is that set of myths invariably accompanied by a statement reminding readers that the United States Civil War involved the death of more soldiers and civilians than all the other wars combined fought by the United States in its entire history anywhere in the world? The Civil War also ended slavery in the United States. Do the Afro-Americans in the United States ever link their ancestors' freedom from slavery to the death of tens of thousands of young boys and men in that conflict? If the post-Zionists would apply their logic to American history they would have to demand that Afro-Americans acknowledge the horrifying circumstances under which their ancestors were freed and declare their willingness to compensate the descendants of those killed in that war. If anyone thinks the Afro-Americans in the United States should do that, no one I know has ever heard about it.

No one reads the vast literature of Hebraic–Judaic "myths" without understanding beyond a shadow of a doubt that the undisguised, explicit purpose of these myths was to support hope and optimism, to provide an electrifying idea that could rally a tired, driven and persecuted people, rather than adding to the ocean of pain that already flooded so much of Jewish life.

The widespread disparagement of the messianic dream among super-rationalists from various ideological camps, including PZ writers, also reflects a basic flaw in their grasp of the Biblical Prophets. Secular socialist Zionists in Palestine/Israel were particularly vehement in their abhorrence of Judaic messianism because they identified messianism completely with the notion of Divine intervention in history and the exclusive reliance on the Messiah for redeeming Jewry from Exile, all of which they attributed to Judaism and to religious Jews.

There is ample documentation to show that the prohibition against attempting to restore Jewry's sovereignty over Palestine did not dominate Jewish religious thought for most of Jewry's long sojourn in *Galut*. Even as late as the seventeenth century it had not obtained complete acceptance by world Jewry, although many famous rabbis opposed human initiative in the matter. That fact is more than evident in the enormous popularity of Shabbetai Zvi's (1626–76) bid to collect a large army and reconquer Palestine for the Jews from the hands of the Ottoman Empire in the face of rabbinic injunctions. But rigid rejection of "pushing the end" (i.e. trying to redeem Jewry from Exile through human agency) gradually came to dominate Orthodox Jewry during the past three centuries, after numerous attempts over the course of earlier centuries to regain control of Palestine ended in tragedy. On the one hand, religious thinkers negated the legitimacy of any expectations of Jewish restoration to Palestine. They removed it from the realm of history and placed it almost entirely in the realm of the Divine will. On the other hand, outspoken assimilationists, as well as Reform rabbis and theologians in Germany and the United States in the nineteenth and early twentieth centuries, also opposed the idea of Jewish "redemption" from Exile. To subscribe to the idea of an ultimate "redemption" from Exile meant that Jewry rejected social and economic assimilation into the dominant Christian society. It also implied that Jews did not necessarily affirm their complete acceptance of the national identity of the country where they resided. That unequivocal affirmation was precisely what Napoleon demanded, and received, at his famous convocation of a mock "Sanhedrin" in France, in February 1807.

Ironically, many (though certainly not all) of the secular socialist Zionists who denounced religious Judaic messianism clung tenaciously to a fantasy-laden, utopian Marxist dream of a "just" (i.e. materially equal) society in the future for the "workers of the world." The more markedly Leftist groups among them also opposed Jewish national aspirations (Lord, 2001; Yariv, 1953). That dream excluded, of course, the bourgeoisie who lived in the fleshpots (that offered precious little to eat) of the little towns of Tel Aviv, Jerusalem or the even smaller town of Haifa in the 1920s and 1930s.

Zionism and the Biblical Vision of the Future

Moshe Meisels (under the pen-name of M. H. Amishai) provided a brilliant explanation of the future orientation of ancient Israel, of the Torah and the Prophets, and of Zionism as heir to the prophetic heritage. A glimpse of Amishai–Meisel's penetrating depiction of the Bible's remarkable concentration on the future is set out below (Amishai, 1981).

The earliest roots of the Biblical message of the future as the most important dimension of existence actually precedes the advent of the ancient Hebrews. Unlike the myths of other nations, no Hebrews were present at the time of the "myths of origin." The first man, Adam, was not a Hebrew. Moreover, the Biblical pre-Hebraic myth paints a picture of a world inhabited by many nations and languages existing before the Hebrews emerged in history, totally unlike the myths of the world around them that focused exclusively on their own people, and particularly on the role of the ruler's connection to the gods. The few remnants of the mythological literature produced by the pre-Israelite Hebrews that appear in the first few chapters of Genesis, depict an awareness of a vast social world whose diversity is explained in the myth of the Tower of Babel and the subsequent divergence and dispersion of peoples and languages. Out of this diverse world of peoples and cultures emerges the figure of Abraham.

The covenant with Abraham is the prototypic Hebraic worldview whose classic document in the book of Genesis is largely directed toward the future, at least on its latent level, not always obvious on the manifest level. Its message is one of comfort and hope for Abraham that his descendants will inherit "the Land" in perpetuity, for all future time. What Abraham received, or in more contemporary terms, what he anticipated or expected from his life of trial, after uprooting himself from his homeland and going to an unknown land that God "showed him," was to guarantee his descendants' future. He lived with a consciousness of being the "father of a nation." As such, his every act was devoted to perpetuating the nation-to-be and safeguarding its future.

Abraham's consciousness of his descendants' nationhood and its future was not occupied solely with the future as physical time in the natural world, but as a historic–cultural–consciously created and designed dimension of human existence, as the unfolding of the Divine and human will. It was not the danger of having his descendents' future terminated suddenly that concerned Abraham, nor was it the search for happiness taught by the ancient Greeks. Without the ability to fulfill the Divine will in the future, to live out our collective and individual history into the future, the present and the past become devoid of meaning. For Abraham, the father of the Hebrew nation, concern for the future expresses the fundamental purpose of existence. Abraham's covenants with God all focus on existence-into-the-future for which each person and each nation, including the Hebrew nation-to-be, bears responsibility. This sense of historical responsibility reaches explicit formulation in the amazing words of Deuteronomy (5: 9–10):

> For I the Lord thy God . . . visiting the guilt of the fathers upon the children, unto the third and fourth generations of them who hate me, and but showing kindness to the thousandth generation of those who love me and keep my commandments.

These verses convey the message that generations of people are responsible for one another, or what can be called "historical moralism." The concept of historical moralism stands in sharp distinction from "historical materialism" which is best renamed "materialist sociology" without the word "historical" because Marxist ideology had, in fact, little or nothing to do with history. Three thousand years after Abraham and 2,500 years after the Prophets of Israel, historical moralism has finally caught the attention of many nations and individuals in some parts of the world in the wake of the awareness of nuclear and ecological dangers threatening the continuity of the human race. The Prophets' warnings and promises about the future focused exclusively on events in the real world, not on any otherworldly, supernatural vision.

For Abraham and for all of Israel, the Land of Israel is the Promised Land, the land of Jewry's future. The Land and the People of Israel are indivisible because the land is the location of the People's future, namely its existence. Zionism's return to the Land is an affirmation of Jewry's future. Its long history in Exile is over, although not forgotten by any means. It is no longer possible for the Jewish People to live in the *Galut*, in Exile. The *Galut* has been destroyed, meaning that Jews who live outside of Israel in countries where they cannot have collective political representation or sovereignty, can no longer survive as a collectivity. The Jewish People can never again go into *Galut* and survive as a nation: That is the unequivocal conclusion to be reached from Jewry's history in the modern world, and in particular from the catastrophe of World War II that put a near-total end to the Jewish community of Europe whose origins go back to the second century BCE or earlier.

The nation of Israel, like all other nations, is, of course, subject to the powerful influences of contemporary world culture fixated on the present that includes just a few years into the future. Israel must not follow suit and slough off its responsibility for its long-term future. Zionism can and must continue to perform its historic role as Jewry's medium for striving to secure its collective future, in both its spiritual–cultural and histor-ical–national sense. Zionism has always been the road into the future for Judaism. Our future is our salvation (Schweid, 1996). Getting lost in the present by rejecting or forgetting the past on which Israel has built its future can be our damnation. To strive to reach upwards from our past in order to achieve our unique spiritual-cultural future will secure our existence on a perpetually higher plane. Jacob's ladder "was placed firmly on the ground, but its top-most rung reached to the sky" (Genesis 28: 12–15). Years later Jacob became Israel!

National History as a Universal Value

In all countries, people teach their offspring their national–cultural history and the meaning they attribute to the continuity of generations through the course of time. No nation entertains any doubts or hesitation in this matter. The citizens of the United States scrupulously consult the inten-tions of the "founding fathers" when it comes to understanding the Constitution and its application to contemporary public and legal dilemmas. One cannot overlook the extent to which the cultural heritage of Germany, France, China, and other countries emphasizes the meaning for the present of the deeds of their forebears centuries or longer beforehand. In some cases, these ancestors lived in what can be objectively called "mythological" times because there is very little or no documentation about the lives of the people involved. King Arthur was a British chieftain who won a decisive battle against the Anglo-Saxon invaders ca. 500 CE. The figure of Arthur always exerted great influence on the development of English cultural identity. The legends about Lancelot, the Knights of the Round Table, or Merlin the Magician, are myths that emerged many centuries later but are all closely linked to the figure of King Arthur in the English collective memory. The Vikings of the eighth, ninth, and tenth centuries did exist and affect history, but our knowledge of their lives is still very limited. Nevertheless, they are viewed as the ancestors of the Danes, Swedes and Norwegians who collect every scrap of archaeological evidence found about them. The twelfth century poem "La Chanson de Roland" exerted a powerful influence on French history, language, culture and identity even though none of the events or figures portrayed in that remarkable poem ever existed, except for Charlemagne himself. Nor did the Nibelungen ever exist, and yet they form an indelible part of German identity and cultural "history." All of these myths are draped in the clouds of time that hide their empirical–historical reality, were there ever such a reality. Nevertheless, the French attribute great significance to *La Chanson de Roland*, as the Germans do to the stories of Siegfried, Brunhilde, Wotan, etc. as the foundation of their identity and language. Most, if not all, of the *dramatis personae* of the Homeric epics – such as Agamemnon, Iphigenia, Achilles, Hector, Priam, Cassandra, Hercules and so forth – probably never walked the earth. These characters have been household names in the Western world for millennia. The question of their historical existence is a matter for antiquarians. The reality of Homer's heroes is not a matter of historical accuracy. The same can be said about how the peoples of China, India, Thailand, Vietnam, or Cambodia would react to questions about the stories of the life of Buddha or of Confucius. In the Far East, the stories of the life of Buddha wield enormous influence on the behavior of many millions of people, on public behavior and religious practice. Buddhists would dismiss questions about the historical authenticity of these legends as irrelevant.

In the case of the Jews, the situation is almost reversed. Jewry's historical record is supported by massive documentation. There is abundant written material from antiquity (1,200 BCE to 200 CE), most of it in the form of historical narratives or legends, as well as an enormous collection of religious and legal works, the extensive writings of the Hebrew prophets, the Wisdom literature, the books of the Apocrypha, Josephus, the Dead Sea Scrolls, etc. Of course, that does not mean that we can establish that there was indeed a specific person such as Abraham as depicted in the Bible. Yet, his "life history" is imprinted on the collective memory of the Jewish People, and on the memory of countless non-Jews, for all time. These works were followed by a vast number of texts produced over the 1,800 years of Jewish history after the Bar Kochba rebellion (135 CE) against Roman control in Palestine. Almost all of these works are accessible to anyone who wishes to read them. There is also an enormous amount of corroborating evidence from the archival and published documents in many countries, as well as from archaeology. Jewry has always been a historically conscious people about itself and about many of its neighboring nations. Any comparison of Judaic history (including myths) to that of other Western and even Far Eastern nations highlights the relatively well-documented historicity of Jewry's collective saga as a nation since antiquity. Of course there is a rich store of "myths" that form part of this historical heritage.

The most common sources of myth for Christians is, and remains, the Evangelists, Paul's Epistles, the writings of the Church Fathers and so forth, as is the Koran for Muslims. Post-Zionists would never presume to utter reservations about the inter-generational transmission of these texts, where history and myth are inextricably interwoven, as they have about the texts of the Jewish People.

Post-Zionism is Anti-Semitic in Essence

The denunciation of Jewry's behavior in certain cultural and political domains when these same standards or patterns are typical of most nations and individuals in the world is one of the common denominators of all classic manifestations of anti-Semitism. Yehezkel Kaufmann identified four salient characteristics for recognizing anti-Semitic statements (Kaufmann, 1939).

1 **Fabrication** – Accusing Jews of crimes/sins they never committed (the "Blood Libel" being one of most infamous examples).
2 **Generalization** – Holding all Jews responsible for the acts of an individual.
3 **Judaization** – Asserting that only Jews commit crimes/sins that are regularly committed by non-Jews.
4 **Discriminatory harshness** – Acts not considered to be crimes when performed by non-Jews are considered to be crimes when performed by Jews.

The major example of the first criterion mentioned above indicative of post-Zionist works is their assertion that famous Hebrew writers and historians were commissioned agents of the Zionist Organization. That assertion is pure fabrication, as we argued earlier in this essay.

The second criterion of anti-Semitism attributable to post-Zionist works (point 3, above) is their negation of the meaning that Jews in general and Zionists in particular attribute to Jewish history as a rationale and/or explanation for their contemporary behavior. For the post-Zionists, Zionism created a myth of historical continuity to "justify" or explain its current policies.

Thirdly, the post-Zionists' ideology is anti-Semitic not because it advocates animosity toward Jews as individuals, which is the meaning commonly attributed to the term "anti-Semitism," and not because they claim that the Jewish People is different from other peoples in religion, language, culture and behavior, which is no revelation to anyone because each nation differs from all others in some or all of these characteristics. The post-Zionists' negativism is directed toward Jewry as a collectivity and is embodied in their view that Jews differ from other nations in terms of what they may think and do! For the post-Zionists, the efforts made by Jews, including those of the Zionist enterprise, to transmit a sense of historical continuity and responsibility to the youth of Palestine/Israel and elsewhere for the fate of the Jewish People as an ethnic-national group constitutes an invasion by a collective ideology into the life of the individual. It also testifies to the ethno-centrism of Jews and Judaism. It matters not that teaching the public, young and old, about its historical heritage as part of the effort to transmit its messages to future generations is accepted as the unassailable right and duty of each and every nation or group. That is the very essence of the term universalism, not global uniformity! Would the post-Zionists condemn the entire world for what is universally agreed to be a positive, necessary and highly valued practice that lies at the heart of civilization itself? There can be no clearer indication of the post-Zionists' anti-Semitic orientation than its defamation of Zionism by accusing it of this universal act as if it were a crime. Simultaneous with this position, the PZs affirm the authenticity of the "tradition" of Arab nations or groups in and surrounding Israel who claim to replace Jewry's ownership of the Land of Israel.

It is transparent that the post-Zionists wish to disseminate a myth of their own, the myth of anti-Zionism woven out of the strands of deconstructionist nihilism and academic anti-Semitism. The negation of Judaic and Zionist history, culture, aspirations and vision, as preached by the post-Zionists, would effectively deprive Israel of its soul and leave it an aimless, haphazard mass of immigrants that the PZ writers claim it is. The super-liberal eschatologist Francis Fukuyama, for whom the democratic liberal state is the *summum bonum* of human statecraft and the end of the need for additional political conflict, admitted that his own logic led to the conclusion that postmodern liberal individualism was socially bankrupt. Societies without faith in their identity founded on their collective past, without aspirations for a collective future as a historical culture, had little prospect of social survival (Fukuyama, 1992).

Zionism's Reconstruction of Jewish Life and History

Zionism viewed through the Post-Zionist prism is bound to focus on death and destruction. Nihilism cannot conceivably concede the vast constructive Zionist enterprise in all walks of life: in the unique and unprecedented assemblage of Jews from all the countries of their dispersion and the enormous steps taken toward the reconstruction of Jewish life following its unfathomable decimation and degradation. Zionist Israel accomplished that, however incompletely, in a remarkably short span of time and in the face of relentless harassment, both from within and from outside the country. The post-Zionists, and other Jewish groups who believe they thrive on pure spirituality (the extremists among the ultra-Orthodox *Haredim*, some fringe Reform or even Conservative religious groups scattered in the United States, some Jewish academics in Western universities, and the remnant Marxian materialists), would prefer that Jewry remain encased in the clouds of ancient myth. Israel should not "dirty its hands" by tinkering with the real world so obviously over-laden with huge impediments and bitter disappointments (Fackenheim, 1978).

Remember! The very first Hebrew myth about human kind that dates from over 3,000 years ago teaches that once people mature and emerge from Paradise into the light of the real world, there is no return to the protection of our childhood dreams. All human societies have no choice but to cover their shame and build their life into the future the best they can. Myths continue to flourish only in our unrequited aspirations.

Notes

1   Two recent books deal extensively with other aspects of post-Zionist writings. Efraim Karsh evaluates revisionist historians in his *Fabricating Israeli History*, London: Frank Cass, 1997 (second revised edition, 2000); and the role of socialism and of some Israeli writers in developing the post-Zionist perspective is discussed by Amnon Lord in *The Israeli Left: From socialism to nihilism*, Tel Aviv: ACPR Publications and Tammuz Publishers, 2000

(Hebrew). These excellent volumes do not treat the works of post-Zionist sociologists that are the subject of the present work. Earlier works in Hebrew by Yehezkel Kaufmann present a scathing criticism of the ideas of Socialist Zionists in Europe and Palestine/Israel. See Kaufmann's *Golah v'Neichar* (Exile and Alienation), vol. 2, 1932; *B'chevlei Ha-zman* (In the Throes of Time), 1936; and *Bein N'tivot* (Between Paths), 1952.

2   The well-known figures (excluding politicians who held official positions in various institutions) mentioned (directly or by implication) in Almog's book, who allegedly served as commissioned agents of Zionism (just "who or what" in Zionism is not stated) include the following: Yitschak Lamdan, Sh. Shalom, Uri Zvi Greenberg, Haim Nachman Bialik, Ephraim Shmueli, Ben-Zion Dinur, Eliezer Rieger, Reuven Grossman, Eliezer Steinman, Avraham Broides, Baruch Ben-Yehudah, Sh. Ben-Zion, Z'ev Vilnai, Avraham Shlonsky, and others. (See the list of educators mentioned on page 57 of Almog's book.)

References

Almog, Oz, *The Sabra – A profile*. Tel Aviv: Am Oved, 1997 (Hebrew).

Amishai, Moshe, *Essays on Zionism*. Jerusalem: The Zionist Library of the World Zionist Organization and the Bialik Institute, 1981 (Hebrew).

Becker, Yakov (Ed.), *The Teachings of David Ben-Gurion*. Tel Aviv: Yavneh Publishing Co., 1958 (Hebrew), p. 28.

Ben-Yehuda, Nachum, *The Masada Myth: Collective memory and mythmaking in Israel*: Madison, WI: University of Wisconsin Press, 1995.

Cassirer, Ernst, *The Philosophy of Symbolic Forms, vol. 2: Mythical thought*. New Haven: Yale University Press, 1925/1955 (translated from the German).

Collingwood, R. G., *The Idea of History*. Oxford: Oxford University Press, 1946/1993. pp. 218–19.

Fackenheim, Emil, *The Jewish Return into History*. New York: Schocken Books, 1978.

Fukuyama, Francis, *The End of History and the Last Man*. New York: The Free Press, 1992.

Kaufmann, Yehezkel, *Exile and Alienation*. Tel Aviv: Dvir, 1930–2 (Hebrew).

——, *In the Throes of Time*. Tel Aviv: Dvir, 1936 (Hebrew).

——, "Our Redemption and the Evaluation of Ourselves." *Moznayim* 43, 1939, (Hebrew), pp. 129–54.

Kaufmann, Yehezkel, *The History of Israelite Religion, vol. 1*. Jerusalem: Mosad Bialik and Dvir, 1952 (Hebrew).

——, *Between Paths*. Haifa: The Reali School, 1952 (Hebrew).

Ohana, D. and Wistrich, R., "Introduction." In D. Ohana and R. Wistrich (eds.), *Myth and Memory: The transformations of Israeli conciousness*. Jerusalem and Tel Aviv: Van Leer Foundation and the Kibbutz Hameuchad, 1996 (Hebrew).

Schweid, Eliezer, "Myth and Historical Memory in Modern Jewish Thought." In D. Ohana and R. Wistrich (eds.), *Myth and Memory: The transformations of Israeli consciousness*. Jerusalem and Tel Aviv: Van Leer Foundation and the Kibbutz Hameuchad, 1996 (Hebrew).

Shmueli, Ephraim, *The History of Our People in Modern Times*. Tel Aviv: Yavneh Publishing Co., 1950 (Hebrew).

Tudor, Henry, *Political Myth*. London: Pall Mall Press, 1972.

Zerubavel, Yael *Recovered Roots: Collective memory and the making of Israeli national tradition*. Chicago: University of Chicago Press, 1995.

3

Israeli Intellectuals and Israeli Politics

EDWARD ALEXANDER

In his essay of 1838 on Jeremy Bentham, J. S. Mill wrote that "specula-tive philosophy, which to the superficial appears a thing so remote from the business of life and the outward interests of men, is in reality the thing on earth which most influences them, and in the long run overbears every other influence save those which it must itself obey." Of course Mill was not always willing to wait for the long run and was often tempted by shortcuts whereby speculative philosophers and other intellectuals could make their influence felt upon government. Frightened by Tocqueville's observations of American democracy, Mill sought to prevent the "tyranny of the majority" by an elaborate scheme of plural voting which would give everybody one vote but intellectuals a larger number; when he awoke to the folly and danger of such a scheme he switched his allegiance to propor-tional representation as a means of allowing what he calls in *On Liberty* the wise and noble few to exercise their due influence over the mindless majority.

By now we have had enough experience of the influence of intellectuals in politics to be skeptical of Mill's schemes. To look back over the major intellectual journals of this country in the years prior to and during World War II – not only Trotskyist publications like *New International* or Dwight Macdonald's *Politics*, but the highbrow modernist and Marxist *Partisan Review* – is to be appalled by the spectacle of the finest minds of America vociferous in opposition to prosecuting the war against Hitler, which in their view was just a parochial struggle between two dying capi-talist forces. The pacifism of English intellectuals in the late thirties led

George Orwell to declare that some ideas are so stupid that only intellectuals could believe them; and in one of his *Tribune* columns of 1943 he said of the left-wing rumor in London that America had entered the war only in order to crush a budding English socialist revolution that "one has to belong to the intelligentsia to believe something like that. No ordinary man could be such a fool."

If we look at the influence of Israeli intellectuals upon Israeli policy in recent decades, and especially during the Yitzhak Rabin–Shimon Peres and Ehud Barak governments, we may conclude that Mill and Orwell were both right, Mill in stressing the remarkable power of ideas, Orwell in insisting that such power often works evil, not good.

Among the numerous misfortunes that have beset the Zionist enterprise from its inception – the unyielding hardness of the land allegedly flowing with milk and honey, the failure of the Jews of the Diaspora to move to Zion except under duress, the constant burden of peril arising from Arab racism and imperialism – was the premature birth of an intellectual class, especially a literary intelligentsia. The quality of Israel's intelligentsia may be a matter of dispute. Gershom Scholem once remarked, mischievously, that talent goes where it is needed, and in Israel it was needed far more urgently in the military than in the universities, the literary community, the arts, and journalism. But the influence of this intelligentsia is less open to dispute than its quality. When Shimon Peres (who views himself as an intellectual) launched his ill-fated election campaign of spring 1996 he surrounded himself with artists and intellectuals on the stage of Tel Aviv's Mann Auditorium.[1]

Three months earlier, he had listed as one of the three future stars of the Labor Party the internationally famous novelist Amos Oz, the same Amos Oz who was notorious among religiously observant Jewish "settlers" for having referred to their organization Gush Emunim (Block of the Faithful) in a speech of June 1989, in language generally reserved for thieves and murderers: they were, he told a Peace Now gathering of about 20,00 people in Tel Aviv's Malchei Yisrael Square "a small sect, a messianic sect, obtuse and cruel, [who] emerged a few years ago from a dark corner of Judaism, and [are] threatening to . . . impose on us a wild and insane blood ritual . . . .They are guilty of crimes against humanity."[2]

Intellectuals in many countries have adopted the motto: "the *other* country, right or wrong," and worked mightily to undermine national confidence in their country's heritage, founding principles, *raison d'être*. But such intellectuals do not usually arise within fifty years of their country's founding, and in no case except Israel have intellectuals cultivated their "alienation" in a country whose "right to exist" is considered an acceptable subject of discussion among otherwise respectable people and nations. As Midge Decter shrewdly put it in May 1996, "A country only half a century old is not supposed to have a full fledged accomplished literary intelligentsia . . . .This is an extravagance only an old and stable country should be allowed to indulge in" (Decter, 1996, p. 7).

The seeds of trouble amongst intellectuals in Zion antedated the state itself. On May Day 1936 the Labor Zionist leader Berl Katznelson asked, angrily, "Is there another people on earth whose sons are so emotionally and mentally twisted that they consider everything their nation does despicable and hateful, while every murder, rape and robbery committed by their enemies fills their hearts with admiration and awe? As long as a Jewish child . . . can come to the Land of Israel, and here catch the virus of self-hate . . . let not our conscience be still" (Katznelson, 1961, p. 18).

But what for Katznelson was a sick aberration would later become the normal condition among a very large segment of Israeli intellectuals. A major turning point came in 1967, when the doctors of Israel's soul, a numerous fraternity, concluded that in winning a defensive war which, if lost, would have brought its destruction, Israel had bartered its soul for a piece of land. The Arab nations, shrewdly sensing that Jews were far less capable of waging the war of ideas than the war of planes and tanks, quickly transformed the rhetoric of their opposition to Israel's existence from the Right to the Left, from the aspiration to "turn the Mediterranean red with Jewish blood" (the battle cry of the months preceding the Six Day War) to the pretended search for a haven for the homeless. This calculated appeal to liberals, as Ruth Wisse has amply demonstrated (Wisse, 1992), created legions of critics of the Jewish state, especially among devout believers in the progressive improvement and increasing enlightenment of the human race. Israeli intellectuals who were willing to express, especially in dramatic hyperbole, criticism of their own country's alleged racism, imperialism, and religious fanaticism quickly became celebrities in the American press. They were exalted by people like Anthony Lewis as courageous voices of dissent, even though what they had joined was, of course, a community of consent.

But it was not until a decade later that the Israeli intelligentsia turned massively against the state, against Zionism, against Judaism itself. For in 1977 the Labor Party lost its 29-year-old ownership of government to people it considered its cultural inferiors, people Meron Benvenisti described as follows: "I remember traveling on a Haifa bus and looking around at my fellow passengers with contempt and indifference – almost as lower forms of human life" (Benvenisti, 1986, p. 70). Such hysteria (which burst forth again in May 1996 when Benjamin Netanyahu won the election) now became the standard pose of the alienated Israeli intellectual, and it was aggressively disseminated by American publications such as the *New York Times*, ever eager for Israeli-accented confirmation of its own views. Amos Oz, for example, took to the pages of the *New York Times Magazine* during the Lebanon War to deplore the imminent demise of Israel's "soul": "Israel could have become an exemplary state . . . a small-scale laboratory for democratic socialism." But that great hope, Oz lamented, was dashed by the arrival of Holocaust refugees, various "anti-socialist" Zionists, "chauvinistic, militaristic, and xenophobic" North African Jews, and so forth.[3] (These are essentially the reasons why it was not until Menachem Begin became prime minister that the Ethiopian Jews could come to Israel.) By 1995 Oz was telling *New York Times* readers that supporters of the Likud party were accomplices of Hamas. Even after spiritual brethren of Hamas massacred almost three thousand people in the United States on September 11, 2001, Oz declared that the enemy was not in any sense the radical Islamist or Arabic mentality but simply "fanaticism," and that in any case the most pressing matter he could think of was to give "Palestinians their natural right to self-determination." For good measure he added the patently false assertion that "almost all [Muslims] are as shocked and aggrieved [by the suicide bombings of America] as the rest of mankind."[4] Apparently Oz had missed all those photos of Muslims round the world handing out candy, ululating, dancing, and jubilating over dead Jews and dead Americans. It was a remarkable performance, which made one wonder whether Oz gets to write about politics because he is a novelist or gets his reputation as a novelist because of his political views.

People like Benvenisti – sociologist, deputy mayor of Jerusalem until fired by Teddy Kollek, and favorite authority on Israel for many years of the *New York Times* and *New York Review of Books* – foreshadowed the boasting of the intellectual spokesmen of recent Labor governments that they were not only post-Zionist but also post-Jewish in their thinking. Benvenisti recalled proudly how "We would observe Yom Kippur by loading quantities of food onto a raft and swimming out with it to an offshore islet in the Mediterranean, and there we would while away the whole day feasting. It was a flagrant demonstration of our rejection of religious and Diaspora values" (Benvenisti, 1986, p. 34).

Anecdotal evidence of the increasingly shrill anti-Israelism (or worse) of Israeli intellectuals is only too easy to amass. Some years ago the sculptor Yigal Tumarkin stated that "When I see the black-coated *Haredim* with the children they spawn, I can understand the Holocaust."[5] Ze'ev Sternhell, Hebrew University expert on fascism, proposed destroying the Jewish settlements with IDF tanks as a means of boosting national morale.[6] In 1969 the guru of Labor Party intellectuals, the late Professor Yeshayahu Leibowitz, began to talk of the inevitable

"Nazification" of the Israeli nation and society. By the time of the Lebanon War he had become an international celebrity because of his use of the epithet "Judeo–Nazi" to describe the Israeli army. When Iraq invaded Kuwait in 1990, he outdid even himself by declaring (in words redolent of what Katznelson had deplored in 1936): "Everything Israel has done, and I emphasize – everything, in the past 23 years is either evil stupidity or stupidly evil." And in 1993 Leibowitz would be honored by the government of Yitzhak Rabin with the Israel Prize.

In third place after Oz and Benvenisti among the resources of intellectual insight into Israel's soul frequently mined by Anthony Lewis, Thomas Friedman, and like-minded journalists is David Grossman, the novelist. Grossman established his credentials as an alienated intellectual commentator on the state of his country's mind in a book called *The Yellow Wind* (Grossman, 1988) an account of his seven-week journey through the "West Bank," a journey undertaken in order to understand "how an entire nation like mine, an enlightened nation by all accounts, is able to train itself to live as a conqueror without making its own life wretched" (Grossman, 1988, p. 212). This is a complicated book, not without occasional patches of honesty. But its true flavor can be suggested by two successive chapters dealing with culture and books, especially religious ones. Grossman first visits the Jewish settlement of Ofra, at which he arrives fully armed with suspicion, hostility, and partisanship, a "wary stranger" among people who remind him, he says, of nothing human, especially when they are "in the season of their messianic heat" (Grossman, 1988, p. 52). In Ofra, Grossman does not want "to let down his guard" and be "seduced" by the Sabbath "warmth" and "festivity" of these wily Jews. Although most of his remarks to Arabs in conversation recounted in *The Yellow Wind* are the perfunctory gestures of a straight man to whom his interlocutors pay no serious attention, he angrily complains that the Jewish settlers don't listen to or "display a real interest" in him. He asks them to "imagine themselves in their Arab neighbors' places" (p. 37) and is very much the angry schoolmaster when they don't dance to his tune or accept his pretense that this act of sympathetic imagination is devoid of political meaning. Neither are the settlers nimble enough to make the appropriate reply to Grossman: "My dear fellow, we will imagine ourselves as Arabs if you will imagine yourself as a Jew." But Grossman has no intention of suspending his own rhythms of existence long enough to penetrate the inner life of these alien people: "What have I to do with them?" (p. 48). His resentment is as much cultural as political. He complains that the settlers have "little use for culture," speak bad Hebrew, indulge in "Old Diaspora type" humor, and own no books, "with the exception of religious texts" (p. 46). And these, far from mitigating the barbarity of their owners, aggravate it. The final image of the Jews in this long chapter is of "potential [!] terrorists now rocking over their books" (p. 51). For Grossman, the conjectured terrorism of Jews is a far more grievous matter than the actual terrorism of Arabs.

The following chapter also treats of culture and books, including religious ones. Grossman has come to Bethlehem University, one of several universities in the territories that have been punningly described as branches of a PLO State. Here Grossman, though he admits the school to be "a stronghold of the Democratic Front for the Liberation of Palestine," sees no terrorists rocking over books, but rather idyllic scenes that remind him of "the pictures of Plato's school in Athens" (p. 57). Bubbling with affection, eager to ascribe only the highest motives, Grossman is now willing to forgive even readers of religious books. He has not so much as a snort or a sneer for the Bethlehem English professor who ascribes Arabs' supreme sensitivity to lyric rhythm in English poetry to the "rhythm of the Koran flow[ing] through their blood" (p. 59). The author's ability to spot racism at a distance of twenty miles when he is among Jews slackens when timeless racial categories are invoked in Bethlehem.

When the Labor Party returned to power in 1992, so too did the Israeli intellectuals and their disciples. People once (rather naïvely) casually referred to as extremists moved to the centers of power in Israeli government and policy formation. Dedi Zucker, who used to accuse Jewish "settlers" of drinking blood on Passover, and Yossi Sarid, who once shocked Israelis by declaring that Holocaust Memorial Day meant nothing to him, and Shulamit Aloni, whose statements about religious Jews would probably have landed her in jail in European countries that have laws against anti-Semitic provocation, all became cabinet ministers or prominent spokesmen in the government of Rabin. Two previously obscure professors laid the foundations for the embrace of Yasser Arafat, one of the major war criminals of the twentieth century, responsible for the murder of more Jews than anyone since Hitler and Stalin. The Oslo process put the PLO well on the way to an independent Palestinian state (a state, it should be added, that commands the allegiance of far more Israeli intellectuals than does the idea of a Jewish one). Amos Oz and A. B. Yehoshua and David Grossman were delighted, with the last of this trio assuring Anthony Lewis that Israel had finally given up its "instinctive suspicion," and that although "we have the worst terrorism," "we are making peace."[7] Benvenisti proved harder to satisfy. He published a book called *Intimate Enemies* (Benvenisti, 1995) the ads for which carried glowing endorsements from Thomas Friedman and Professor Ian Lustick, in which he proposed dissolution of the State of Israel.

Only a few figures within Israel's cultural establishment expressed dismay at what was happening. The philosopher Eliezer Schweid warned that a nation which starts by abandoning its cultural memories ends by abandoning its physical existence.[8] Amos Perlmutter analyzed the "post-Zionism" of Israeli academics as an all-out attack on the validity of the state.[9] A still more notable exception to the general euphoria of this class was Aharon Megged. In June of 1994 this well-known writer and long-time supporter of the Labor Party wrote an explosive article in the newspaper *Ha'aretz* on "The Israeli Suicide Drive" in which he connected the Rabin government's record of endless unreciprocated concessions to a PLO that had not even cancelled its Charter calling for Israel's destruction, to the self-destructiveness that had long before infected Israel's intellectual classes. "Since the Six Day War," Megged wrote, "and at an increasing pace, we have witnessed a phenomenon which probably has no parallel in history: an emotional and moral identification by the majority of Israel's intelligentsia with people openly committed to our annihilation." Megged argued that since 1967 the Israeli intelligentsia had more and more come "to regard religious, cultural, and emotional affinity to the land . . . with sheer contempt"; and he observed that the equation of Israelis with Nazis had become an article of faith and the central idea of "*thousands* [emphasis added] of articles and reports in the press, hundreds of poems, . . . dozens of documentary and feature films, exhibitions and paintings and photos." He also shrewdly remarked on the methods by which anti-Zionist Israeli intellectuals disseminated their message and reputations. Writers like Benny Morris, Ilan Pappe, and Baruch Kimmerling "mostly publish first in English to gain the praise of the West's 'justice seekers.' Their works are then quickly translated into Arabic and displayed in Damascus, Cairo and Tunis. Their conclusion is almost uniform: that in practice Zionism amounts to an evil, colonialist conspiracy . . ."[10]

The minds of the majority of those who carried on the Oslo Process of the Israel government from 1993 to 1996 were formed by the writers, artists, and publicists whom Megged excoriated. Although Shimon Peres' utterances about the endless war for independence which his country has been forced to wage often seemed to come from a man who had taken leave of the actual world, they were rooted in the "post-Zionist," post-Jewish, and universalist assumptions of the Israeli intelligentsia. Just as they were contemptuous of any tie with the land of Israel, so he repeatedly alleged that land plays no part in Judaism or even in the Jewish political philosophy that names itself after a specific mountain called Zion. Like the Israeli intelligentsia, he accused Israel's religious Jews of an atavistic attachment to territory over "spirit," claiming that Judaism is "ethical/moral and spiritual, and not an idolatry of soil-worship".[11] Just as Israeli intellectuals nimbly pursued and imitated the latest cultural fads of America and Europe, hoping to be assimilated by the great world outside Israel, so did Peres hope that Israel would one day be admitted into the Arab League.[12]

Despite the enlistment of then President William Clinton as his campaign manager, and the nearly unanimous support he received from the Israeli and world news media, to say nothing of the herd of independent thinkers from the universities, and the rented academics of the think tanks, Shimon Peres and his Oslo process were decisively rejected by the Jewish voters of Israel. Predictably, the Israeli intellectuals (not guessing that Labor's successors would blindly continue the process) reacted with melodramatic hysteria. David Grossman, in the *New York Times* of 31 May, wailed sanctimoniously that "Israel has moved toward the extreme right . . . more militant, more religious, more fundamentalist, more tribal and more racist.[13]

Among the American liberal supporters of Israel's intellectual elite, only the *New Republic* appeared somewhat chastened by the election result. Having for years, perhaps decades, celebrated the ineffable genius of Shimon Peres and his coterie, the magazine turned angrily upon the Israeli intellectuals for failing to grasp that "their association with Peres was one of the causes of his defeat." "Disdainful of [Jews] from traditional communities, they thought of and called such people 'stupid Sephardim.'" This contempt for Jews from Arab countries expresses itself in a cruel paradox, for it coexists with a credulity about, and esteem for, the Middle East's Christians and Muslims. Such esteem, coupled with a derisive attitude toward Jewish symbols and texts, rituals, remembrances and anxieties, sent tens of thousands to Netanyahu.[14]

The most ambitious attempt to trace the history and analyze the causes of the maladies of Israeli intellectuals is Yoram Hazony's book *The Jewish State* (2000). Within months of its publication the dire consequences of the Oslo accords, post-Zionism's major political achievement, became visible to everybody in Israel in the form of the *Second Intifada*, otherwise known as the Oslo war, a campaign of unremitting atrocities launched by Yasser Arafat when after only 97 percent of his demands, including an independent Palestinian state, had been met by the government of the hapless Ehud Barak.

The Jewish State is a broadside aimed at those Israelis who, in what its author calls "a carnival of self-loathing," (Hazony, 2000, p. 339) are busily eating away at the Jewish foundations of that state. The book's very title is a conscious affront to Israel's *branja*, a slang term for the "progressive" and "enlightened" experts whose views, according to Supreme Court Chief Justice Aharon Barak, should determine the court's decisions on crucial matters. For these *illuminati* have sought to enlist no less a figure than Theodor Herzl in their campaign to de-Judaize the State of Israel. Nearly all the "post-Zionists" discussed in *The Jewish State* claim that Herzl did not intend the title of his famous book to be *The Jewish State* at all, that the state he proposed was in no significant sense intrinsically Jewish, and that he believed in a total separation of religion from the state. Hazony argues (and massively demonstrates) that Herzl believed a Jewish state was essential to rescue the Jewish people from both anti-Semitism and assimilation, the forces that were destroying Jewish life throughout the Diaspora. (Most of Herzl's rabbinic opponents, of course, argued that Zionism was itself but a thinly veiled form of assimilation.)

Hazony's *Jewish State* has two purposes. The first is to show that "the idea of the Jewish state is under systematic attack from its own cultural and intellectual establishment" (p. xxvii). These "culture makers" have not only renounced the idea of a Jewish state – "A state," claims Amos Oz, "cannot be Jewish, just as a chair or a bus cannot be Jewish" (338). The writers who dominate Israeli culture, Hazony argues, are adept at imagining what it is like to be an Arab; they have, like the aforementioned David Grossman, much more trouble imagining what it is like to be a Jew.

If Israeli intellectuals were merely supplying their own illustration of Orwell's quip about the unique susceptibility of intellectuals to stupid ideas, their hostility to Israel's Jewish traditions and Zionist character would not merit much concern. But Hazony shows that they have had spectacular success, amounting to a virtual *coup d'état*, in their political struggle for a post-Jewish state. "What is perhaps most remarkable about the advance of the new ideas in Israeli government policy is the way in which even the most sweeping changes in Israel's character as a Jewish state can be effected by a handful of intellectuals, with only the most minimal of opposition from the country's political leaders or the public" (p. 52).

The post-Zionists have imposed their views in the new public-school curriculum, in the Basic Laws of the country, and in the IDF, whose code of ethics now excludes any allusion to Jewish or Zionist principles. The author of the code is Asa Kasher, one of Israel's most enterprising post-Zionists, who has modestly described his composition as "the most profound code of ethics in the world of military ethics, in particular, and in the world of professional ethics, in general" – so terminally profound, in fact, that an Israeli soldier "doesn't need to think or philosophize anymore. Someone else already . . . did the thinking and decided. There are no dilemmas" (pp. 53, 56).

The ultimate triumph of post-Zionism, Hazony argues, came in its conquest of the Foreign Ministry and the mind of Shimon Peres. Both came to the conclusion that Israel must retreat from the idea of an independent Jewish state. In the accord reached with Egypt in 1978 and even in the 1994 accord with Jordan, Israeli governments had insisted that the Arab signatories recognize the Jewish state's "sovereignty, territorial integrity, and political independence" (p. 58). But the Oslo accords with the fanatically anti-Zionist PLO conceded on every one of these issues; and if the agreement with the PLO was partly an effect of post-Zionism, it was an effect that became in turn a cause – giving respectability and wide exposure to post-Zionist political prejudices formerly confined to academic circles.

Thereafter, Peres and his Foreign Office routinely promoted the interests not of a sovereign Jewish state but of the (largely Arab) Middle East. In a reversal of policy akin to that of the Soviet Foreign Ministry in the wake of Stalin's pact with Hitler, Uri Savir and other Foreign Ministry officials exhorted American Jews who had for decades resisted the Arab campaign to blacken Israel's reputation to support US foreign aid to the two chief blackeners, the PLO and Syria. They – it was alleged – needed dollars much more than Israel. Peres himself, as we observed earlier, carried the post-Zionist campaign for assimilation and universalism to the global level, grandly announcing in December 1994 that "Israel's next goal should be to become a member of the Arab League" (p. 67).

The second (and much longer and more nuanced) part of Hazony's book has a two-fold purpose. The first is to write the history of the ideological and political struggle within the Jewish world itself over the idea of the Jewish state, paying particular attention to how that ideal, which a few decades ago had been axiomatic among virtually all Jews the world over, had so quickly "been brought to ruin among the cultural leadership of the Jewish state itself" (p. 78). Hazony's second aim as historian is to demonstrate the power of ideas, especially the truth of John Stuart Mill's axiom about the practical potency, in the long run, of (apparently useless) speculative philosophy. It was the power of ideas that enabled philosopher Martin Buber and other opponents of the Jewish state to break Ben-Gurion and to undermine the practical-minded stalwarts of Labor Zionism. (Likud hardly figures in this book). The quarrels between Ben-Gurion and Begin have from Hazony's perspective "the character of a squabble between the captain and the first mate of a sinking ship" (p. 79).

Hazony is a masterful political and cultural historian, and his fascinating account of the long struggle of Buber (and his Hebrew University acolytes) against Herzl and Ben-Gurion's conception of a genuinely Jewish state is told with tremendous verve and insight. Buber is at once the villain and the hero of this book. He is the villain in his relentless opposition to a Jewish state; in his licentious equations between Labor Zionists and Nazis; in his fierce anti-(Jewish) immigration stance (announced the day after he himself had immigrated from Germany in 1938). But he is the hero because his posthumous ideological victory over Labor Zionism – most of today's leading post-Zionists claim that their minds were formed by Buber and his bi-nationalist Brit Shalom/Ihud allies at Hebrew University – is in Hazony's view the most stunning example of how ideas and myths are in the long run of more political importance than kibbutzim and settlements. Because Buber understood the way in which culture eventually determines politics and grasped the potency of books and journals and (most of all) universities, his (to Hazony) malignant influence now carries the day in Israel's political as well as its cultural wars.

Hazony argues that since the fall of Ben-Gurion Israel has had no Prime Minister – not Golda Meir, not Menachem Begin – who was an "idea-maker." Even the very shrewd Ben-Gurion and Berl Katznelson (who presciently warned of the dangers lurking in the "intellectual famine" (p. 299) of Labor Israel were slow to recognize the potentially disastrous consequences of entrusting the higher education of their children to a university largely controlled (for twenty-four years) by the anti-Zionist Judah Magnes and largely staffed by faculty he recruited. Magnes, in language foreshadowing the clichés of today's post-Zionists, charged that the Jewish settlement in Palestine had been "born in sin" (p. 203). Moreover, he believed that seeing history from the Arabs' historical perspective was one of the main reasons for establishing the Hebrew University.

Hazony's book is written backwards, something like a murder mystery. He begins with a dismaying, indeed terrifying picture of a nearly moribund people, exhausted, confused, aimless – their traditional Labor Zionist assumptions declared "effectively dead" by their formerly Labor Zionist leaders, most crucially Shimon Peres. He then moves backward to seek the reasons why the Zionist enterprise is in danger of being dismantled, not by Israel's Arab enemies (who gleefully watch the spectacle unfold), but by its own heavily petted intellectual, artistic, and political elite – professors, writers, luminaries in the visual arts.

The material in the early chapters is shocking, and I speak as one who thought he had seen it all: the visiting sociologist from Hebrew University who adorned his office at my university with a PLO recruiting poster; the Tel Aviv University philosophy professor who supplied Noam Chomsky's supporters with a letter of kashrut certifying the "lifelong dedication to Israel" of their (Israel-hating) idol; the Haifa University sociologist active in the American-Arab Anti-Discrimination League (a PLO front group); the contingent of Israeli professors taking up arms on behalf of the great prevaricator Edward Said. But the material Hazony has collected (and dissected) from Israel's post-Zionist and post-Jewish intellectuals shocks me nevertheless. Compared with the Baruch Kimmerlings, the Asa Kashers, the Ilan Pappes, and other protagonists in Hazony's tragedy, Austria's Jorg Haider, the right-wing demagogue about whom the Israeli government kicked up such a fuss not so long ago, is a Judeophile and Lover of Zion.

Hazony carefully refrains from applying the term "anti-Semitic" to even the most extreme defamations of Jewish tradition and of the Jewish state by post-Zionists and their epigones. But surely such reticence is unnecessary when the secret has long been out. As far back as May 1987 the Israeli humorist and cartoonist Dosh, in a column in the Israeli newspaper *Ma'ariv*, drew a picture of a shopper in a store that specialized in anti-Semitic merchandise reaching for the top shelf – on which lay the most expensive item, adorned by a Stuermer-like caricature of a Jew and prominently labeled "Made in Israel." The article this cartoon illustrated spoke of Israel's need to increase exports by embellishing products available elsewhere in the world with unique local characteristics. Israel had done this with certain fruits and vegetables in the past, and now she was doing it with defamations of Israel, produced in Israel. Customers were getting more selective, no longer willing to make do with grade B merchandise produced by British leftists or French neo-Nazis. No, they wanted authentic material, from local sources; and Israeli intellectuals, artists, playwrights, were responding with alacrity to the opportunity.

But Dosh had spoken merely of a specialty shop. To accommodate the abundant production of Hazony's gallery of post-Zionist/post-Jewish defamers of Israel (both the people and the Land) would require a department store twice the size of Macy's or Harrod's. On bargain day, one imagines the following recitation by the elevator operator: "First floor, Moshe Zimmermann, Yeshayahu Leibowitz, and 68 other members of the progressive and universalist community on Israelis as Nazis; second floor, A. B. Yehoshua on the need for Israeli Jews to become "normal" by converting to Christianity or Islam; third floor, Boaz Evron in justification of Vichy France's anti-Jewish measures; fourth floor, Idith Zertal on Zionist absorption of Holocaust refugees as a form of rape; fifth floor, Benny Morris on Zionism as ethnic cleansing; attic, Shulamit Aloni on Zionism (also Judaism) as racism; basement, Ya'akov Yovel justifying the medieval blood libel; sub-basement, Yigal Tumarkin justifying Nazi murder of (religious) Jews. Watch your step, please."

The Jewish State is a formidable but not a flawless book. In his discussion of Israeli writers, Hazony sometimes forgets the difference between imaginative literature and discursive essays or public statements. He also occasionally overreaches himself, as when he drops Aharon Appelfeld into the same political–cultural boat, where I am sure he does not belong, with Amos Oz and David Grossman. In the second part of the book, he lays blame on Ben-Gurion's Hebrew University antagonists for forming the minds of the post-Zionists, but does not account for the fact that the politically most important post-Zionist, Peres, was the personal protégé of Ben-Gurion himself. On one or two occasions, too, he forgets that ideas are radically defenseless against the uses (and misuses) to which they are put. The fact that Shulamit Aloni assigns Buber responsibility for her views does not necessarily mean he entirely deserves that burden.

Although Hazony's argument for the large role played by Israel's professoriat in dismantling Labor Zionism is convincing, it cannot be a sufficient cause of current post-Zionism and post-Judaism. The habitual language of post-Zionists, and most especially their hammering insistence on the contradiction between being Jewish and being human, is exactly the language of European Jewish ideologues of assimilation over a century ago. Gidon Samet, one of the numerous resident ideologues of post-Judaism and post-Zionism at *Ha'aretz*, is not far from the truth when he likens their attractions to those of American junk food and junk-music: "Madonna and Big Macs," Samet says, "are only the most peripheral of examples" of the wonderful blessings of Israel's new "normalness" (Hazony, pp. 71–2). Of course, whatever we may think of those who in 1900 urged fellow-Jews to cease being Jewish in order to join universal humanity, they at least were not promoting this sinister distinction in full knowledge of how it would be used by Hitler; the same cannot be said of contemporary Israeli ideologues of assimilation and universalism **(see chapter 7)**.

Most readers of post-Zionist outpourings have little to fall back on except their native mistrust of intellectuals. Thus, when Hebrew University professor Moshe Zimmermann declares that Zionism "imported" anti-Semitism into the Middle East, it requires knowledge (not much, to be sure) of history to recognize the statement as preposterous. But sometimes the post-Zionists are tripped up by overconfidence into lies that even the uninstructed can easily detect. Thus Avishai Margalit, a Hebrew University philosophy professor spiritually close to, if not quite a card-carrying member of, the post-Zionists, in a *New York Review of Books* essay of 1988 called "The Kitsch of Israel," heaped scorn upon the "children's room" at Yad Vashem with its "tape-recorded" voices of children crying out in Yiddish, 'Mame, Tate [Mother, Father].'" Yad Vashem is a favorite target of the post-Zionists because they believe it encourages Jews to think not only that they were singled out for annihilation by the Nazis but also – how unreasonable of them! – to want to make sure they do not get singled out for destruction again. But, as any

Jerusalemite or tourist who can get over to Mount Herzl will quickly discover, there is no "children's room" and there are no taped voices at Yad Vashem. There is a memorial to the murdered children and a tape-recorded voice that reads their names.[15] Margalit's skullduggery is by no means the worst of its kind among those Israelis involved in derogating the memory and history of the country's Jewish population. But it comes as no surprise to learn from Hazony that Margalit believes Israel is morally obligated to offer Arabs "special rights" for the protection of their culture and to be "neutral" toward the Jews. With such neutrality as Margalit's, who needs belligerence?

In Hazony's book, Israel has perhaps found its latter-day Jeremiah, but given the widespread tone-deafness of the country's enlightened classes (Tuchman, 1984) to their Jewish heritage, perhaps what is needed at the moment is an Israeli Jonathan Swift, especially the Swift who wrote the verses about "gave the little wealth he had/ to build a house for fools and mad;/and showed by one satiric touch,/ no nation wanted it so much."

I began this essay with statements by J. S. Mill and George Orwell about the role of intellectuals and their ideas in politics, and I shall conclude in the same way. The first statement, by Mill, might usefully be recommended as an aid to reflection by the intellectuals of Israel: "The collective mind," wrote Mill in 1838, "does not penetrate below the surface, but it sees all the surface; which profound thinkers, even by reason of their profundity, often fail to d . . ." The second statement, by Orwell, seems particularly relevant as the Oslo war rages on: "if the radical intellectuals in England had had their way in the 20's and 30's," said Orwell, "the Gestapo would have been walking the streets of London in 1940" (Orwell, 1941).[16]

Notes

1   *Jerusalem Post*, April 6, 1996.
2   *Yediot Aharonot*, August 6, 1989.
3   *New York Times Magazine*, July 11, 1982.
4   *New York Times*, April 11, 1995; "Struggling against Fanaticism," *New York Times*, September 14, 2001.
5   *Jerusalem Post*, December 1, 1990.
6   *Davar*, April 15, 1988 (Hebrew).
7   *New York Times*, May 17, 1996.
8   *Jerusalem Post International Edition*, April 15, 1995.
9   "Egalitarians Gone Mad," *Jerusalem Post*, International Edition, October 28, 1995.
10   Aharon Megged, "The Israeli Suicide Drive," *Jerusalem Post International Edition*, 2 July 1994.

11   Quoted in Moshe Kohn, "Check Your Quotes," *Jerusalem Post International Edition*, October 16, 1993.

12   The Arab League contemptuously replied that Israel could become a member only "after the complete collapse of the Zionist national myth, and the complete conversion of historical Palestine into one democratic state to which all the Palestinians will return."

13   "The Fortress Within," *New York Times*, May 31, 1996.

14   "Revolt of the Masses," *New Republic*, June 24, 1996.

15   Ten years later, Margalit reprinted this piece in a collection of his essays called *View in Review*. There he says he has omitted a sentence from the original essay that "had wrong information in it about the children's memorial room at Yad Vashem." But he blames this on "an employee" who misled him. Margalit's sleight of hand here reveals two things: (1) when he says in his introduction to the book that "I am not even an eyewitness to much of what I write about," we can believe him; and (2) the Yiddish writer Shmuel Niger was correct to say that "we suffer not only from Jews who are too coarse, but also from Jews who are too sensitive."

16   In *The Lion and the Unicorn* (1941) Orwell also wrote: "The really important fact about the English intelligentsia is their severance from the common culture of the country . . . In the general patriotism, they form an island of dissident thought. England is the only great nation whose intellectuals are ashamed of their country." This, not to put too fine a point upon it, no longer seems true.

References

Benvenisti, Meron, *Conflicts and Contradictions*. New York: Villard, 1986.

Decter, Midge, "The treason of the intellectuals," *Outpost*, May 1996, p. 7.

Grossman, David, *The Yellow Wind*. New York: Farrar, Straus and Giroux, 1988.

Hazony, Yoram, *The Jewish State*. New York: Basic Books, 2000.

Katznelson, Berl, *The Collected Works of Berl Katznelson*. Tel Aviv: The Israel Labor Party, 1961, VIII, 18.

Orwell, George ,*The Lion and the Unicorn*. London: Secker and Warburg, 1941.

Wisse, Ruth, *If I am Not for Myself: The liberal betrayal of the Jews*. New York: The Free Press, 1992.

4 The Frankfurt School and Post-Zionist Thought

HANAN A. ALEXANDER

Post-Zionism is an intellectual movement that has had considerable influence over the post-Zionist "new historians" in Israel who challenge the prevailing "myths" of Zionist historiography. According to the accepted "myths," Zionism is a socialist-democratic movement of national liberation. Many advocates of this new perspective conceive Zionism as a colonialist movement that imposed Western hegemony on the native Arab peoples of Palestine (Cohen 1987; Morris 1989, 1990, 1993; Sternhell 1998). Controversial history textbooks influenced by post-Zionist ideas were introduced into the state secular schools during the Barak administration, despite opposition from the Education Committee of the Knesset, that were later removed when the Sharon administration took office (Naveh 1995).

The philosophical assumptions of several prominent post-Zionists reflect the influence of the Frankfurt school of neo-Marxism pervasive in the postmodern zeitgeist. These assumptions are examined here in light of recent trends in moral and political philosophy and epistemology. Post-Zionists that embrace these assumptions have not presented a coherent philosophical doctrine. The results of their collective writings have political consequences that threaten liberal democracy in Israel and the integrity of the Jewish state. Not surprisingly, these post-Zionists see Zionism as the threat to democracy and their own view as the antidote to this threat. Whatever their intentions, their logic is influenced, directly or indirectly, by a neo-Marxist heritage that leads to conflict with important democratic assumptions.

It is also argued here that these radical post-Zionist threats to democracy originate in part from extensions of, not departures from, some of the basic assumptions of classical Zionism, particularly in its socialist formulation. The achievement of both a Jewish and democratic state, as is called for in Israel's Declaration of Independence, requires not only a rejection of these post-Zionist positions, but a reformulation of several principles of Zionist thought as well.

Post-Zionism and Neo-Marxism

Post-Zionism is a complex intellectual tradition that reflects a variety of intellectual influences. Certainly not all post-Zionists are neo-Marxists. However, several key concepts that shape the arguments of many post-Zionists such as "cultural hegemony," "colonialism," "imperialism," "false consciousness," "ideological determinism," "cultural narratives," "native peoples," "the injustice of the powerful," and "the rightness of the oppressed," bear a striking resemblance to the ideas of Max Horkheimer (1996) and Theodor Adorno (1973), founders of the Frankfurt school. This reflects the extraordinary influence of critical theory in contemporary intellectual discourse. Moreover, a number of post-Zionist authors of works on education (Gur Zeev, 1999; Zuckerman, 1993, 1999), make direct reference to the ideas of the Frankfort school.

Whether or not critical theory influenced post-Zionist arguments directly or indirectly, they are subject to many of the conceptual problems that plague the Frankfurt neo-Marxist school. To understand these difficulties, it is useful to recall how Horkheimer and Adorno adapted Marx and their impact on post-Zionist thought.

Marx interpreted the Hegelian dialectic in terms of conflicts between socio-economic classes. In Marx's view, the workers of the late nineteenth century were alienated from the products of their labor because capitalists owned what laborers produced and used that ownership to control the workers. The primary tool that capitalists use to this end was ideology, which always reflects the power interests of the ruling capitalist class, but which is passed off as "objective knowledge," "correct morality," and "true religion" (Marx, 1977). According to Marx, there is no "objective knowledge," "correct morality," or "true religion." Knowledge, values, and faith are always grounded in power interests expressed in terms of political ideologies, i.e. Marxian thought is one embodiment of radical relativism. These ideologies promote false consciousness, which prevents workers from seeing how the capitalists control and enslave them. The workers are doomed to servitude unless they awaken from their ideological slumber and see that they require a more authentic ideology that reflects their interests rather than those of the capitalists (Marx and Engels, 1947). This analysis leads to a "hermeneutic of suspicion" that reveals how the exercise of power is found throughout the structure of society.

The Frankfurt school built upon these doctrines by introducing the concept of culture into the discussion. Power, argued Horkheimer and Adorno (1972), is manipulated not only by means of the social–economic–political order. It is also, and perhaps even primarily, a product of culture. Those with power use the mechanisms of culture to dominate and control. Critical theory adopted the term "hegemony" to refer to cultures that dominate in this way. Hegemonic cultures use not only the false consciousness of knowledge, morality, and religion to manipulate the powerless but all of that which we call culture. This includes language, literature, media, theater, dress, food, music, architecture indeed all of the elements of daily life. One important tool for cultural domination is to be found in schools that purport to communicate knowledge, morality and values (Hoy and McCarthy, 1994).

The educational strand of critical theory, critical pedagogy, sees the educational task as freeing students from hegemonic domination. This is accomplished by exposing the hidden assumptions and social structures that reinforce oppression. Once they see how society has held them in chains, people can be initiated into an ideology that reflects their true socio-economic and cultural interests rather than those of the ruling classes and dominant cultures (Apple, 1990, 1995; Giroux, 1992; Gur Zeev, 1999; McLaren, 1989).

Hegemonic cultures spread by means of a variety of mechanisms in addition to schools and media. One of these is known as colonialism. Colonialism involves the movement of a group who represent a culture of power from their land of origin to another land, which is not theirs. In this new land the culture of power dominates and ultimately oppresses the native peoples in order to plunder its resources and return them to the country of origin. Today, in an era of global communications, hegemonic cultures can colonialize and oppress native peoples by means of the electronic media that homogenize all popular culture to conform to the patterns of the dominant West. Television, cinema, popular music, music video, video games, multimedia web sites, clothing styles, fast food, and more are all mobilized toward this end (Said, 1978, 1979, 1994).

The core post-Zionist claim that bears the mark of the Frankfurt school is that the "Zionist project" entails the colonialization of historic Palestine by an alien hegemonic culture that imposed itself on the native Arab people, thereby alienating the local Palestinian Arabs from socio-economic, political, and cultural power in their own land. This process of colonialization "privileges" the Jewish – Zionist, Hebrew-speaking, modern, secular – culture over the traditional Arabic-speaking culture that existed in Palestine prior to the Zionist "invasion" and "occupation." To rectify the situation it is necessary to recognize that the "Zionist narrative" is but one account of the events that transpired in Palestine over the past one hundred years. There is another narrative, that of the oppressed Arab peoples, that also deserves to be heard and to receive a position of power in the political constellation of the region. This can be accomplished by transforming the State of Israel from one that privileges Jews to a state of "all its citizens" and by creating a Palestinian Arab state free of Zionist settlement on the West Bank of the Jordan River and in the Gaza Strip (Silberstein, 1999).

This analysis is widely disseminated today among intellectuals and on college and university campuses in Israel, Europe, and North America, in the print and electronic media, and among many political leaders who supported the principle of land for peace basic to the failed Oslo process. Perhaps its greatest influence is found among many so-called "New Historians" who seek to debunk the myths of Zionist historiography and to understand the violation of fundamental human rights inherent in the Zionist project (Sternhell, 1998). This violation is evidenced in Jewish confiscation of Arab property since the first Zionist settlement in the land of Israel in the late nineteenth century. It is symbolized in naming former Arab villages with Hebrew names. It can be seen also in the forced expulsion of Arabs from Palestine in 1948 – which the Arabs refer to as their *nakba* or national catastrophe – and in the manipulation of the Holocaust – the "parallel" Jewish tragedy – to justify the persecution of Palestinian Arabs (Gur Zeev, 1999).

It is easy to understand why this account is appealing. Palestinian Arabs have suffered both before and after the establishment of the State of Israel. All decent people must be moved by the plight of people who have lived in refugee camps for three or four generations. This radical theory draws attention to that suffering and offers a way to address it. Unfortunately the cure inherent in this analysis is worse than the disease. The result of this radical account will always be intensified violence that increases rather than alleviates suffering. This is because the theory falls prey to three fallacies rooted in its neo-Marxist background: one political, one moral, and one epistemological. Each of these fallacies undermines crucial assumptions necessary to any coherent theory of democracy.

The political fallacy embraces government based on absolute rather than distributed power. The moral fallacy adopts a form of determinism that undermines moral agency and responsibility. The epistemological fallacy entails a radical relativism that precludes the possibility of criticizing those in power and that leads to justifying any means on the basis of utopian ends.

The Fallacy of Absolute Power

In Marx's view someone was to be allocated absolute power. The question is who. Karl Popper (1945) pointed out that Marxist politics are grounded in Plato's political theory. Plato (1987) argued that power in a just society ought not to be granted to tyrants and oligarchs, since they use it only to further their own interests. Nor should it be allocated to the majority because it could always elect a tyrant. Plato believed that power should be given to philosophers who understand the nature of justice.

Marx too thought that power should be given to those who understand the nature of justice, namely those who would represent the oppressed and the downtrodden. In Marxist political theory there are essentially two categories, the powerful and the powerless. Since those who have power always abuse it, preference should be granted to those who do not. Justice in this view always sides with the less powerful.

According to the radical critique of Zionism, secular, Hebrew-speaking, culture succeeded in imposing its colonial hegemony over "historic" Arab Palestine.Those who enjoy the fruits of this hegemony have obtained power. They use this power to retain control over the land, and impose their will on its native people. Justice dictates that this power should be broken and granted once again to those who were oppressed by Zionist colonialism.

Popper pointed out, however, that Marx's reading of Plato accepts a "theory of unchecked sovereignty" according to which absolute power should be allocated to the best and the brightest who understand justice. This presupposes that there is only one correct understanding of justice, that the philosophers or politicians (in the name of the "downtrodden") comprehend justice properly, and that they will implement that understanding without error. That assumption is patently false.

There are numerous plausible interpretations of justice as well as of Plato's theory. There is no *prima facie* reason to prefer the interpretation of the downtrodden and oppressed over other interpretations. Nor is it by any means obvious that such an ideology represents the clearest understanding of oppression or how it might be alleviated. Moreover, even were the ideology of oppression the preferred theory of justice, there is no guarantee that the political leaders that espouse it properly understand this theory. The recent *Intifada* suggests, for example, that the current Arab–Palestinian leadership, or Arab leadership for the last century for that matter, did not adopt an effective response to what they perceived to be oppression. Finally, even if that interpretation were to be more promising, there is no guarantee that Arab Palestinian leaders, now or at any time, would not err in its implementation. The socio-economic condition of Palestinian Arabs is certainly worse today than it was two years ago at the beginning of the *Intifada*.

Moreover, whatever possibilities may exist for error on the part of the leaders of the oppressed, Marx's view does not allow for criticizing those in power in order to correct those errors. Rather, Marxist theorists would take absolute power away from one tyrant and grant it to another! But why should we suppose that the tyrant who claims to represent the oppressed would be more just, or open to critique, than the oligarch who represents the powerful? The Bolsheviks and Maoists were no less oppressive than the rulers that preceded them, at the very least.

Radical politics is not a solution to the problem of oppression. It only replaces one oppressed people with another. Classical Zionism taught that Diaspora Jewry could not attain social, economic, political, and cultural power in an environment dominated by a non-Jewish population. Herzl's Zionist solution was to extricate Jewry from its condition as a minority lacking collective political representation by returning to the ancient homeland of the Jewish people to re-establish Jewish political sovereignty (Hertzberg, pp. 204–25). Zionism succeeded beyond the wildest imaginations of those who conceived it.

Now that Jews have regained the power of national sovereignty, this same radical position is adopted by the post-Zionists to assert that Jewry should relinquish it. What would happen if Israel were to accede to this demand and allow Israel to become "a state for all of its citizens" within the current boundaries of Israel, and to agree to the creation of a Palestinian state in Judea, Samaria and Gaza? Once again Jewry would become powerless. Witness the treatment of Christian minorities in Lebanon, in the Palestinian Authority, and throughout the Arab world (Ye'or, 2002).

Or consider the reawakening of anti-Semitism in Europe and throughout the Muslim world. Radical politics suggests nothing that would protect Jews from this racist hatred. On the contrary, they feed it, justifying terror against Jews as a necessary means for the Palestinian Arabs to achieve self-determination. Anti-Semitism of this kind is one of the main forms of Jewish alienation to which Zionism responded (Pinsker, in Hertzberg, 1969). Yet the radical politics espoused by post-Zionists influenced by the Frankfurt school does not allow the same right of self-definition to Jews that it affords Palestinian Arabs. Instead, it defines Zionism as racism against Arabs and advocates replacing one form of hegemony with another that would result in returning the Jews to their pre-Zionist condition of subservience in the Christian and Muslim nations (Ye'or, 2002).

Alleviating the "oppression" for one group by denying liberty to another seeds violence not democracy. Open, liberal society requires systematic opposition to oppression, which is not possible when absolute power goes unchecked. Therefore, the task of political theory cannot be to decide who gets power. Popper argues that its role must be instead to figure out how to protect individual citizens from the mistakes of even the best, brightest, and most well intended leaders. That requires a theory of "checks and balances" that lies and the very heart of open, liberal democracy that is completely missing in neo-Marxist political theory.

The Fallacy of Determinism

The second fallacy found in the radical critique of Zionism has to do with its very moral critique of oppression. According to neo-Marxist doctrine, ideology and culture determine belief and behavior, which are in turn inexorably tied to power interests associated with socio-economic class. Oppressed people, who accept the hegemonic ideology representing the powerful forces that conspire to oppress them, live in false consciousness. To be liberated from this false consciousness, they need to embrace a more authentic ideology that reflects their true socio-economic and cultural interests.

Zionist ideology, say the PZ writers, represents a form of false consciousness, especially when it is imposed on Arabs who are citizens of the State of Israel. Post-Zionists of the neo-Marxist stripe assert that an alternative Palestinian ideology is required to liberate Palestinian Arabs from the oppression of Zionism and to achieve a just resolution of the Palestinian problem. This is the ideology that should be taught in the schools of the Palestinian Authority, in order to make children aware of the false consciousness that has been imposed upon them and to introduce a more authentic consciousness in its place. Israeli schools require counter-education rather than education. Palestinian ideology allows Jewish as well as Arab children who are citizens of Israel to see the errors of Zionist oppression in order to prepare for a "state of all of its citizens." Zionist ideology, on the other hand, is a form of violence that forces youngsters to embrace the hegemonic ideology of Zionism.

There are two difficulties with this view. First, it is hard to fathom how the allegedly "authentic" ideology that replaces false consciousness has a liberating effect, given that belief and behavior remain ideologically determined. To say that belief and behavior are determined by ideology means that the individual does not possess the liberty to choose. Even if the oppression of a particular group or class is ameliorated by the acceptance of this new ideology, there is no guarantee that the plight of the other group whose ideology was replaced will be improved, or that the freedom of particular individuals will be enhanced. Moreover, if the individual has no choice in selecting this ideology, his or her freedom is severely restricted. And if the freedom of the individuals within a group or class is restricted rather than enhanced by the new ideology, then it makes little sense to say that the group comprised of those individuals has been liberated (Alexander, 2002).

One response to this argument would be to claim that this concept of individual freedom is part of the very modern, hegemonic, Western ideology that is to be overturned by the new authenticity. The liberty experienced in this case is cultural and collective rather than individual. This new ideology does not suffer from some of the narcissistic individualism of Western liberalism.

However, this response fails to offer an account of what it would mean for the group to be liberated, if the freedom of the group's members remains restricted. Instead, just as Marxist political theory replaces one absolute tyrant with another, Marxist ideological determinism replaces one false consciousness with another. The new false consciousness promises liberation, but in the end allows the individual no greater degree of freedom than the previous one. It is inevitable that an individual or group will grab the reins of power afforded by this new false consciousness and use them to advance their own interests even when they are in conflict with the very oppressed people whose liberation is being sought. In fact, Marx's own political theory endorses just such a power grab in the form of the dictatorship of the proletariat (Marx, 1977).

The second problem is even more troubling. The injustice of oppression is central to the neo-Marxist argument. It is the moral bite of this injustice that provides the emotional energy to radical politics. Yet, if belief and behavior are determined by ideology, it is difficult to fathom what it could mean to say that anything is morally wrong. This is because moral discourse requires the assumption of free will. If external forces such as society, history, ideology, biology, or the gods, rather than people, are the agents of attitudes and actions, then it makes no sense to speak of right and wrong or justice and injustice (Alexander, 2001).

Moral concepts assume that people can be held accountable for their behavior, so it is relevant to instruct them to think or act differently. But if thinking and action are controlled by ideology, then it is not people but ideology that should be addressed in an effort to right a wrong or alleviate injustice. But it is just this ideology that is said by the neo-Marxists to be determined by the conditions of socio-economic class. How then can false consciousness be altered if it is not the individual who is to discover that his or her views are false and in need of change? And it is precisely this individual control over belief and behavior that is denied by neo-Marxist ideological determinism.

The neo-Marxist claim that oppression is unjust rings hollow. Not only does radical politics replace one injustice with another, ideological determinism guts radical moral outrage of any significant ethical content. In doing so it denies the moral agency and personal responsibility required of democratic citizens. What remains in this analysis is only raw power – the never-ending battle between warring factions each of which claims the right to attack the other based on its own righteous anger. Post-Zionism of this variety does not offer a way to ameliorate Palestinian Arab suffering. It promises rather unending violence with no means of adjudicating between various points of view or resolving differences through dialogue!

The Fallacy of Relativism

The third fallacy of Frankfurt school post-Zionism is epistemological. According to the critical theorists, there is no such thing as objective knowledge or correct morality. What is called knowledge or ethics is in fact nothing more than an expression of the ideological interest of those in power.

The privilege afforded in Israel to the Zionist narrative in recounting the history of the Arab-Israeli conflict must be rectified to recognize that there are two narratives, each of which reflects different power interests. A so-called "balanced" presentation would grant equal weight to the Palestinian Arab version of these events. So too, to condemn terror against Israeli civilians as a means of advancing the political agenda of the Palestinian narrative is to impose the moral standards of the Zionist, Western narrative, on an Arab narrative. To many Palestinian Arabs, suicide bombers are not terrorists; they are freedom fighters. It is important to note that many post-Zionists who embrace neo-Marxism would recoil from such a defense of terrorism, though some have not. It is, nevertheless, a logical consequence of the assumptions they have adopted.

One problem with this sort of strong relativism is its incoherence. This can be seen in the critique of the privilege afforded the Zionist narrative. If the truth of a narrative is relative to power interests, on what grounds can we criticize the privileging of a hegemonic narrative? Is not the narrative on the basis of which this privilege is criticized also relative to power interests, and thereby also subject to the same criticism? If the critique of hegemony is justified, in other words, then it is not justified. Were this critique to withstand criticism, it must also be registered against itself, in which case we would be in a position of both accepting and rejecting the grounds on which hegemony is to be criticized. Under these circumstances, it is impossible to understand what such a critique could mean (Norris, 1997; Siegel, 1987, 1997).

A second problem is that this sort of relativism immunizes everything from criticism because it obliterates any possible difference, however small, between truth and falsehood. Consider the claim that Zionism is a form of colonialism. "Colonialism" usually refers to people of power coming from their homeland and invading the land of another people to suppress its natives, plunder its resources, and return them to the homeland. Little in this model applies to the Zionist case. The Jews who left the lands of their birth to come to the Land of Israel were not people of power and often were not considered an integral part of the prevailing ethnic-national population in those lands, and certainly did not represent them in any way. Nor did they understand themselves to be coming to a foreign land to exploit its resources for the benefit of their original homeland. Rather, they were returning to their historic home. They did not subjugate the natives; they claimed to be the natives.

Moreover they did not plunder resources. There were precious few resources in the Land of Israel until the Zionists began to create them. The creation of these resources encouraged the migration to Palestine of Arabs from places that offered fewer opportunities. Nor were these resources shipped back to the lands in which the early Zionists were born. These resources remained in the Land of Israel, which in part created additional attraction for Arabs to partake of its new prosperity.

According to the relativist doctrine, however, the colonialist claim is immune from critique because it is part of the Palestinian Arab narrative. Its repudiation based on "facts" should not be taken seriously since there are no facts independent of the narratives within which they are formulated. Hence, there is no way to adjudicate between these two perspectives.

This epistemological problem has profound moral consequences. When standards that distinguish between truth and falsehood are blurred, criteria to differentiate between right and wrong are also affected. The moral difference between terror and freedom fighting is obscured, for example, since it is impossible to criticize one narrative on the basis of the assumptions of another. Yet, as we have seen, whatever it is that the Palestinian terrorist is fighting for, one would be hard pressed to call it freedom. Similarly, the Arabs and PZ neo-Marxists believe they can refer with impunity to Zionism as racism, when Zionism provides a response to anti-Jewish racism.

The blurring of criteria for epistemological and moral evaluation leads to the third problem with this sort of relativism – its agenda of intolerance hidden behind the guise of tolerance. By protecting competing views from "unfair," "anachronistic" critique, many relativists aimed to promote tolerance among people of conflicting perspectives. The version of relativism inherent in the neo-Marxist rhetoric found in post-Zionism, however, is not intended to foster tolerance. Criticism of hegemony on the part of the oppressed is permitted, in this view, even while critique of the ideology of the oppressed is protected from criticism. This does not place the Palestinian narrative on par with Zionism. It aims to replace Zionist hegemony with the narrative of the oppressed Palestinian Arabs.

The appeal to two equivalent narratives *is* a deception. There is a privileged narrative according to this view. The narrative of the oppressed is more truthful than that of the powerful. This narrative is protected from the very critique imposed on the so-called hegemonic view, such that any means can be justified to enable advocates for the oppressed to acquire the power they desire. Consider the case of the so-called massacre in Jenin, Samaria, in April 2002. There was a rush to judge the Israeli Defense Forces because they represent hegemonic power. It was assumed by many that war crimes must have been committed despite considerable evidence to the contrary. Yet in many circles, the massacre of innocent Israeli civilians by Palestinian terrorists was not subject to critique, since the terrorists are fighting for the freedom of the oppressed, and allegedly they have no other means to advance their cause.

The consequences of this thinking are nothing short of catastrophic for democracy and the rule of law. According to this logic, any means is morally justifiable to achieve any political end so long as it is held passionately within the context of a national or cultural narrative of the oppressed. The oppressed are allowed to do anything they like to those whom they accuse as their oppressors in order to achieve the power they see as rightfully theirs. The horrors perpetrated by people on one another using this sort of reasoning during the twentieth century by ideologists of both the right and the left wing are well known.

The absence of evaluative criteria leads to yet a more insidious, fourth and final problem – protection of the true oppressors. Jordan ruled the Arabs of the West Bank and Gaza for nineteen years from 1948 until

1967. Lebanon, and by extension Syria, rules those north of Israel's borders to this very day. What have these countries done to alleviate the suffering of their Palestinian brothers and sisters residing within their borders? Nothing! Over five million Jewish refugees, including close to a million Jews from Arab lands, were resettled after World War II. The Palestinians are the only group to remain in refugee camps located in Arab countries. These people are being used as pawns in the hands of the despotic Arab regimes. The true oppressors of the Palestinians, in this view, are Arab dictatorships, not Israel's democracy. Yet the dual narrative theory protects these despots from the international criticism they so richly deserve. Radical relativism in this view hides and reinforces rather than alleviates oppression.

Zionism Reconceived

But is this critique of neo-Marxism in post-Zionist thought not itself an ideological statement embedded in power interests? The answer is yes, so what? The problem is not whether power interests are reflected in a particular point of view. They undoubtedly are. Rather, the question is whether those interests are justified and whether competing interests are addressed fairly. Yet, it is precisely moral categories such as justice and fairness that are ruled out by the dichotomization of the powerful versus the powerless. The powerless are not always right, and the powerful are not always wrong. In fact, it is not at all clear who are the oppressed and who the oppressors in the Middle East. To determine which views ought to be embraced requires a framework that enables conceiving the nature of justice and fairness. Nor can that framework be arbitrarily restricted to certain elements in the foreground of the news media, while all other elements comprising an essential part of the larger historical-political picture be ignored for the sake of political convenience. The relative isolation of Israel on the international scene, partiularly in the Arab dominated United Nations, hardly provides a basis for a view of Israel as an oppressor surrounded and outnumbered by hostile Arab nations who support the Arab Palestinians.

For moral concepts such as these to have meaning, we must accept at least three assumptions called conditions of moral agency and ethical discourse. We must assume first that people have freedom of choice within reasonable limitations. We are the agents of our actions, not history, or society, or nature, or the gods. We are, therefore, responsible for our mistakes and to be credited for our achievements. Second, we must also assume that we have moral intelligence that is the capacity to distinguish between right and wrong according to some moral tradition or theory. Hence we have not only the freedom of will to chart our own course, but also the capacity to understand whether or not that course is a good one. Finally, we are fallible; we make mistakes. We err in what we believe and in the actions we choose to take on the basis of those beliefs. So if we do good or evil, it is not because it is our nature to do so, but because we have chosen to act on the basis of our understanding of the circumstances (Alexander, 2001).

Without these assumptions it makes no sense to speak of moral categories. It makes sense to address me with ethical imperatives only if I am responsible for my actions. If external agents such as history, society, nature, or the gods, determine my actions, then why address me? Rather we should address the relevant external agent. And if I cannot be supposed to understand the difference between the choices that lie before me, or if I can do no wrong, or no right, then how is it possible for me to make a meaningful, non-arbitrary choice? Ethical concepts such as justice and fairness require free, intelligent, and fallible agents. Yet, it is precisely these that are precluded from neo-Marxian analysis. Neo-Marxism promotes determinism rather than freedom, absolutism rather than falliblism, and a form of relativism that obliterates the difference between right and wrong.

Unfortunately these ethical pre-conditions can be found no more readily in classical than in post-Zionist thought. Classical Zionism was also deeply influenced by Marxist notions of power, determinism, and relativism. According to the Zionist analysis, Diaspora Jews are alienated from their cultural heritage because they cannot cultivate their own culture and language that gives expression to Jewish historial-national identity. Jewish life is abnormal and under attack in the Diaspora because Jews lack adequate control over their social–economic–political–religious environment. The solution is to acquire Jewry's control over its environment by reclaiming the Jewish land and recreating the Jewish nation-state.

Zionism emphasized the enormous influence on Jewish life and consciousness exercised by the surrounding culture and the decisive role of Jewish solidarity in counteracting this influence. From this fundamental position it concluded that Jewry can detrmine its historical–cultural fate only under conditions of Jewish social–political solidarity and sovereignty. Clearly, the concept of sovereignty entails reference to the subject of national–ethnic power or powerlessness regarding the collectivity's environment. Assumptions of the post-Zionists regarding the subject of Arab power or powerlessness are not, therefore, a dramatic departure from classical Zionist thought. Rather radical post-Zionists apply some of the principles learned from the Zionist heritage on this subject. However, in the view of the PZs, Jews in the Zionist State of Israel have switched their position from what they had been in the *Galut*. The Jews are now the powerful people perceived, almost automatically, as oppressors, especially if we totally disregard the larger geo-political picture and focus attention exlusively on Israel, including Judea, Samaria and Gaza. In the latter very limited veiwpoint, the Palestinian Arabs can be depicted in a position of powerlessness, and hence are the oppressed.

However, is it possible to re-conceive Zionism in which moral categories such as justice and oppression make sense without falling prey to dogmatic absolutism or determinism on the one hand, or to radical relativism on the other? To answer it is useful to note that the origins of this Marxist influence lay in the impact of European romanticism, in particular French and German Enlightenment figures such as Rousseau and Hegel. This influence leads to idealization of the romantic self on the one hand and the romantic nation on the other. Each takes the form of an absolute, which results in untenable extremism. The romantics also saw themselves as discontinuous with the past. So too, Zionism of this variety sees itself either as a rebellion against or a messianic fulfillment of Jewish history.

An alternative would understand Zionism in light of Enlightenment figures such as John Locke in England and James Madison in the United States. Rooted in critical rationality and liberal communitarianism, such a Zionism would constitute neither a rebellion against nor a fulfillment of Jewish tradition, but rather a modern reformulation and continuation of that tradition. Zionism in this view is not a break with Jewish history. Rather it is a development within Jewish history in which Jews reassert political independence and responsibility, regain control over their past, and ultimately reshape their future.

Democracy can be understood as that form of society that promotes, protects, and defends moral agency and the conditions of ethical discourse: freedom, intelligence, and fallibility. These ideals are grounded in Biblical and Rabbinic traditions. Conditions for Jews in nineteenth- and twentieth-century Europe, North Africa, and the Middle East made it impossible for Jewish life to continue to embrace these values. Zionism can be understood, then, as a reaffirmation and reorganization in the modern context of that democratic culture that has historically always been part of the Jewish ethos, and which is based on a mixture of Jewish ethnic-nationalism and individualsm, not on one without the other.

In this view, the reference to a Jewish and democratic state in Israel's declaration of independence is a principled aspiration not a political compromise. Israel is a young state, and its democratic institutions are still very fragile. But the culture of public debate and critical analysis required for democracy – of personal responsibility and collective morality, of justice, fairness and solidarity – are deeply rooted in Biblical and Rabbinic texts and in the varieties of communal organizations throughout Jewish history. We require not a post but a renewed Zionism, freed from the conflicts and contradictions of Marxist and neo-Marxist ideology, and filled instead with the historical Jewish commitment to free will, moral intelligence, and fallibility. These presuppositions lead to faith in the rule of law and to a society grounded on justice and fairness that are the hallmarks of both democracy and Jewish tradition.

References

Adorno, Theodore W. (1973) *The Jargon of Authenticity*. Translated from the German by K. Tarnowski and F. Will. Evanston: Northwestern University Press.

Alexander, Hanan A. (2000) Education in the Jewish state. *Studies in Philosophy of Education*, 19:5, pp. 489–505.

—— (2001) *Reclaiming Goodness: Education and the spiritual quest*. Notre Dame, ID: Notre Dame University Press.

—— (2002) Education as spiritual critique: Dwayne Huebner's *Lure of the transcendent*. *Journal of Curriculum Studies*, forthcoming.

Apple, Michael W. (1990) *Ideology and Curriculum*. New York: Routledge.

—— (1995), *Education and Power*. New York: Routledge.

Cohen, Mitchell (1987) *Zion and State: Nation, class, and the shaping of modern Israel*. Oxford: Oxford University Press.

Giroux, Henri (1992) *Border Crossings: Cultural workers and the politics of education*. New York: Routledge.

Gur Zeev, Ilan (1999) *Philosophy, Politics, and Education in Israel*. Haifa: University of Haifa Press (Hebrew).

Hertzberg, Arthur (1969) *The Zionist Idea: A historical analysis and reader*. New York: Athenaeum.

Horkheimer, Max (1996) *Critique of Instrumental Reason*. New York: Continuum.

——, and T. W. Adorno (1972) *Dialectic of Enlightenment*. New York: Herder and Herder.

Hoy, David and Thomas McCarthy (1994) *Critical Theory*. Oxford: Blackwell.

Marx, Karl (1977) *Capital: A critique of political economy*, translated from the German by B. Fowkes. New York: Vintage.

——, and F. Engels (1947) *The German Ideology*. New York: International.

McLaren, Peter (1989) *Life in Schools: An introduction to critical pedagogy in the foundations of education*. New York: Longman.

Morris, Benny (1989) *The Birth of the Palestinian Refugee Problem, 1947–1949*. Cambridge: Cambridge University Press.

—— (1990) *1948 and After: Israel and the Palestinians*. Oxford: Clarendon Press.

—— (1993) *Israel's Border Wars, 1949–1956: Arab infiltration, Israel's retaliation, and the countdown to the Suez War*. Oxford: Clarendon.

Naveh, Eyal (1995) *The Twentieth Century: The century that changed the world*. Tel Aviv: Tel Aviv Books (Hebrew).

Norris, Christopher (1997) *Against Relativism: Philosophy of science, deconstructionism, and critical theory*. Oxford: Blackwell.

Plato (1987) *The Republic*. Translated by D. Lee. London: Penguin.

Popper, Karl (1945) *The Open Society and its Enemies*. London: Routledge and Kegan Paul.

Said, Edward (1978) *Orientalism*. New York: Pantheon Books.

—— (1979) *The Question of Palestine*. London: Routledge and Kegan Paul.

—— (1994) *The Politics of Dispossession: The struggle for Palestinian self-determination*. New York: Pantheon Books.

Siegel, Harvey (1987) *Relativism Refuted: A critique of contemporary epistemological relativism*. Dordrecht: Reidel.

—— (1997) *Rationality Redeemed? Further dialogues on an educational ideal*. New York: Routledge.

Silberstein, Laurence J. (1999) *The Post-Zionism Debates: Knowledge and power in Israeli culture*. New York: Routledge.

Sternhell, Ze'ev (1998) *The Founding Myths of Israel: Nationalism, socialism, and the making of the Jewish state*. Princeton: Princeton University Press.

Ye'or, Bat (2002) *Islam and Dhimmitude: Where civilizations collide*. Teaneck, NJ: Farleigh Dickenson University Press.

Zuckerman, Moshe (1993) *Shoah in the Sealed Room: "The "Holocaust" in Israeli press during the Gulf War*. Tel Aviv: Author's publication (Hebrew).

—— (1999) "Culture Industry, Authoritarianism, and the Individual." In Ilan Gur Ze'ev (ed.), *Modernity, Postmodernity, and Education*. Ramat Aviv: Tel Aviv University, pp. 87–100 (Hebrew).

5 The Leftist Media and the al-Aqsa Uprising

DAVID BUKAY

This chapter discusses the connections between the media, the Left, and Arafat's terror, using a new concept that I will refer to as pseudo-Zionism. Zionism represents the following structure: Jewish people – Jewish state – Land of Israel. In other words, there is a Jewish people; the Jewish people, like all other peoples, is entitled to and worthy of a homeland; and this homeland can only be in the Land of Israel. Anyone who omits one of the ingredients of this structure is not a Zionist, but an anti-Zionist, as in the *Bund* movement in Poland, which believed that there was a Jewish people, and also that it was worthy of a homeland, but favored a different homeland than the Land of Israel. Within Zionism there is a familiar, legitimate debate, throughout the political spectrum, concerning the borders of the state, the status of the Jewish religion within the state, and the state's political–social–economic and, particularly, cultural heritage. But there is no debate as to those basic ingredients of Zionism.

On the other hand, post-Zionism stresses the following elements on the theoretical level: acknowledgment of lack of objectivity; preparedness to pass judgment; use of relevant comparisons; choice of neutral and non-emotionally laden terms; and use of methodological tools of political science (Morris, 1991; Pappe, 1993). In practice, this approach contradicts all the most fundamental values of Zionism, severely criticizes the nature of the Jewish state in unprecedented fashion, and in many cases accepts the claims of the enemies of Israel, which put its existence in question and aim at annihilating it. Post-Zionism indeed credits itself with debunking myths, yet itself creates many myths with a low standard of evidence. It has been strongly criticized by Efraim Karsh, who blames it for devising flimsy theories, distorting historical facts, and creating fashionable myths without a factual basis (Karsh, 1997).

Positioned between these two there is, I assert, an ideological stance, essentially lacking in wisdom, of pseudo-Zionism. It is espoused by people who are within the Zionist camp yet harshly criticize its policy, while being blind to the claims and aspirations of its enemies. Instead the pseudo-Zionists focus on Israel and its policy without seeing the whole picture, certainly without recognizing and understanding the positions of its enemies. They oppose Jewish nationalism, referring to it as chauvinism (whereas Palestinian nationalism is legitimate); they are prepared to downplay the flag and the national anthem, as if these symbols have become outmoded, without considering the intensification of nationalism in the world and the strengthening of the state (whereas the Palestinians are permitted to wave their flag and to proudly sing their national anthem). Their attitude is characterized by an exilic low-profile mentality, a preoccupation with "What will the *goyim* say?" (whereas the Palestinians are permitted to be vociferous and to externalize their goals with unprecedented violence, since they, of course, are dispossessed).

The pseudo-Zionists' attitude toward Israeli policy is so critical that they are prepared to accept the demands of Israel's enemies in compromises that pose existential danger to the state. Moreover, they are proclaimed secularists in outlook and oppose the Jewish religion (while being prepared to respect other religions). Thus, for example, they concur that the Temple Mount is sacred only to the Muslims and hence should only be referred to as *Haram al-Sharif*, whereas since the Western Wall is but a collection of rocks they are prepared to relinquish the Jewish presence there. Anything of a Jewish historical character is invalid and improper. The main trait of the pseudo-Zionists, however, is that they regard themselves as "people of the great world," internationalists, whose activity is primarily motivated by the principle of how the world will react and not by the existential interests of the State of Israel. Paradoxically they accept a key Jewish religious concept, but in reverse: the Jews are indeed a "special people" and must serve as a "light unto the nations," but in the sense of creating moral, suprapolitical modes of activity. As they see it, Israeli must not act like all other peoples, certainly not like the other countries in the international system that emphasize their patriotism, proudly flaunt their nationalism, and actively struggle to maintain their national power and political integrity, even at the price of war. The basic right, after all, is to kill and not be killed. That is how states were established throughout history, and that is how they maintain their status (Waltz, 1959).

If Zionism is determined activity to maintain the national honor, and a sense of pride that the Jewish people, after two thousand years of exile, has succeeded in returning to Zion and securing its basic right to live in an independent state, then pseudo-Zionism represents contrasting notions. The pseudo-Zionists live in Israel on condition, and they have no problem with trading in their loyalty to the country and living outside of Israel.

What are the implications of this phenomenon for analyzing the media-leftist complex and the *al-Aqsa Intifada*, and how is the pseudo-Zionist outlook related to Arafat's success? I will argue that this complex bears significant responsibility for the fact that for the first time in world political history, a ceaselessly violent terrorist movement stands to triumph and establish a state. The reason for pseudo-Zionism's supporting the Palestinian Authority and the values it represents is not, in fact, identification with Arafat and his cronies, but rather a peculiar ideological disposition to understand and sympathize with Israel's most determined enemies, who have set their hearts on its total eradication. Without doubt the heritage of the Jewish exile comes into play here – the desire to flatter, to tattle, to win approval from the Gentile. This runs counter to the common behavior of most citizens of the countries of the world. There are few other cases of such severe opposition to serving governments and their policies. Certainly this may reflect the fact that the Jewish people was in exile for two thousand years, dealing with all areas but very little with politics, its outlook being shaped by its experience as a persecuted minority.

Owing to a messianic and utopian mindset, devoid of all responsibility and understanding, the great serial arch-terrorist, Arafat, was brought here together with his corrupt cronies, after being rescued by the skin of his teeth by Nasser from "Black September" in Jordan in 1970; after being driven out of Beirut by Israel in September 1982; and after being expelled from Lebanon in utter humiliation by Syria in "Black December" in 1983.[1] At the same time, the Israeli media granted its total sponsorship to the Oslo agreements, making the "sages of Oslo" the country's leading celebrities. These processes together add up to a great crime against the Jewish people in independent Israel.

Much has been written about the close links between the media and international terrorism. Researchers on the subject have observed that: the media is the terrorist's best friend; the act of terror is nothing in itself – the publicity is all; publicity through the media is the mother's milk of the terrorist; terrorism ideally suits the needs of television; if it had not existed it would have had to invent it; without publicity, terrorism is the weapon of the impotent; the media is the terrorists' best propaganda agent; without television terrorism is like a tree that falls in a dense forest; television has reinforced the effects and enhanced the spread of terrorism more than any other factor.

These are a few of the analysts' insights about the interconnections between the media and international terrorism. Indeed, there are few instances in scholarly inquiry where there is such broad agreement about one factor's responsibility for the success of another factor. Ted Koppel was on the mark when he noted that television and the terrorists essentially have a symbiotic relationship (Nacos, 1994; Schmid and Paletz, 1992). Why does this happen? What causes these relations to form, when it is not a matter of cooperation through identification or even of agreement? The explanations lie in the functions of the media.

The media is a social institution, a central part of the modern state, which satisfies vital societal needs such as: coverage and analysis of the news; providing entertainment to the public; and conferring status and prestige on individuals and institutions. The most important aspect of the media's functioning, however, is the economic one. The media is comprised of profit-seeking corporations whose main source of income is publicity. The media is an economic enterprise (Herman, 1999, pp. 11–42). Achieving maximum profit means achieving maximum dissemination, via maximum publicity. That is, the focus of attention is the socioeconomic elite, which does the publicizing and hence also the profiting. The viewing, reading, and listening public almost totally acquiesces to this elite's categorization of the issues and how it is reflected in what gets printed and broadcast.

In addition, the media wants to sell advertising by highlighting what is most in demand, namely the out-of-the-ordinary and the producers of violence. Hence terrorist incidents are especially suitable for television coverage, since they involve heartrending drama and gripping human tragedy (Gerbner, 1992, pp. 94–107; Hoge, 1982, pp. 89–105). Terror is a main item in the ratings.

The problem has two principal dimensions (Mcquail, 1998). First, the media constitute part of an extensive economic network. They produce a product, which, from their perspective, constitutes information, and tries to sell as much of it as possible. Second, it wields enormous power and constantly makes use of it. The media is a superpower, and its power is more dominant than that of any other element in modern society. Butler's (1992) survey of the election campaigns in Britain since 1951 devoted two chapters to the media and reached an equivocal conclusion: they are not content with description and objective analysis of events, but instead work actively and dynamically in the political system and influence policymaking and the political and public agenda.

The competition between the different media, and the race for "scoops" and sensations to garner publicity and ratings, are the media's two main concerns. In this regard the media do not just cover the news but create the news, and highlight the issues they deem appropriate according to the "frequency principle," in which the crucial factor is the media people's positive or negative perception: the more an issue and the people associated with it suit the predilections of the media and the views they seek to convey to the public, the greater the chances that they will be intensively and positively covered, and vice versa (Galtung and Ruge, 1970). Thus the Left is portrayed as positive, wise, thoughtful, intelligent, cultured, and moderate, while whoever does not belong to the Left is portrayed as the opposite. And the sympathetic/hostile coverage, the positive/negative treatment, are in accordance with the "frequency principle."

In Israel the print and electronic media are almost completely controlled by the Left, in its radical, pseudo-Zionist form. The media are one-sided and act, even if unintentionally, against the interests of the State of Israel via hostile, fear-inducing coverage of the reality it reflects. To add insult to injury, however, the media feign innocence and injured virtue by making the claim, which can easily be refuted, that their activities are balanced. In this regard there is a simple test: the editorial positions, the presentations, the interviews, and the analyses can be transferred to the hands of others, while the existing media people maintain the same channels of expression, and it can then be determined if there is really no difference, even a dramatic one, in the prevailing balance.

Terrorist incidents are a wonderful sales promoter for the media: they constitute a tragic drama that evolves in a live, overblown broadcast. Terror is romanticized and its capacities are enhanced, instead of showing its perpetrators as the death-deserving savages that they are. The terrorists' ability to win achievements depends on publicity, and terror becomes a form of psychological warfare: the terrorists choose the presentation (i.e., the location of the event), the actors (random victims), and the form of presentation via the media. Terror, contends Crelinsten (1979), should not be understood only in terms of violence but also in terms of propaganda. The violence is intended to alter behavior by coercion, and the propaganda by persuasion. Terror combines these two dimensions. Indeed, the media has become an effective tool for the perpetrators of terror. It provides a wide audience of viewers for the human drama; publicity for the terrorists' complaints and demands; an opportunity to gain status, prestige, and followers; and proof that the government is impotent and cannot provide security.

The connections between terror and the media can be described in the following schema. In the first stage, the terrorist organization carries out a terrorist act against a desired target. The random victims have no significance; the process of dehumanization renders them worthless. The aim is publicity and conveying the message. In the second stage, the media reports extensively and dramatically and creates an image of the organization as having enormous destructive powers. This occurred, for example, in regard to the Symbionese Liberation Army (SLA) in the United States that kidnapped Patricia Hearst. For half a year the media dealt obsessively with this organization's activities, and publicized its manifesto and the profiles of its members. Only later did it become clear that this was not even a terrorist organization but a gang of criminals, bank-robbers. In the third stage, the publicizing efforts of the media succeed in creating strong public awareness, in three different spheres:

1 The threatened public, which is supposed to pressure the government to change its policy. A notable example is Israel's panic-stricken withdrawal from Lebanon without an agreement.
2 World public opinion, which receives extensive information about the organization, its complaints and desires. A notable example is the terrorist strike at the Munich Olympics in 1972, which exposed the PLO to hundreds of millions of viewers.
3 The native population of the terrorists, among whom the organization wins prestige and status as well as new members. A notable example is the increased volume of those joining the Islamic fundamentalist terror organizations.

The media and terrorism, then, have a symbiotic relationship, where each side supplies the other's needs and even helps it grow and flourish. The media sells the event to the public in return for ratings, which raises the costs of the publicity, and terrorism exploits this to become an important political phenomenon – as in the paraphrase: "If I appear on television, I not only exist, I am important." By the same token, whatever is not broadcast on television not only is not important but simply does not exist.

Along with this manifestly symbiotic relationship, there exists a media–political connection between the media and the socio-economic elite, which shapes the political agenda. This phenomenon has reached unprecedented dimensions in Israel, where a few rich families control a high percentage of the print and electronic media. The concentration of the media in the hands of a few threatens democratic freedoms, especially the freedom of expression. In practice, what the general public receives is the perspective of the economic interests of the powerful families who control the media rather than objective and honest programming. Furthermore, the geographic location of the media and the social status of its mandarins play a major role in shaping Israel's political agenda. In addition to this frightening concentration, cliques of journalists have developed, in association with elements in the political system, almost to the point of creating a monopoly that rides roughshod and sanctimoniously suppresses other opinions and views, while subverting all public debate on issues critically important to Israeli society's functioning.[2] The media is mostly controlled by trend-setting, salon leftists, a coterie of well-heeled "yuppies" who are happy to declare nonchalantly that they are part of the "peace camp" and the brotherhood of nations (that is, of those in the nations who are like themselves). This is a coalition of political opportunists, "people of the great world," for whom the interests of their state do not necessarily come first (Bukay, 2001; **chapter 7**).

So far we have shown the symbiosis between terror and the media, and the links between the media and the socioeconomic elite. The question now is: what is the media's operative significance for the success of terrorist acts? We will consider two aspects that have a common outcome. The first aspect involves pressures to constrain the battle against terror and seek compromises and settlements instead; the second involves "humanizing" terrorism, both by emphasizing the threats it poses to the victimized population, thereby enhancing its power, and by highlighting the misery and misfortune of the population whose leaders resort to and justify terrorism. The common outcome of these two aspects is "paradoxical opposed reciprocity," entailing a contagious effect of success: a hardening of resolve among the population whose leaders employ terrorism, and damage to the national fortitude and morale among the victimized population.

1 *Constraining the government's anti-terrorist policy.* Broad media coverage is terrorism's main achievement: it increases the impact of its messages while paralyzing the government's activity and disrupting its decision making and reaction capacity. The goal is not military but rather psychological defeat, by wearing down the national morale and will. The immediate result is frustration and despair, since "there's nothing to be done" and "terrorism can't be defeated." From the terrorist organizations' standpoint the outcome is demoralization and chaos, sharpening disagreements, growing doubt and uncertainty, intensifying public anxiety, and disruption of the patterns of life. Terror deals in fraud and deception, and does so via interviews and articles in the media for purposes of psychological warfare, meant to sow confusion of concepts and values. The goal is to destroy the faith in and legitimacy of the government and bring about a change in policy.

How do these aspects pertain to the inhuman terror that Arafat has employed since the end of September 2000, known as the *al-Aqsa*

Intifada? The Israeli media's main message is to frighten the public, both by highlighting the terror organizations' proclamations and publicizing dismaying pictures, which underline the notion that "the war is at the gate"; the conclusion is that one must exercise restraint and give in, since "terrorism can't be defeated." Israel, therefore, must also discuss the "right of return" and divide Jerusalem. Thus a band of journalists have determined that terrorism cannot be militarily defeated, and that even after retaking the territories Israel will have to discuss an agreement resembling the offers of former prime minister Barak. Israel, it is said, must either conduct negotiations even under fire on full peace at a heavy price, or occupy the Palestinian Authority at high risk of a comprehensive regional war at terrible cost. The mantra was drummed in incessantly that Sharon is the one who has torpedoed any chance for a political settlement, and is acting now to attain what he has long sought – war. The Sharon government is said to be dragging the people into Lebanonization, into a trap that leads only to killing and murder. This, in turn, is said to be a sure prescription for the suicide of the national-religious coalition. The message is: it is not Arafat, the father and mother of international terrorism, who is responsible for the situation, but rather the national–religious coalition in Israel, led by Sharon; that the Israeli government not only is not doing enough to end the cycle of violence but is in fact exacerbating it. For some pseudo-Zionists, Arafat's terror is justified in light of the circumstances.

2 *Resisting the draft.* The second message concerns the phenomenon of refusal of military service, which leads to a weakening of the national fortitude and a sharpening of the controversies among the public, while constituting dramatic evidence of Arafat's triumph. This phenomenon obtains giant headlines and great resonance in the media, without any reference to the actual number of refusers, and goes hand in hand with grave moral accusations against the army's actions. Thus, one of the refusing officers was granted a huge interview in the Friday supplement of Israel's largest-circulation newspaper *Yediot Aharonot*, and in the next edition his compatriots stated that he was a combination of Dreyfus, Socrates, and Galileo, "a real hero in this unfortunate country." The timing and manner of publication of such messages in the media, and their magnitude relative to the size and influence of the group, indicate that this is actually political activity in the direction of insurrection, to the benefit of hostile, anti-Semitic international elements. Thus, some political actors in Israel have acknowledged that the officers' refusal to serve is a great achievement for Arafat. The media has published lengthy articles on movements and organizations that take radical positions toward Israel's policy. Many sources have reported that circles in the Palestinian

Authority closely follow the phenomenon of refusal to serve, and that Arafat is strongly encouraged by these developments to continue in his terror, assuming that, as occurred in Lebanon, the phenomenon will strengthen pressures within Israel for a withdrawal.

Indeed the public discussion of this issue, which the media magnifies immeasurably, serves one of the most cherished goals of terror. Thus Israel falters in its path and its faith weakens, amid surmises that perhaps it is best to give in and compromise. Arafat's feelings of triumph intensify, both in regard to the victims of terror as well as the psychological, economic, and social damage that he is causing to Israel.

Another aspect of the refusal to serve in the military is the visits to Arafat by members of Knesset and Israeli personalities, aimed at encouraging him. This reached its peak, however, with a visit by hundreds of Israelis who received Arafat with fervent applause and tears, crying: "Soldiers go home!" Later groups of ruffians went even further and painted slogans of actual incitement on tanks, such as "army of murderers." These acts undoubtedly constitute support for the enemy in wartime as well as incitement and insurrection; yet, of course, nothing was done, since for members of the leftist elite and the media all is permitted. After all, they have absolute justice on their side, and incitement to violence exists only on the right side of the political map, whereas they themselves are entirely innocent of incitement and insurrection.

The third message concerns the issue of the "targeted killings." The media has long claimed that the policy of targeted killings has failed severely and in fact led to an increased number of terrorist attacks, which only those who conduct the policy do not realize. Thus a group of cinema people, who live at the taxpayers' expense, severely protested the blowing up of the Voice of Palestine station, "which has no connection to the struggle against terror. Bombings, targeted killings, and encirclements will only lead to escalation, and the Israeli government is responsible for this reality." The issue of the targeted killings received its greatest boost, however, from two former heads of the General Security Service, Ami Ayalon and Yaacov Peri. Ami Ayalon is a prime example of a war hero who is a recruit to the peace project. But what is most problematic is that one of the more effective tools in the war against international terror is now, in Israel, the subject of a fervent public controversy, which makes it difficult to use consistently and significantly.

The effects of terror were bolstered still further in propaganda and international terms when several members of Knesset, Yael Dayan, Naomi Chazan, and Mussy Raz, tabled a bill in the Knesset stating that Israel "will not be able to carry out targeted killings of Palestinians, and will not execute them without a trial." For an added legal touch, the legal adviser Eyal Gross asserted that Israel is not a democracy engaged in self-defense, and "in regard to the targeted killings the occupation is what is being defended." But the height of humiliation and disgrace was reached by the journalist who made a comparison between the sanitized rhetoric of the spokesmen of the Wannsee Conference regarding the annihilation of European Jewry and the terms "targeted killing," "ticking bomb," and "clearing territory." As he stated: "Sixty years after, and with all the necessary distinctions, it is worth recalling that the sanitized rhetoric of the present is likely to dirty our hands and silence our conscience."

Thus the pseudo-Zionist group engages in its intensive activity that damages and endangers Israel. The use of intolerable words, such as Nazism and apartheid, lends justification to the international system in acting against Israel and constitutes a great propaganda boon for the country's most odious enemies. Anyone who has studied or experienced, even only a little, the Nazi ideology or the policy of apartheid can only marvel and stand amazed at such a comparison. But the pseudo-Zionists are not cautious about their words, and do not understand their effect on Israel's image in the international system. One need not engage in apologetics to assert that there is no more moral state than Israel in the international system. There is no army that observes the "purity of arms" (even though weaponry by definition is not in fact "pure") as Israel does. A brief analysis of the actions of Britain, the United States, France, and the other democratic countries will reflect on the uniqueness of Israel and its policy. But nothing stops the pseudo-Zionists, until they reach the edge of the abyss.

The most recent example is the killing of Salah Sh'adeh, who set up the military wing of Hamas and was responsible for the murder of hundreds of Israeli civilians. He is a prime example of a terrorist of the worst kind whom it is obligatory to eliminate. Nothing could be more justified than his killing, even at the price that was paid. Yet whoever observed the chorus of hypocrisy in the media, which sang in one voice about "the terrible blunder" and "the intolerable price," could only wonder at their irresponsibility. Only one question is relevant: if you, a moral and refined media person, had been among the policymakers, and you had had responsibility for public security – what would you have done? It is very easy to criticize in the media; it entails no responsibility. But the great rule, always, is "If someone comes to kill you, kill him first." But the preening media orchestra will say, yes, Salah Sh'adeh deserved to die, but how can one act in a way that endangers children? Indeed, the price of harming children is an appalling one. Yet they should open their eyes to the fact that the terrorist gang surrounding Arafat, and in all the organizations, shield themselves with children as much as possible. Children have served them as hostages for over a year. What, then, does one do? Is it acceptable that they continue to kill us with a savage terror unprecedented in history while taking cover behind children? The only mistake – and it is part of a long string of Israel's failures to explain itself – is that Israel does not inform and warn world opinion about this form of child exploitation. The whole world should know how the master-terrorists use children as hostages.

Finally, the media magnifies the threat of terrorism and undermines morale. In the present era of Arafat's terror, the media publishes in lead headlines the statements of the terrorist organizations on the revenge they will exact against Israel, and flaunts photographs of the terrorists, their deeds, and their proclamations. It takes pains to publish the terrorists' lists of individuals slated for assassination, and creates a dire feeling of intolerable terror. This dangerous policy of the media is highly effective. The media addresses not only public opinion, but also directs defiant questions at the decision makers: would it not be wise to relent so as to forestall revenge attacks? Would it not be prudent to capitulate and withdraw? In this way the identity of those who instigate the terrorist activity is forgotten, and instead it is the antiterrorist activity that is questioned, rather than showing resolve in the struggle against terrorism.

Thus the pseudo-Zionist members of Knesset have asserted that the violence and terror since September 2000 constitute "a war for the well-being of the settlers," that Israel behaves like the terrorist organizations, and that its preventive efforts constitute murder. Moreover, journalists have published articles claiming that terror as a means based on violence is one of the methods used by the racist State of Israel.

The discussions and debates that are held in the media only reinforce these tendencies, and constitute encouragement to terrorism by showing that it has a positive yield. The reality, of course, is different. By acting resolutely against terrorism, by eliminating its leaders, by blocking the channels of its funding, one succeeds in overcoming it. Proofs of this abounds in Europe, in Japan, in South America. This pertains both to the nationalist and the religious organizations, such as the Kurdish PKK following the arrest of Oçalan; the Islamic Jihad after the assassination of Shekhaki; and the religious terrorist organizations in Egypt and Russia. Thus, in the Land of Israel in the late 1930s, Britain fully succeeded in crushing the Palestinian terror of al-Qassam. But terrorism disrupts sound thinking, sows doubts, and undermines national cohesion via publicity in the media. No less grave is the way in which the media gives the feeling that the "cycle of revenge" is widening, and that it is the media's moral duty to close it.

What is important, however, is not closing the "cycle of revenge" but rather the clear realization that criminal terrorism exists and must be destroyed, and that every state is obligated to conduct an antiterror policy if it values life. The aim is to assert power as the basis for an agreement, not to capitulate to terror through negotiations. The state is always more powerful than the terrorist organizations, and only faint-heartedness and feebleness, reinforced by the media, prevent the achievement of these goals. Particularly important are General Amos Gilead's statements that the Israeli media serves terror, reveals military and operational secrets, distorts reality in the other side's favor, and has no red lines.

3 The "humanization" of terror and the exaggeration of its power. This involves defining terrorists as freedom fighters, patriots, and guerrillas, as well as granting them broad media coverage in the form of photographs and quotations of their words, interviews and their taped suicide proclamations, images of their families in mourning – whatever gives them legitimacy and respectability. At the same time, close-ups of the victims, interviews with people who express fear, coverage of major places that have become devoid of people – these are some of the ways the media causes harm. The most dangerous aspect is the media's tendency to display "intellectual objectivity," which views the law-abiding citizen and the terrorist, the state and the terrorist organization, as two equal sides in a morally symmetrical struggle. The media gives them equal time for coverage and interviews, and treats terrorists courteously and deferentially. Instead of being denied airtime they gain respectability, and are accorded legitimacy and decency. What stands out in the coverage of terrorism is the inability to distinguish between the inhuman attacks on civilians and the right of a country to defend itself. Yet terror is so evil and so ugly that no journalistic treatment can prettify it. It is a duty to fight it and eradicate it.

An attempt is also made to explain the sources of fanatic terrorism in economic terms. The postmodern style of thinking is, however, entirely erroneous and creates "moral equivalency" between fanatic, immoral terrorism and the war against terrorism as a legitimate form of self-defense. This is based on the image of the hapless terrorist whose acts stem from deprivation, having been left no other way to achieve his legitimate objectives. And here perhaps lies the greatest error of the media, its greatest misconception. Terror never and nowhere stemmed from poverty and deprivation. The leaders of the terrorist organizations are middle-class, university graduates, and urban. Poverty leads to crime and not to terrorism. Ideology and fanaticism lead to terror. The number of doctors, engineers, and professors among the leaders of terror organizations is remarkable. There is no evidence, from anywhere in the world, that misery and poverty are what leads to terror. The statistical data are unequivocal:

of the 120 suicide murderers in Israel from October 2000 to June 2002, over 85 percent had a high school and university education and 65 percent had a full university education. All nineteen of the suicide murderers in the United States on September 11, 2001, had a higher education and a strong economic status. All the leaders of the terrorist organizations are economically well-off and educated, and there are long lists that show this. Those in the refugee camps are not relevant at all, merely serving as justification and as fodder for the kingpins of terror. The poor want to exist and survive. Terror wants to destroy and kill.

But the media continues to peddle its bad merchandise, as if eliminating poverty and deprivation will prevent violence and terror. This issue was resolved in Europe in the 1970s, and there is broad agreement on it even in scholarly research. Yet in Israel, in idiotic folly, it is still discussed, its implications still debated. Indeed the media, which takes pains to be impartial between terror and the state, and acts according to the politically-correct principle, magnifies the achievements of terror and, on the educational and economic issue, outdoes even itself.

Furthermore, the media does not understand that even if the terrorist makes a bad impression or is negatively portrayed, he has achieved his objective. The problem is not what he says, which is a performance for publicity and part of psychological warfare, but what he does. What terror says to the media is entirely different from what its activity aims at. The terrorist may express conciliation and goodwill, or he may express hostility and rage. The terrorists do not care how they are portrayed, so long as they garner publicity. Sometimes in fact they want to be seen as "evil," "cruel," and "without human feelings" (Clutterbuck, 1981).

The media can carry out terrorism's mission even inadvertently by means of negative coverage. It exaggerates the effects of terror on the functioning and well-being of society. The dramatic reports create an image of menacing power that is far greater than the real danger, and severely weakens the national resolve of the population. The public becomes inured to the horrific acts, and there is a creeping readiness to understand the terrorists' deeds, to seek a compromise arrangement, just so long as there is quiet.

How are these aspects manifested in Arafat's terror in the *al-Aqsa Intifada*? In a project of pure propaganda and unprecedented psychological warfare, front pages and Friday supplements of the Israeli press have featured wide-ranging interviews with senior figures in the Palestinian Authority such as Mohammed Dahlan, Jibril Rajoub, Abu-Allah, Saeb Erekat, Abu-Mazen, Nabil Sha'ath, and many others, some of them several times, so as to convey Arafat's mendacious messages directly to the Israeli population and thereby sow doubts and stoke controversies.

The main messages of the psychological warfare are: that the Palestinians are demanding only 22 percent of their historical homeland; that the Israeli government serves the army, which is an extreme, warmongering element; that the Israeli government is exclusively responsible for destroying the peace that was achieved with Arafat, and exists even now; and that at Camp David there was no Israeli offer, and what was told the Israeli public is a crude lie and deception.

But most of all, the media magnifies the scope of the terrorist threats. Thus, when the media enters the refugee camps it broadcasts over and over small groups of masked people who are preparing for a miniwar against Israel, projecting their power, violence, and lust for revenge and thereby scare the Israeli public and deter the decision makers. Again and again, the spotlight is on the intensity of their wretchedness. Yet when the Israeli army enters the refugee camps, the reaction of these "heroes" is to flee in panic – as in the Tulkarm camp where six hundred people turned themselves over to Israel security forces, and as in Ramallah when Israel entered it in late March 2002. These are the "heroes" whom the media portrays as girding themselves for the revenge they will inflict on Israel. Instead of displaying every one of them in a close-up and letting them send greetings to their families, it would make more sense to show the abject-ness of their military level and not foster a myth of the bravery of these masked terrorists among the Palestinians. Yet the media stresses the fear that they sow in the streets of Israel and not the cowardice of their crim-inal acts, in which they stand in crowded places and shoot in every direction, on the competence level of retardates. The media reaches the height of perversity in covering the acts of the suicide bombers. Instead of showing the perpetrators as the scum of the earth, miserable cowards who seek to kill and injure young people in places of entertainment and gaiety rather than fighting against an army, it immediately presents their filmed "testimony" and the statements of the leaders of the terrorist organiz-ations in direct broadcasts to the Israeli people. Soon the media shows the terrorists' families in their makeshift huts for mourning, further under-lining their wretchedness. Thus the media exacerbates fear and dread – which is, indeed, the goal and *raison d'être* of terrorism.

Israel is the only democracy in the world whose media constantly presents, in television and newspaper interviews, the representatives of the terrorists and the representatives of the government as equal interlocu-tors. And the terrorists are treated politely and questioned courteously, thereby transmitting their messages. The Israeli media wants to reinvent the wheel in regard to its role in national security, ensuring that only in Israel, among all the democracies, do the public's worst enemies appear regularly before it: spokesmen of Hamas and Islamic Jihad, the suicide bombers with rifle in hand, and Bin Laden, addressing the people with their sophisticated messages.

If we look at the media coverage of terrorist incidents in Western democracies, we find the following realities. In Britain, the BBC adheres to strict rules: as little blood as possible, without shocking pictures of corpses including covered ones. In regard to the IRA – choirboys compared to the PLO and the fundamentalist Islamic organizations – the rules are very stringent: up to 1995, viewers had no exposure to their images or voices. Even the image of the IRA political leader, Gerry Adams, was blurred and his voice dubbed. Generally the media was under governmental pressure not to publicize the terrorist organizations and not to criticize the struggle against terror. Rule 3 of the regulations prohibits giving the IRA interviews and a public forum without governmental approval. Broadcasts by outside actors were censored, blocked, or reedited. And all this at a time when the IRA posed no existential threat to England.

Germany was the first country to try to regulate the media–government relationship in regard to terrorist incidents. There is a tradition and even a public consensus there on restricting information related to terrorism. The coordination was not just based on rules of censorship but, rather, active coordination in real time. This is one of the important factors that enabled the destruction of the Baader-Meinhof organization. The media-government coordination also proved effective in regard to the 1974 kidnapping of Peter Laurenz, leader of the Christian Democrat Party in Berlin, and the 1977 kidnapping of industrialist Martin Schleier.

In France, the rules of coverage are derived from a strict legal system for protecting privacy. Photographs of victims of terror attacks and other shocking pictures are prohibited by the Law of Individual Freedoms. Concerning the media's coverage of terror there is a strong consensual tradition with the government.

Particularly noteworthy is the media's behavior in the United States since the Bin Laden attacks and the warfare in Afghanistan. But these countries are, after all, "just" democracies. Only in Israel do we find the "public's right to know," meaning the media's right to supply the unfortunate public with the verities that it postulates.

Arafat's strategy works by "warfare on two fronts": gaining the support of world public opinion, and eroding morale in the internal Israeli system. For both of these strategies the media plays a critical role. Arafat was at his best in the pleasantries that he published in the United States, in which he expressed three things: condemnation of the terror of the fundamentalist organizations; an understanding of Israel's fears about the "right of return," with a readiness for creative solutions to end the refugee problem; and the notion that Palestinian well-being requires an Israeli return to the 1967 borders with Jerusalem as the capital of the two peoples. On that very date, however, he reiterated in Arabic his *shuhada'* speech, in a version asserting that one *shahid* from the Palestinian people is worth seventy *shuhada'* and that the Palestinian people would march to Jerusalem with millions of *shuhada'*. In reply to an inquiry he event sent a detailed statement to the United States to prove that he was fighting terrorism, and even took responsibility for the *Karine A* weapons ship – despite the fact, he claimed, that he had not known about it. Yet on the same day on which that reply was publicized, Arafat acted on behalf of severe terrorist attacks, including suicide bombers and *Qassam* missiles that were seized, and gave a fiery speech in Arabic titled "To Jerusalem Go Millions of *Shuhada'*."

Yet in Israel the silly debate about Arafat's responsibility and role continues.[3] Nothing was ever so clear-cut as the fact that Arafat is a serial terrorist who has never changed his ways. Only in Israel does the debate go on and intensify, sponsored by those who in the past sang to "Father Stalin, Sun of the Peoples," the greatest murderer in history. The Israeli media does not want to learn and internalize the fact that the Palestinian national movement is a fascist movement in its tenets, goals, and means, which sanctifies blood and death in conceptual totalitarianism, and that Arafat is active mainly in the industry of the death of young people. He did not care about the destruction of Arab capitals, and killed tens of thousands of his own people and others in Arab countries in the 1970s and 1980s; and he certainly does not care about sacrificing thousands of his people today, dispatching them with stones to shield his praetorian guard. Arafat, who has received billions of dollars from the international system, has not rehabilitated even a single refugee family; yet the pseudo-Zionists blame Israel for their situation. Arafat is indifferent to life and death, and he has but one goal – the liberation of all Palestine.

But the problem is graver. Only under the aegis of the media, which innocently protests that it is "just asking," and "just raising topics for discussion," and "just trying to examine the issue," did the sages of Oslo gain the status of media heroes and celebrities. And they receive unprecedented airtime and coverage, and every nonsensical statement they make wins a huge and immediate resonance. And, indeed, they set the political agenda. Sponsored by the media, its direct and senior partner in the calamities of Oslo, of which we are just at the beginning, their statements are treated as wisdom incarnate, as ultimate messianic tidings. In March 2002 Ron Pundak, one of the leading Oslo sages, who displays messianic folly, complete mental closure, and total blind obstinacy, stated that "if there is a political horizon, the Tanzim itself will break up its violent factions."

Wonderful indeed. Thus also Chamberlain, after the Munich agreement with Hitler, proclaimed that he had brought peace not only for his generation but for the coming generations as well. And these words of nonsense prove that the media is always ready to supply a media stage for the Oslo celebrities. Why blame Arafat? The Israeli media have no better friend.

Thus former Member of Knesset Shulamit Aloni said in January 2002, after visiting Arafat in Ramallah, that she trusted him more than the prime minister of Israel, Sharon, and the chief of staff, Mofaz. Arafat, she stated without blushing, had invested $2 billion in infrastructure development, and did not want to launch the *Intifada*. As for the *Karine A* arms ship, Arafat claimed he had nothing to do with it, and she believed him. And she did not flinch. She said these things notwithstanding published assertions by Bashar Assad that Arafat was an incomparable liar, and that Syria had had no trust in him since the 1970s. Such assertions could also be made by King Hussein and President Sadat, as well as other Arab Middle Eastern leaders.[4]

But Shulamit Aloni and the pseudo-Zionists in fact trust Arafat despite the extensive intelligence information that he is terrorism personified, and despite the harsh statements coming from government spokesmen in the United States. Notwithstanding the diplomatic niceties and obligatory restraint owing to its general interests in the region, the United States blames Arafat in unequivocal terms: President Bush is "very disappointed in Arafat . . . I was considerate of him and declared support for a Palestinian state, and in return Arafat escalates the terror, and lies brazenly." If Arafat does not show that he is serious about fighting terrorism, the United States will impose sanctions against him. "We're sick and tired of Arafat . . . [we should] give him an ultimatum." Arafat behaves as a terrorist. Vice-President Cheney stated: "We don't trust Arafat." "Arafat is a lost cause, and we should cut off contact with him immediately." "As far as I'm concerned, you can hang Arafat." Senior officials in the government and the White House: "Arafat is mentally disturbed," "a liar," "we're tired of him," "it's a waste of time, there's no point talking with Arafat." The emissary Zinni: "Arafat is an incorrigible liar. He lied to me brazenly. We're talking about a completely untrustworthy person. Arafat is mentally unbalanced." "Arafat is a Mafia chief." And former head of the CIA Woolsey: "Arafat needs to undergo a total change of the heart and the mind."

Shulamit Aloni and her pseudo-Zionist friends will continue to act against Israel's existential interests on different claims and pretexts, defending and trusting Arafat at his wod, and will even attack the United States if it moves against Arafat and the Palestinian Authority, so long as they can sustain their contorted utopian dreams. That is why one of the senior academics in Israel, Ze'ev Sternhell, counseled Arafat on how to wage his terrorist struggle against Israel, and advised him to attack male settlers in the territories while refraining from attacks within the 1967 borders. Ron Pundak declares in mental blindness and in an unwavering march of folly that Arafat "is the person one has to talk to," and that a settlement can be reached with the Palestinians on "one hundred percent of the territory and one more meter, with Israel absorbing a quota of a few tens of thousands of Palestinians." And Beilin, who is funded by unknown European donors, and is interviewed in the Israeli media with amazing frequency, achieves new and unmatchable heights of audacity and brazenness in averring that Oslo alone is the path and the way, and only Sharon is responsible for the outbreak of the *al-Aqsa Intifada* and for the ongoing terrorism as well.

A young journalist, who in his youth undoubtedly sang the *International*, is angry about the comparison between "Arafat, leader of an occupied people, and Bin Laden, a psychopathic fanatic." It is very difficult for him to absorb that Arafat is the father and mother of international terrorism, who will be found at every juncture over the past forty years. But why just him? If Arafat is not terrorism incarnate, then Stalin really is the "Sun of the Peoples." A prime example of the success of Arafat's terrorism, of submitting to violence in favor of the hedonism of the moment, is a comparison by one of the court journalists of the Oslo sages, Akiva Eldar, between the Palestinian "right of return" and the Israeli "law of return": "Can any *al-Aqsa Intifada* cancel the realization of the idea of two states for two peoples, a fair solution to the refugee problem, and a just division of Jerusalem?" And the journalist Yoel Marcus elaborated: "There will be no agreement with Arafat unless we withdraw to the 1967 borders including Jerusalem, and agree to the right of return." And when that happens, and the State of Israel is on the way to its demise as a political entity, we are sure to find Marcus and his friends somewhere in cultured Europe, sitting over a cup of coffee. Previously he expressed bewilderment that "no one foresaw that the weapons we gave him would be turned against us with lethal terror and mortar fire." Indeed – no one foresaw? Does the sun rise in the east? But Marcus, Eldar, and their friends have learned nothing, not even the Palestinian political language, whose basis is *Hudeibiyah* (the agreement the prophet signed with the Meccans in 628, which he violated after two years); and *jihad* (a holy war on behalf of Allah) – as Arafat has proclaimed on hundreds of occasions. Nor have the media people in Israel learned that the phenomenon of the suicide bombers began solely in the period of Arafat's rule in the territories. And they have not learned that Arafat is terrorism incarnate, so that it is the height of absurdity to demand that he fight terrorism.

Only an insane person can be demanded to fight against himself. And Arafat is not at all insane.

Thus arose the media mantra of the somnambulant post-Zionists – that Camp David was an exercise in deception, and Arafat is the victim and not the recalcitrant party. But it is worth reading the words of Abu-Mazen, who took part in the Camp David talks: "East Jerusalem must return to us, and West Jerusalem must be an open city . . . we will not agree that you will have a presence at the Western Wall . . . [except] for holding religious ceremonies . . . there are four million refugees all of whom come from the soil of historical Palestine, and it is their right to return to their homes." And Hasan A'sfur, who was a member of the Palestinian delegation at Camp David: "From our standpoint there is no option of conceding the total and far-reaching right of return." But the media-leftist complex has cultivated, and the pseudo-Zionists are indeed raising, the idea of multiculturalism.

It is most important that we attend to this issue. There is no country in the world that does not have national, religious, and ethnic minorities. It is worth considering countries such as the United States, and Britain, and France, no less democracies than the enlightened Israeli democracy. Have they changed their national anthem in deference to their minorities? Have they changed the national institutions? The flag and the national symbols? And what does one have to say, in how much time, and with which testimonials, to obtain American citizenship? And in what language does one swear allegiance? And what is done every morning in the educational institutions, if not singing the national anthem and raising the flag? And what is done in France, which proclaims that it is "a state of all its citizens" yet requires all minorities to accept its national symbols and institutions? And on the flags of Switzerland and the Scandinavian countries, one finds a cross. Are they acting to change this in deference to their minorities? And Italy and Spain are Catholic countries. Are they acting to change their religious status because of the minorities within them? Australia and Canada, which were immigrant-absorbing countries, began a stringent selection process. Did they replace the national institutions, the national anthem, and the flag according to the desires of the immigrants? And perhaps the pseudo-Zionists and post-Zionists should begin with the Arab states, those enlightened democracies and perfect upholders of human rights? And perhaps they will act resolutely to subvert the insane dehumanization practiced by the fascist Palestinian national movement toward Israel?

The main source of the *al-Aqsa Intifada* and its salient features was the great success of Hizbullah, which brought Israel to make a panicked withdrawal from Lebanon without an agreement. Bernard Lewis, in an interview he gave to the post-Zionist Yaron London, analyzes the developments: "I think Israel was right to enter Lebanon . . . the later withdrawal, as it was carried out, without an agreement, while abandoning friends and weaponry, was interpreted by the Palestinians as a sign of weakness. From the experience of Hizbullah they deduced that the Israelis are soft, pampered, and if they're attacked – they'll give in. The Palestinians said these things explicitly. . . . The withdrawal from Lebanon had a great influence on the Palestinians' decision to renew the armed struggle." These things were said by Ahmad Jibril, head of the Popular Front terrorist organization, in his meeting in Amman with Member of Knesset Hashim Mahamid. This is also what Nasrallah, the Hizbullah leader, said to the Palestinians in January 2000.

And now the great question, which was so foolishly debated in the media, has also been answered: will the Shi'ite guerrilla, who expelled the Israeli army in a panicked stampede from Lebanon, continue to march toward Jerusalem or stop at the border? The situation at the Lebanese border is explosive, and war could break out there any moment, despite Israel's total withdrawal in agreement and coordination with the United Nations. Thus Arafat, after Camp David, found that he was able to act on the same basis. He dropped all restraints and began to emulate Nasrallah, using unprecedented terrorism, to achieve the same objective of Israeli withdrawal, under the auspices of the hedonistic and prettifying media and the pseudo-Zionists. The picture, however, was so one-dimensional that no one examined it as a whole. Southern Lebanon is not disjunct from the wider reality of the region. Nasrallah became a hero of Palestinian culture and activism. For the first time in Israel's history the enemy was able to overcome it, now that its resilience, under the public pressure exerted by and through the media, had eroded beyond recognition.

And the reality in Lebanon is one of a gigantic "black hole" that is waiting to explode. So far Israel has restrained itself and has not done anything in the face of the Hizbullah provocations. Yet their menacing process of feverish armament continues, including ten thousand long-range missiles that pose a threat to Haifa. In the political and intelligence dimension, according to Foreign Minister Peres, Hizbullah has forged deep links with the Palestinian Authority and serves as a bridge to Iran, while also developing a network of mobilization and activity among the Israeli Arabs. Indeed, Hasan Nasrallah was right when he said that "Israel is weak as a spider's web." It fled from Lebanon in disgrace and betrayal of its allies, and brought the *al-Aqsa Intifada* upon itself. And when the fog dispersed, what emerged was the deal between Arafat and Iran: weapons and money for Hizbullah activity in the territories. This was in addition to ongoing support and extensive funding of the Hamas and Islamic Jihad organizations.

The principal blame, however, for the greatest terror and violence in the history of the State of Israel lies with the Oslo process, and the bringing of Arafat, together with 150,000 of his corrupt cronies, from Tunis to the territories. Arafat is a murderous, terrorizing ruler and a serial violator of every agreement, just as he was in Jordan in 1970 and in Lebanon in 1982. It began with the agreement of May 1969, which entrenched his status in Lebanon, and from there on the history is clear and unequivocal. Only in Israel have the messianic sages of Oslo failed to master it. But those who are familiar with Arafat and his sojourns in Jordan and Lebanon, where he sacrificed Arabs and Palestinians and caused the destruction of Amman and Beirut, know that his inner world is one of terror and war only. Yet the euphoric vision of the Oslo sages was too lovely to be tarnished, and, with the help of their compatriots in the media, any possibility of criticism was drowned in a chorus of derision. In total fervor the media proclaimed that peace was at hand while all who thought otherwise were warmongers, who must be denied a media forum lest they poison the well of life. Israel is immersed in the "Beilinism syndrome."

The Oslo sages tried to devise a "new order" in Palestine. Although they harshly reproved those who sought to make a "new order" in Lebanon in 1982, for them it was permitted. A set of gamblers without restrictions, messianic hedonists whom Shabbetai Zvi would have envied, arrogantly decided they had found the way to redeem the people of Israel, and imported Arafat without learning about his personality and his psychopathology, while ignoring his deeds in Jordan and Lebanon and his violent value system, not even grasping the significance of the military uniform he wore at all times. Oslo was not a political process, but a state of mind among dreamers of dreams and peddlers of illusions who misled an entire people. And they were well served by the media, which did not permit any public discourse and mocked those who failed to perceive the vision of redemption. A fatal sort of "mutual admiration society" developed: the Oslo sages gave the media "scoops" of dreams, a chimera of peace, and the media turned them into celebrities whose army of peace it was worth joining. All the rest, of course, were warmongers.

Yet Arafat did not conform to expectations, constituting a one-man "rejectionist front" in the political domain and using the political process as the continuation of war by other means; he is, indeed, a serial terrorist, he is a patrimonial leader who controls the flames, the height of the flames, and the intensity of the flames; he is estranged and apathetic toward all the civil matters of managing a state and society. His inner world is a world of war and violence. He has sacrificed even his private life to this project. Arafat is impervious to all but the realization of his goals. He is the greatest refuser of all. Any political arrangement arrived at with him will collapse at one point or another. He acts via political settlements, takes a break to use violence and terror, goes back to political settlements, then takes another break at the next stage of the national struggle. Nothing interests him except a "solution to the Palestine problem" as an integral national symbol, even at the expense of total wars in the Middle East, even at the expense of the suffering, despair, and even lives of the Palestinian people.

Whoever sought in him a partner such as Saad Haddad found him at the height of his international power in the form of the Durban conference. Removing Arafat, however, is an interest of the first order for all the players in the system – both the regional system of the Arab states, particularly Egypt and Jordan, and the international system. Removing him can prevent a regional explosion that would emanate beyond its immediate environment, and is certainly in the existential interest of Israel. His continued presence will likely mean that Israel will forfeit the peace agreements with Egypt and Jordan, and be unable to reach a political settlement with Syria. Ejecting him is indeed an obligation, because he is the gravest, ultimate strategic enemy who has ever arisen against Israel. Although with British delicacy, Bernard stated unequivocally that the idea of bringing Arafat from Tunis was mistaken. Arafat has never concealed his aim of realizing the "right of return" to all Palestine, and he wants Jordan as well.[5]

What, then, needs to be done about the symbiotic relations between terror and the media? This question has long been asked in scholarly research, and still no clear, agreed answer has emerged. The Pulitzer Prize-winning columnist George Will has pondered the systematic irresponsibility of the media, which stems mainly from the "Watergate syndrome," an event that became a paradigm for successful journalism. Yet the time has come, Will asserts, to soberly consider the relationship between "the public's right to know" and "the public's need to know," or, more accurately, "the public's right to be protected." Does the public need to know everything? yes. Does it need the media as the "watchdog of democracy?" Yes. But does it need to know everything immediately, in real time, and with no connection to the dangers of terrorism? no. In this regard, the media has become "an electronic megaphone for terror."[6]

The media plays a critically important role in democracy. Damaging it is likely to mean damaging the most basic freedoms. The government is not allowed to act against it and circumscribe it; instead, the media itself must exercise self-supervision and fairness in reporting. Back in 1981 an ethical code was determined in the United States, in the form of certain guidelines regarding terrorist activity: restrained, discreet coverage – providing facts only; not to report on rumors, speculations, and conjectures; not to broadcast live and in real time; to maintain a low, discreet profile at the site of an incident, it being clearly forbidden to mediate or take an active part; not to ask or broadcast critical questions, such as setting a deadline; not to provide information that could aid the terrorists; and to deny them propaganda publicity. The CBS network prepared a guidebook for covering terrorist acts on television: reporters were to avoid live coverage of the terrorists' aggression; avoid disrupting the activity of the security forces in the field; and avoid using words or measures that might exacerbate the situation (Gallimore, 1991, p. 106; Montgomery, 1991, p. 63).

Although the rules were not always observed in covering terrorist incidents, after the Bin Laden attacks the media learned its lesson. American patriotism was now regnant, and nothing was done to pique public opinion. Thus the journalist Yitzhak ben-Horin reported that "something strange is happening to the American media, which is adjusting itself to the patriotic spirit that prevails among the public. The American flag covers the screen; whoever speaks against the president is punished; American national pride is at its peak." Likewise the weekly magazine *Time* decided to crown the mayor of New York, Giuliani, as Man of the Year, and not Bin Laden, because it rightly assessed the mood in America. Is such a situation conceivable in Israel? The fatalities in the attack in the United States are the equivalent of less than 150 fatalities in Israel. Up to mid-July 2002, Israel had suffered 550 fatalities in the *al-Aqsa Intifada*. It seems, then, that one cannot escape the conclusion that the Americans are a people who love life, whereas the Israelis have gotten used to the "victim syndrome."

The Israeli media must understand the significance of its enormous power and take responsibility. It can and must take a stance, but it must also be honest and responsible. It must ask questions and even uncover surprises, and it must prevent the government from acting without surveillance. But, to the same extent, it must not help the forces of darkness defeat the state. On the issue of terror, as in war, moderation and responsibility are required, and so is judgment. If that is good for the citizens of the United States, which despite everything is not existentially threatened, it certainly is good for the State of Israel, which is fighting for its life, in three internal and regional spheres of threat, notwithstanding the lunatic mantras of the pseudo-Zionists.

Has the *al-Aqsa Intifada* achieved its objectives? Although it is still, to be sure, ongoing, an intermediate assessment is possible. The answer is positive. Arafat has succeeded in advancing his goals via terror, and the price the Palestinians are paying in casualties and economic damage is not at all perceived as in democratic regimes. In authoritarian regimes the question of the human and economic cost is only in the eyes of the leadership and according to its considerations. This is true of Saddam Hussein in Iraq, and of Arab states that participated in the wars against Israel. It is true wherever there are patrimonial leaders. Arafat's terror is winning, because the struggle is over a balance of forces: who will impose his *modus operandi* on whom? He is winning at a time when debates in Israel have intensified; when a sharp public controversy has developed on what sorts of action to take; when there is a cognitive transfer of blame for the terror from the Palestinians to "the occupation and the settlers"; when the desire to bring about peace is stronger than the desire for national survival by eliminating terror; when doubts arise about the justice of one's own path while the tendency grows to understand the motives of the terror and its perpetrators.

Arafat has succeeded in disrupting life in Israel. He sows fear and anxiety, and the renewed resolve that emerged at first, which stemmed mainly from a stunned surprise among the Israeli public, quickly turned into pressure on the political system by the media-leftist complex and the pseudo-Zionists, while raising perplexing questions about the rightness of the path. Next, central planks of the Zionist ethos will come up for discussion: the "right of return" (UN Resolution 194, December 11, 1948) and the Partition Plan (UN Resolution 181, November 29, 1947). And again the Jews' longing for exile awakens, the main question being not whether the Jew has left the exile but whether the exile has left the Jew. And thus, likewise, the basic Arab premise will prevail: not only that there is no such thing as a Jewish people, but that Palestine is not the solution to the Jewish problem. And if the Jews stand firm, a new wave of terror will emerge – the "Palestine *Intifada*," in coordination with the Israeli Arabs, who will be supported by the media–leftist complex and the pseudo-Zionists in their claims of discrimination, rather than focusing on issues of their loyalty to the State of Israel.

The ideological–messianic notion, however infantile, that the problems in the Israeli-Palestinian conflict lie in Israel's control of the territories leads the media-leftist complex, in blatant national irresponsibility, to concentrate on blaming Israel rather than the Palestinians' attitudes and goals. Thus Member of Knesset Yossi Sarid averred that "the Israeli occupation is the root of the whole problem, and the settlements are the worst calamity that has befallen the Zionist enterprise." The refusal movement, for its part, spawned an unprecedented slough of harsh censures of Israel and the occupation. Israel Prize winner Efraim Kishon gave this ringing rebuke: "Israeli journalists and writers traipse about the world, revile the state, talk about the suffering of the Palestinian people, and for this receive prizes." Indeed, at the time of the largest reserve mobilization since the Lebanon War, the media seeks out refusal, grumbling, and opposition to entering the territories, and finds a solid wall of statements about a "war of no choice," and willingness to be mobilized because "the war is for our homes."

Member of Knesset Yossi Sarid has outdone himself in likening the situation to Kosovo and asserting that a Kosovar reality requires a Kosovar solution. This represents an extreme of Jewish self-belittlement, but also of a dearth of knowledge and understanding. Kosovo was taken over by international forces under UN auspices. A UN high commissioner sits in Kosovo. Is that what Sarid seeks? And what solution? Separation? Will the international force protect Israel from the most savage terror in history under the direct command of Arafat? And will they succeed, even if they want to, in keeping suicide bombers out of Israel? And what has Mr. Sarid internalized about the performance of the United Nations in keeping peace, in Lebanon for instance? And when will he learn that an international force can make a certain contribution, however small, only when the two sides willingly agree? The example of the Israeli-Syrian border is indicative: both sides support and want a settlement; hence the United Nations plays its role. Is that the situation with the Palestinians?

And the media does not understand the phenomenon of the suicide bombers, which, according to one journalist, "is gathering an insane momentum among the Palestinians, something appalling, heretofore unknown, inconceivable, and indigestible. It is a phenomenon without comparison and without precedent . . . The phenomenon is widening, women are joining as well as men . . . parents bless the death of their children and the deaths they have caused. . . . The official Palestinian voice exalts and glorifies [the bombers] to the level of saints . . . " And the media has learned nothing about the Arab–Islamic political culture.

And a prominent political analyst says with the total conviction of an expert historian and strategist that the Israeli policy of retaliation, which Sharon has been conducting for forty years, is bankrupt. Since the 1950s it has not succeeded, and it will not succeed with the Palestinians. And of course it is to blame for the burgeoning of suicide terrorists. As he put it: "What the IDF has succeeded in doing in recent weeks is to establish a mass, deadly army of suicide bombers . . . " Even if Sharon takes over all the territories, "nothing will change. The suicide bombers will continue to proliferate. Eventually all the Palestinians will volunteer to commit suicide in Israel."

Among such people, Arafat's terror has succeeded. And Arafat is the main beneficiary, both of the experience gained from Israel's panicked flight from Lebanon in May 2000, and of the experience he himself has gained since 1993 in deceiving and deluding the Oslo sages with false stances, and in unleashing unprecedented terror since September 2000. Yet the media-leftist complex has learned nothing, and the pseudo-Zionist "ship of fools" sails on.

Notes

1   Syrian president Hafez al-Assad did not want to see or meet with Arafat since 1983. That is the firm attitude of most Arab leaders today, who loathe and despise him but have to pay lip service to Arabism. In the 1982 war Arafat was abandoned by all, and Qaddafi even advised him to fight to the last drop of Palestinian blood. Bashar al-Assad humiliated Arafat when he took pains to send him back after Arafat had already boarded his plane to fly to Damascus. And the prime minister of Lebanon did not let Arafat transmit his broadcast speech to the Arab heads of state who had gathered in Beirut for an Arab summit conference in late March 2002.

2   See the series of articles by the independent investigative reporter, Yoav Yitzhak, in *Ma'ariv*, 2001, and also articles by Ari Shavit in *Ha'aretz* and by Ben-Dror Yamini in *Yediot Aharonot*, July 26, 2002.

3   It has been possible for over thirty years to study the brilliant tactics of Arafat, as a recurrent ritual, a regular display to the media of his policy of terror and condemnation. One hand does deeds of inhuman terror, the other condemns. Thus he behaved in Jordan and Lebanon, regarding dozens of agreements that he signed and then violated immediately, only to beg pardon and swear that it was worth signing a further agreement with him, which he would indeed uphold. Indeed, Arafat has four masks that he uses simultaneously, with blatant lies and trickery: the masses, whom he uses as raw material that can be squandered in large quantities; his terrorist fighters, who are called an army and police force, and stand at his beck and call; his political cronies, who speak fluent English and whose role is only to talk in positive terms and verbalize the dream of an imminent peace; and Arafat himself, as a lovable grandfather who only seeks for his unfortunate people a small piece of land, and, of course, compromise and affection from their fellow humans.

4   In his last visit to the Middle East, Clinton quoted Mubarak as saying that "Arafat is an unbearable type," and Abdallah, King of Jordan, said that "Arafat is responsible for the tragedy of the Palestinian people" (*Yediot Aharonot*, January 25, 2002).

5   On this matter there were resolutions of the Palestinian national councils, inspired by the rejection-front organizations in the PLO. The above quotation is from the words of General Amos Gilead (*Yediot Aharonot*, December 26, 2001); in regard to these statements Peres said that Gilead was turning Arafat into a genius (*Ma'ariv*, December 28, 2001); and the director-general of the Foreign Ministry, Avi Gil, "is leading the struggle against the militarization of the national assessment" (*Ma'ariv*, January 4, 2002).

6   A classic example of the crude use of the media at the time of a terrorist attack
     was seen in the Elon Moreh incident on March 28, 2002, when Israeli tele-
     vision's Channel 2 gave continuous information in real time about what had
     happened there via the settler leader Benny Katzover.

7   See Letters to the Editor in the *Yediot Aharonot* supplement, February 8,
     2002. See also the article by Dan Margalit on the reactions in the Meretz
     movement to the issue of refusal, and the claim by former attorney general
     Michael ben-Yair that Israel is a fascist state (*Ma'ariv*, March 22, 2002). See
     also the statements of former Member of Knesset Shulamit Aloni in enthusi-
     astic support of refusal, and that Meir Kahane was small game compared to
     Avigdor Lieberman and Effi Eitam (*Ma'ariv*, March 24, 2002).

References

Bukay, D. "The Bold and the Beautiful – the Israeli Left: Politics of Ignoring and
     Imperviousness," *Nativ* 3 (80), June 2001.

Butler, D. *The British General Elections of 1992*. Hampshire: Macmillan, 1992.

Clutterbuck, R. L. *The Media and Political Violence*. London: Macmillan, 1981.

Crelinsten, R. *Hostage-Taking*. Lexington, MA: Lexington Books, 1979.

Gallimore, T. "Media Compliance with Press Guidelines for Covering
     Terrorism." In Y. Alexander and R. G. Picard (eds.), *In the Camera's Eye*. New
     York: Brassey's, 1991.

Galtung, J. and Ruge, M. "The Structure of Foreign News." In J. Turnstall (ed.),
     Media Sociology. Urbana: University of Illinois Press, 1970.

Gerbner, G. "Violence and Terror in and by the Media." In M. Raboy and B.
     Dagenais (eds.), *Media, Crisis and Democracy*. London: Sage, 1992.

Herman, E. S. *The Myth of the Liberal Media*. New York: Peter Lang, 1999.

Hoge, J. W. "The Media and Terrorism." In A. H. Miller (ed.), *Terrorism, the
     Media and the Law*. New York: Transnational, 1982.

Kahan, M. *Media as Politics*. New Jersey: Prentice-Hall, 1999.

Karsh, E. *Fabricating Israeli History: The new historians*. London: Frank Cass,
     1997.

Mcquail, D. *Media Policy, Convergence, Concentration and Commerce*. London:
     Sage, 1998.

Montgomery, L. F. "Media Victims: Reaction to Coverage of Incidents of
     International Terrorism Involving Americans." In Y. Alexander and R. G.
     Picard (eds.), *In the Camera's Eye*. New York: Brassey's, 1991.

Morris, B. *The Birth of the Arab Refugee Problem: 1947–1949*. Tel Aviv: Am
     Oved, 1991.

Nacos, B. L. *Terrorism and the Media*. New York: Columbia University Press,
     1994.

Pappe, I. "The New History of the 1948 War," *Theory and Criticism* 3 (1993),
     pp. 99–114.

Schmid, A. P. and Paletz, D. L. *Terrorism and the Media*. Newbury Park, CA:
     Sage, 1992.

Waltz, K. *Man, the State and War*. New York: Columbia University Press, 1959.

New York Times, February 1, 2002.

6

Post-Zionism and Democracy

RAYA EPSTEIN

Post-Zionism as Ideology and Reality

Post-Zionism is not just an ideology that seeks to replace the preceding, prevalent ideology, or a new theory that aspires to represent more humane, moral, and democratic values than Zionism, which it sees as reactionary, antidemocratic, and immoral. Post-Zionism is also the reality in which the State of Israel functions and in which its citizens live and face the threat of being murdered by Arab-Palestinian terrorists. This terrible fact is closely and directly related to the emergence of the post-Zionist reality.

The assertion that post-Zionism is a reality, and not just a point of view or a particular ideology, in no way contradicts the fact that it is also a point of view and an ideology. It is only important to note that the post-Zionist ideology and views seek to replace Zionism. Clearly, Israel Jewry confronts a deep ideological struggle that has, and will have, palpable effects on its social and political life.

From the democratic standpoint the debate is entirely legitimate. The problem, however, is that the defense of post-Zionism usually involves denying the democratic legitimacy of Zionism. The devotees of post-Zionism do this by attempting to identify their own view with the essence of democracy, while often presenting Zionists as anti-democratic and even as fascist nationalists.

The New Democracy as Post-Zionism and Post-Judaism

The following passage by Eliezer Schweid (1996) relates to post-Zionism/post-Judaism:

> In the wake of the Six Day War a trend arose in Israeli society of return to Jewish roots, and its varied manifestations lasted longer than the manifestations of nationalist enthusiasm that were awakened during the war. . . . However, a counterprocess also began that intensified in the 1980s and finally succeeded in overcoming the yearning for Jewish roots: the polarization of the conflicts surrounding religious Zionism and "religious coercion," and the polarization of the debate surrounding the "Greater Land of Israel" led to granting liberal democracy and its scale of values the status of a comprehensive worldview that forms the personal identity and way of life of those on the secular Left. This was an alternative response that fights against the religious Jewish identity on the one hand and the national Jewish identity on the other. (Schweid, 1996: 52)

Schweid characterizes the change in terms of the fact that previously "Israel was a national democratic state that was designed according to the European national model. The Left has now posited an alternative definition of democracy in the spirit of American liberalism: civil rather than national democracy, with religion consistently separated from the state" (Schweid, 1996: 52)). However, the change effected by post-Zionism is more profound than the replacement of one model of liberal democracy with another. In the United States, the Democratic party does not play the role of representing the unquestionable ideology of the state, as a one and only truth that requires the existing political parties to act according to it. It is inconceivable that in America one party calling itself "Democratic," which defines its ideology as liberal, would try to impose its views on the Republicans. And even if the latter won the elections, they would not force them to act and run the country according to the Democrats' ideology, and abandon the positions that brought them to power. No political party in the United States would dare arrogate to itself a monopoly on democracy and propagate the notion that the other party or parties should bow to its imperatives or else be denounced as a danger to American democracy. If it would do so, its own democratic legitimacy would immediately be denied.

But Israel's Left has done exactly that. It has done so not only with regard to the Likud and the religious parties, but also against Israel's Jewish character and its Zionism: "Liberal democracy has now been presented not only as a structure and normative basis of the nation's government, but as a comprehensive worldview and way of life"

(Schweid, 1966). The Left has not settled for liberal democracy as merely "a worldview that forms its personal identity and way of life." Not for that unavailing purpose did it devise its ingenious method aimed at permanently neutralizing the hated national side of the Israeli political map, the old Zionism, and the new spirit of Judaism that arose in the wake of the Six Day War. The transformation that it effected did not merely replace the patriotic and collectivist Israeli values with neo-liberal, individualist principles, but rather with the demand that its principles and values alone – whatever their conceptual content[1] – be presented as the embodiment of democracy and that "the religious and national values be subordinated to them . . . the aim is that democracy (as the Left, and only it, interprets it) should dictate the public sociocultural way of life in the State of Israel . . . Thus emerged radical secular *post-Zionism* that is a manifestation of the essence of *post-Judaism*. On that basis appeared the new version of the Israeli identity: not a national realization of the Jewish identity but rather its comprehensive replacement" (Schweid, 1996: 52).

In other words, after the Six Day War the Israeli Left did not replace one model of liberal democracy with a model of its own. It replaced liberal democracy, whatever its shortcomings, with an ideological democracy that can be defined as an "ideocracy," or as totalitarian democracy. Talmon (1952) saw the basis of this trend "in the assumption that there exists a one and only truth in politics." Ironically, this truth was formulated according to a liberal conception. The one and only truth of totalitarian democracy that took control in Israel following the Six Day War is a complete antithesis of religious Judaism, of nonreligious Jewish identity, of liberal democracy, and of Zionism.

Totalitarian Democracy

The last devotees of socialist Zionism who try to defend themselves against the post-Zionist attack by accusing post-Zionists of replacing "the old, patriotic and collectivist Israeli values with neoliberal, individualist values," fall into the trap that was prepared for them in advance. They confirm (without being conscious of it) the post-Zionist claim about the existence of totalitarian characteristics in the old Zionism and give retroactive legitimization to those characteristics without discerning those very characteristics in post-Zionism. Hence they are unable to reconcile Zionism with anti-totalitarian principles. They try to return Israel to a socialist-collectivist Zionist path that no longer exists, rather than striving to develop a renewed, revised concept of Zionism based on the conservative Anglo-Saxon model of liberalism, instead of the French model with its pronounced totalitarian tendencies (Hayek, 1944; Talmon, 1952). The classical liberal model and Judaism are not contradictory. On the contrary, to a large extent classical liberalism has its roots in the Jewish biblical foundation of Protestant Christianity. Socialist Zionism, however, just like its post-Zionist enemy, is anchored in the totalitarian French model, which is hostile to Judaism.

There are ideologies that exist alongside the given reality, reconcile themselves with the existing order, aim only at improving and amending it and not at destroying it completely. The followers of these ideologies favor developmental-reformist activity that does not shatter the spontaneity of ordinary life. They are not in a hurry, and have the tolerance and patience to wait until their corrective activity bears fruit. That may not happen in their lifetimes, but rather in future generations.

There are, however, other ideologies and views whose authors and implementers are not satisfied with amending the existing order gradually. They are fueled by a messianic energy that has enormous religious power, even if their ideas and beliefs are completely secular. The followers of these secular religions are not at peace with the given reality (Mannheim, 1936) which they perceive it as totally evil. They do not see any possibility of amending it via a gradual evolutionary change. They are not reformists but, rather, revolutionaries. These utopians want a "brave new world" here and now, and they aim at utterly destroying the "old world."

This utopianism was not born in Russia at the time of the 1917 revolution, nor did it disappear with the rise of postmodernism which sees itself as the incarnation of democracy that has finally defeated its rivals and foes. In a seemingly paradoxical manner, it is precisely those ideologies that regard themselves as most democratic that will likely be the ones to destroy the implementation of democracy in the real world. This phenomenon is already familiar from the days of Jean Jacques Rousseau[2] (Avineri, 1992) and has appeared in our time as well **(chapter 7)**.

Yaacov Talmon (1952) referred to this phenomenon as totalitarian democracy. He also called it by a number of other names that constitute the basic tenets of his theory, such as: political messianism, secular religion, totalitarianism of the Left, and of course, utopia. This trend in its modern form first emerged in the French Enlightenment movement of the eighteenth century, in the course of that movement's bold, uncompromising, and militant struggle against the Christian church and against any religion whatsoever. Its followers championed values that were emphatically liberal-humanist, while in actuality they justified the imposition of ideas and political tyranny as a necessary and inevitable means to achieve their lofty objectives. The first attempt to implement utopian liberalism in this form was made in the Jacobin republic of Robespierre.[3]

After this mode of thought underwent certain changes, though not major ones, in the doctrine of Karl Marx and in the Russian version of Marxism, the totalitarian communist regime made its attempt at implementation, which lasted more than seventy years.

Regarding the phenomenon of totalitarian democracy, it is highly significant that the communist regime collapsed not primarily because of economic or political circumstances but rather because of a gradual process of the demythologization of Soviet society, namely the disintegration of the public's blind faith in the utopia on which the totalitarian state of the Soviet Union based itself. There still are some who believe that this inhuman regime was a product of the specific circumstances of Russia alone. Peter Berger wrote with some sarcasm yet in full seriousness, that Western intellectuals will stop being deeply impressed by the socialist myth only when Western societies are taken over by socialist regimes (Berger, 1977). He was referring to the enormous influence of leftist ideas over the West throughout the modern era. In the 1970s and 1980s it seemed as if this influence had finally waned, and the victory of conservative liberalism would never again be questioned. It soon became clear that this was an illusion, and that Western societies are indeed being conquered if not by socialist regimes then by a uniform regime based on renewed leftist tenets that constitute a transformation of the old socialist myth. As always, within the trend of totalitarian democracy the renewal, however apparently dramatic, is expressed in ideas only, while the totalitarian pattern of thought, which the ideas that replace each other sometimes display, remains stable and unchanging.

After World War II, a rich and varied critical literature was written in an attempt at theoretically addressing the phenomenon of totalitarianism and finding a way to prevent its realization in the future. Most thinkers deal with the totalitarianism of the Right, while relatively few focused on the totalitarianism of the Left. One reason for the lack of interest in the ideas underlying that kind of totalitarianism is that the inquiries are conducted by Western intellectuals who are susceptible to the influence of those very ideas, as we know not only from Berger's insights. Another, no less important reason for that lack of interest lies in the magical, enchanting name that refers to and conceals the most dangerous phenomenon of leftist totalitarianism, the name "democracy."

Two Errors of Yaacov Talmon

Totalitarian democracy, as Talmon showed, emerged from the French Enlightenment movement of the eighteenth century, and has continued to exist in its different incarnations throughout the modern era. It manifested itself not only in the visions or abstract theories of Western intellectuals but also in murderous regimes, such as the Jacobin democracy and the former Soviet communist state. However, Talmon erred in his optimistic conclusion that political messianism, a later incarnation of the trend in question, "ceased to be a danger after it failed to become a sort of world church whose followers, in various countries, would be inspired to form a revolutionary army that takes orders from a supreme war headquarters." He erred both in regard to the general intellectual aspect of the issue and in regard to its specific Israeli aspect.

The world church of totalitarian democracy has not died

On the international level, Talmon's conclusion may seem to be justified, but only if it is applied to the internationalist orientations of Marxist ideology and the far-reaching programs of the former communist bloc, which is precisely what he originally intended. His error stems from his paradoxical failure to take into account what his own theory asserts about the nature of totalitarian democracy. Talmon claimed and demonstrated that democracy of this kind is not characterized by belief in a certain idea (for example, the communist idea). He maintained that its uniqueness lies in the fact that it rests on a one exclusive truth, in the belief in single pre-eminent idea, whether a communist, social-democratic, or ostensibly liberal-capitalist idea. "Ostensibly" because true liberalism, as he defines it, cannot at all be reconciled with belief in a sole, exclusive idea even if it is the liberal idea itself. True liberals, as they define it, cannot demand that the rest of society believe in what the liberals believe. Anyone who mandates such a thing, and further claims that those who do not heed his behest constitute a danger to democracy, in fact has a pronounced totalitarian mindset, even if he regards himself (or is regarded by those with a totalitarian mindset like his own) as an enlightened liberal.

Currently it is discernible that the new secular world church is arising not in Russia and Eastern Europe but, rather, in the West. Its followers in various countries are supposed to toe the line that no longer issues from Moscow but rather from Paris, Brussels, or Bonn. The obedient soldiers of its army do not take orders from a war headquarters but, rather, from a peace headquarters. Talmon could not have predicted that after the dissolution of the communist bloc a new totalitarian church would arise in enlightened Europe that, like the old one that expired, would conceal its totalitarian nature under a guise of putative democracy. The new church inherited from its predecessor the total identification with the PLO murderers and adopted the same anti-Semitism behind the mask of anti-

Israelism. It is the very same anti-Semitism that was championed by the former communist church.

The roots of the new world church

It is also worth noting that even though this new world church began to form after the fall of the communist regime, its earlier roots were in the "student rebellion" against the existing social order that arose in Europe and America in the late 1960s and early 1970s. This protest was led by movements called the New Left in English-speaking countries, and referred to as "leftism" (*Gauchism*) or "extreme leftism" (*Extreme Gauche*) on the Continent. These movements espoused revolutionary-totalitarian ideologies (Trotskyism, Maoism, neo-Marxism, anarchism, etc.), and they fulfill Talmon's (1960) criteria of "political messianism." Members of these rebllions were self-declared nonconformists who lived at the margins of society. Subsequently it emerged that their influence on Western society was profound. Many of the former leftist rebels eventually assumed key positions in the Western world in commerce, academia, politics, the organizations of the United Nations, and so forth. Although there is not enough space here to provide a detailed demonstration of that claim, suffice to point out the blatant similarity between the stances of the United Nations, which once served to extend the influence of the world communist bloc, and the policy of the European Union. This unholy resemblance is most clearly manifest in the common pro-Palestinian and anti-Israeli stance, which is a clear-cut continuation of the anti-Israeli policy of the former Soviet Union, even though initially the policy of the now-irrelevant communists was taken by Arab countries. Clearly, even if there is an element of economic-pragmatic benefit in this stance (trade relations with the Arab states, etc.), it plays only a relatively small role compared to the political-ideological aspect. The goal of today's utopians is the establishment of a global society in which, similar to the "communist society" that was the objective of Karl Marx's messianic vision, all differences between nations and national cultures are erased and what emerges instead is a united, undivided humanity that enjoys social justice, social equality, affluence, humaneness and morality.

Another parallel with Marxism is the fact that the devotees of the EU and other internationalists regard the wish to maintain national uniqueness as politically incorrect. That is not to say there is no difference at all between the old model and the new one. The countries of the former Soviet Union, where Marxism was implemented, have not yet developed the elegant and efficient dissent-silencing system of political correctness. Thus far, these countries have adopted various methods that were not as refined and liberal as those of today's enlightened Europe, in order to achieve the same goals.

It is only natural that the question of the Jews can be resolved as well in the context of the future postmodern humanity, which is already being established, more or less in the same form as the old Marxist vision proposed. Except that in the role of the wandering Jew who cannot be entirely assimilated, there appears instead the Jewish nation-state. One European Union leader commented about Israel that "the world does not know whether to swallow it or vomit it." Both literally and metaphorically, Europe forged an alliance of blood with the Muslim world that is fighting a war to the death against the State of Israel and the entire Jewish people. From Europe's perspective, the nation of Israel and the Jewish People have no right to exist in the "brave new world" that it is building. It is worth remembering that Karl Marx's futuristic vision was exactly in this spirit, though not regarding the Jewish state that did not yet exist, but "only" regarding the Jews such as they were. The matter has not at all ceased to be relevant.

The resemblance here, however, is not only to the Marxist position. The common EU–UN stance of virulent anti-Semitism toward the Jewish state adds the new, brutal anti-Semitic elements to the Marxist ideology and the attitude of the already-defunct communist bloc, all of which brings it to the verge of resembling Nazi anti-Semitism.

After the break-up of the communist bloc and Western democracy's great victory over it, why is Europe reverting to the Marxist model in an altered form and succeeding to do what the communists were unable to do? In my view the main reason, albeit not the only one, is that after World War II the world conducted a process of de-Nazification, and later even went so far as to identify nationalism with chauvinism, racism, and Nazism. Any national, particularist matter, whatever its nature, became entirely illegitimate. This attitude essentially accords with the communist attitude and is considered to be very successful in coping with the totalitarian-Rightist danger and a way of preventing its realization in the present and the future.

History, and especially in the twentieth century, has clearly proven that the danger of totalitarianism is not limited to the Right. The danger of Leftist totalitarianism is no less grave. It is only to be expected that both the European and Israeli Left, which control public awareness, preferred to ignore the second kind entirely. No "decommunization" was ever performed in any country. The universalism of Marxist doctrine is abstract and devoid of all nationalism or particularism. Not only did Marxism not lose any of its previous legitimacy but even became the one and only unquestioned ideology, the credo of the religion of totalitarian democracy, in its renewed, though no less fundamentalist, form that emerged in the current purportedly "post-ideological" era.

The European "leftist" generation, formed in the turbulent rebellion of the 1960s, have outgrown and replaced their Maoism or Trotskyism with views more fashionable and relevant to the present, but they have not succeeded in changing their previous mode of totalitarian thinking. It is not at all accidental, then, that the *Gauchist* generation, with its totalitarian thought patterns, could undermine the old liberal democracies of the West and replace them with totalitarian democracy under a renewed disguise. It is the same, familiar totalitarian democracy of the past, with a change of outward form only. In all its various versions the great and glorious utopia remains its essence. Along with the eighteenth century Enlightenment in France, and with Marx and Marxists in the nineteenth and twentieth centuries, the leftist globalists of the early twenty-first century aim at building a new world order, a "brave new world" that is to rise on the ruins of the old world. The difference is that in today's renewed version, achieving the sacred goal and fulfilling this supreme idea requires not just individual human victims, but entire nations as victims. The first among them is the Jewish people.

The local church of totalitarian temocracy: Post-Zionism

Talmon also erred in regard to the internal Israeli aspect of the problem by concluding that totalitarian democracy had "ceased to be a danger." His error on this level is less surprising than his error on the external level, since in Israel the self-declared liberals in the Western sense of liberalism often end up taking part in entirely non-liberal processes often unaware that they are doing so.

Talmon did not ignore the less than democratic aspects of the Ben-Gurion socialist regime. It seems that he applied his general conclusions about the necessary link between utopia and totalitarianism to Zionism, which he viewed as a utopia. In this regard one can dispute or accept his claims, but the real problem lies elsewhere. In the course of criticizing the totalitarian aspects of Ben-Gurion's rule, Talmon did not devote sufficient attention to the totalitarianism of Ben-Gurion's critics to his left. Although Talmon disparaged the Jewish nationalist movements that were founded after the Six Day War as a manifestation of totalitarian political messianism, he did not seem to see the pronounced political messianism and utopian nature of the left-wing peace movement. Indeed, Talmon himself was in the forefront of those seeking a utopian peace. Moreover, there is a paradox in Talmon's stance: He was a classical liberal, intensely critical of the totalitarian Left. Yet, in the local Israeli context, he was no less leftist than some of the most prominent totalitarian leftists in the country. Talmon's position on Israeli issues faithfully served those opposed to the Land of Israel movement. Eventually, this opposition emerged as the group that prepared the ground for post-Zionism and post-Judaism (Schweid, 1996). This movement bore out Talmon's main insights about a necessary link between political messianism and totalitarian democracy, between utopia and totalitarianism in practice, between totalitarianism of the Left and Jews who repudiate their Jewishness.[2] The movement bore out these insights when, thirteen years after Talmon's death, the secular messianic religion established the Oslo regime, a regime whose terrible totalitarianism has not freed the Jews of Israel from its utopia of blood to this very day.

Talmon did not live to see the appalling Israeli proof of his conclusions. Would he have agreed with the assertion that the world church of postmodern Europe, whose establishment he could not have predicted, and the Oslo regime that embodies a post-Zionist ideology to which he made a significant conceptual contribution, essentially constitute the same totalitarian phenomenon? Would he have reached the conclusion that an international totalitarian regime of the West has emerged that cooperates with Arab-Muslim terrorism in its war against the Jewish people? Would he have realized that the Oslo regime, whose essence is to replace the Jewish identity of the citizens of Israel with a Western-abstract identity, is an organic and central part of this totalitarian war against the Jewish people? Would he have been prepared to apply his profound theory of totalitarian democracy to our existential struggle against totalitarian post-Zionism, which has become post-life, a justification for the murder of the Jewish people?

Post-Zionism in the Modern and Postmodern Contexts: The Jews and Democracy

The universalist utopia in the modern and postmodern eras

According to Talmon, the totalitarianism of the Left as opposed to that of the Right, rests on the belief in liberal values and principles of freedom, individualism, rationalism, and universalism. Both his theoretical doctrine and concrete historical reality show that the secular universalist utopia, which lies at the basis of totalitarian democracy, has recurred throughout the entire modern era. It began with the French Enlightenment of the eighteenth century, and continued in the politica–messianic movements of the nineteenth century, in the Russian communist regime, and, today, in the vision of a new world order that is taking shape in the postmodern era. To repeat: The element common to all of them is the unrestrained, essentially messianic, yearning for the unity of peoples, or even their utter erasure within the totality of humanity. The individuals who constitute that totality, like the totality itself, are nothing but an abstract idea of abstract people who are not dependent on anything.

The issue of the Jews as a particular people, by definition and by nature, is linked to the history of the universalist utopia, both in the modern and postmodern eras, almost no less tragically than it was linked to the history of the nationalist mythology, which, at the end of the humanist, modern, enlightened, and rational period, fostered a Holocaust. The true name of the story is venomous and murderous anti-Semitism. What differentiates the postmodern era from the modern one is that the current anti-Semitism wears the guise of anti-Zionism and of the struggle against "the occupation," together with the notion of extending the boundaries of the "unity of peoples" in the universalist utopia. There is, indeed, a bit of problem here, namely, that it is hard to believe in the possibility of unity when one component is the postmodern *International* of Europe, and the other component is national Islamism (Ye'or, 2002), clearly the heir of German national-socialism. But when there is a common enemy, even absolute opposites can unite. Needless to say this common enemy is the State of Israel, and along with it the Jewish people as a whole.

Auto-anti-Semitism in the modern and postmodern eras

Within the State of Israel itself, the forces of destruction linked to the universalist world utopia of our times, are very vigorously active. The ease with which they were able to become part of the utopian anti-national trend without relinquishing the older "modern" universalist utopia of the socialist ideology, is itself evidence of the common foundation of the two. They share a common nature in the fact that the communist and socialist universalism of the modern era and the struggle against Jewish nationality, are but manifestations of a single universalist utopia.

The universalist forces of destruction in Israel are driven by a tremendous messianic energy that again aims at building a "brave new world." As in the old days of the Marxists-communists, these circles believe without question in the sacred principle of the utopian international religion. Their motto is "We will destroy the old world utterly (i.e. the Zionist entity)." Most significant of all, Israeli post-Zionist ideology is a version of the universalist utopia of the postmodern era which is virulently anti-Semitic (Sharan, 2001) similar to the doctrine of the anti-Semitic Jew Karl Marx.

However, both then and now, it is not a case of the "primitive" anti-

Semitism of the masses who are fueled by xenophobia, nor of the Nazi right-wing anti-Semitism that draws its dark power from the appeal of ancient myths. Here we are speaking of an intellectual anti-Semitism of the Left: The self-proclaimed progressive, enlightened, moral and rational Left. In fact, the Left regards authentic Jews and Judaism as the primitive and reactionary forces of darkness, who disrupt progress and form an obstacle on the path to fulfilling the purpose of history. The inevitable result of this messianic approach is the striving (conscious or unconscious) to erase Judaism as a particular identity from the map of history. In other words, the "brave new world" of the universalist utopia in its two versions is a new world without the Jewish people.

Just as in the building of the new Jew-free world by the Marxists, so also in the building of the new, Jew-free world by the architects of the postmodern era, the participation of the Judaism-hating Jews is essential. What makes the current situation different is that this time the Jews have a nation-state of their own, in which Jews who are devotees of the universalist utopia can finally fight against Judaism and make their fine contribution to creating a Jew-free world much more effectively than at any time in the past. Furthermore, the struggle to eradicate Judaism is now waged under the guise of democracy. The Marxist, postmodern and post-Zionist pseudo-liberal views on democracy lead back to the totalitarian democracy of the French Enlightenment, in which anti-Semitism formed an essential ingredient.

Anti-Semitism as a benchmark of affiliation with post-Zionism

In a seminal article, Aharonson (1997) discussed the structural anti-Semitism of post-Zionism and the worldview of the eighteenth-century French Enlightenment, as well as the link between the two. During those days of the growth of the Oslo utopia, it was not yet known that Israel would face an eruption of the anti-Semitism of peace, the combination of Arab and Western anti-Semitism that hardly bothers anymore to don its guise of anti-Israelism and anti-Zionism.

In one regard only should Aharonson's article be amended in light of recent events. It has emerged that the real post-Zionists are not only those people who have written and published books and articles that openly espouse this position. The *al-Aqsa Intifada* exposed an important benchmark to determine whether a given individual is actually a post-Zionist. That benchmark is the overt or covert justification of murderous anti-Semitism. That anti-Semitism is revealed in the European–Muslim alliance that seeks to eliminate the Jewish character of the State of Israel (Ye'or, 2002). Finally, it is manifest in the manipulative use of the concept of "liberal democracy" in both the European and Israeli contexts, when in fact it is the system of totalitarian democracy that is being implemented to accomplish the goal of annihilating the State of Israel and, thereby, the Jewish people as a whole.

Similarly, using the benchmark of anti-Semitism that was revealed against the background of the Oslo war, one may distinguish between real post-Zionists, i.e. auto-anti-Semites, and those whose completely legitimate purpose was (and perhaps still is) the criticism of Zionism, not the annihilation of the Jewish state. Indeed, one of the first post-Zionists in history, Benny Morris, has done some stringent soul-searching and "repented"; whereas political intellectuals who never vocally took post-Zionist stances, and even proclaim at every opportunity that they are the real Zionists, now reveal their actual post-Zionist views via covert and overt cooperation with the anti-Semitic crusade being waged against the State of Israel and the Jewish people in and outside Israel. As only one example of the latter, one can cite the recent participation of some Jewish-Israeli professors in the European initiative to exclude Israeli scientists from research grants offered in Europe, from scientific conferences, and so forth.

The Common Denominator between Socialist Zionism and Post-Zionism

Auto-anti-Semitism is central to the post-Zionist ideology. Aharonson (1996) sums up its basic premises and conceptual definitions. "Post-Zionism means the negation of Jewish nationality, the abrogation of its ties to the Land of Israel, or casting grave doubt on their legitimacy . . . " Some of the post-Zionists are characterized by the wish "to get rid of what is bad in Judaism, particularly the notion of the election of the Jewish People (The concept of 'The Chosen People')." Some even "go further and envisage a society in which Jewish nationality will disappear, since it stands no chance within the Arab spatial domain." Aharonson also notes that post-Zionist anti-Semitism has deep roots in the history of Jewish society in the Land of Israel and in Europe: "To be sure, all these assertions are not new, and were closely tied to Zionism almost from its birth, and now have been adjusted to the current prevailing language and conditions. Furthermore, it was a historical criticism of Judaism itself, and hence was implanted and passed into Zionism . . . "

The question remains to what extent can the critics of post-Zionism among the old Zionist Left in Israel allow themselves to be truly objective and nonmobilized, and to avoid, willfully or unconsciously, the undeniable points of continuity between the socialist–Zionist Establishment that ruled Israel without challenge up to the arrival of post-Zionism, and post-Zionism itself? That kind of continuity indeed exists, and is linked to the universalist utopia that was already discussed above. Socialist Zionism was based more on this utopia than on the concept of Jewry's election. It aimed more at making the Jews a nation like all the others than at developing the particular Jewish nationality grounded in authentic Judaism. It was concerned more with satisfying the need to establish a country of refuge for the persecuted Jews than with profoundly connecting the Jews who came here to the Land of Israel. That is the real reason for the seemingly strange fact that the liberation of the Temple Mount, Jerusalem, and parts of the historical Land of Israel in the Six Day War, prompted the socialist Left immediately to adopt the goal of "returning the territories" to the Arabs "for peace." It is also the reason for the seemingly no less strange fact that the liberation of the land underwent an immediate verbal transformation, both by the ruling establishment Left and the oppositional radical Left, into the unchallengeable, unofficial term "occupation." Although everything did not occur at once, the fact is that today, during the cruel war that the "partners in the peace process" are waging against us, we are still blaming ourselves ("One must not rule over another people," "Occupation corrupts," and the like), and whoever questions this self-blame and instead blames the enemy is almost certain to be perceived as an extreme rightist, fascist, messianist, enemy of democracy, and enemy of peace.

It was not the post-Zionists but in fact the socialist Zionists who invented the mendacious "occupation" code word, though by now it has penetrated so deeply into the collective consciousness that apparently the general public, too, believes its veracity. All the post-Zionists did was to logically and consistently extend this notion, and proclaim that Zionism and the State of Israel as a whole are "occupied territory." It was not the post-Zionists, but in fact the Zionists of the ruling establishment who provided our Arab and Western anti-semitic enemies with this pernicious weapon of defining the Jewish presence in the Land of Israel as "occupation." The post-Zionists, of course, have done well in riding this Trojan horse toward achieving the essentially anti-Semitic goal of negating the legitimacy of the State of Israel.

Transforming the Jews living in Judea and Samaria into enemies of the people is also a totalitarian project primarily of the Zionist Left, and only subsequently of the post-Zionist Left. One can accept or criticize Gush Emunim and its ideology, but the Jewish people's links to the Land of Israel are not artificial ideological links. They do not exist by virtue of the

Yesha (Judea, Samaria, and Gaza) Council or of any other official body for that matter. Rather, Jewry's tie to the Land of Israel consists of real historical links, both existential and spiritual. They are non-instrumental links that touch the soul of every Jew no matter who he is, via the historical memory of every one of us, and hence via the collective soul and memory of the Jewish people.

An Alternative to Post-Zionism – Returning to Ourselves

The key slogan in demonstrations of the "peace coalition," which has been the standard-bearer of post-Zionism and post-Judaism during the Oslo war, is the passionate call to "return to ourselves." Even though, not only apparently but actually, there is at present a divide between the Zionist Left that fights the enemies of Israel and the radical Left that cooperates with them, this call expresses a profound common denominator between the two. Hence it may well be that at some other time, when the illusion of a utopian peace emerges once again, the differences will vanish. Even today the difference is not clear-cut, since neither group wants to take part in the "war of occupation," though one views the operations called Defensive Shield or Determined Path in that light, whereas the other sees them as a "war to defend our homes."

Stock phrases such as "return to ourselves," "war of occupation," "war for our homes," "war for the settlements," and so on may seem to be casual slogans without value or meaning. In fact, they are likely to serve as components of the Orwellian language of the totalitarian utopia, which gives them an inverted meaning and uses them as tools of a perniciously powerful mental coercion. First and foremost, we must clarify to ourselves the positive or negative, tacit or manifest meaning, of the post-Zionist position. Failing to do so, we will not comprehend and confront the common denominator of the views expressed by Leftist Zionists and by the post-Zionists. That confusion will prevent any attempt to come to grips with the existential problems of Israel and of the Jewish people as a whole.

Does "return to ourselves" mean to return to the beautiful, small, liberal Israel announced from the stage by the once-popular singer Yaffa Yarkoni that fits neatly with the stance of Prof. Ze'ev Sternhell regarding the legitimacy of the armed struggle of the Palestinians in the "territories?" (Sternhell's view leads directly to the conclusion that it is permissible for the Arab-Palestinian "freedom fighters" to murder Jews, be they civilians or soldiers in the Israeli "occupation army"). This slogan will not help the Jewish people become more moral and humane, perhaps even the opposite. Nor will a "return to ourselves" help us live and survive. Moreover, the essential justice of the struggle for our existence cannot be based on a "return to ourselves," which means a return by Zionism to a renewed Uganda Project, the settling of the Israelis, i.e. the former Jews, in a self-administered prison in a gray expanse without name, roots, history, or identity. In short, anywhere except in the Land of Israel!

If we do not know how to arrive at this not-so-simple truth by ourselves, the enemies of Israel are there to rise up against us and murder us. It is the mendacious blaming of "the occupation," a term that Israeli Jews invented and invigorated, that serves as a justification and goad to the genocide of the Jewish people by the Arabs and their political associates. They murder us not just as individuals, but as a people. That murder is not physical only, but is moral, spiritual, and existential as well. This lie of ours murders our soul. Yet, the murderers of hundreds of Jews (at the beginning of January 2003, the number stood at 694) over the period of less than two years alone (2000–2002), not to speak of the past few decades, are still regarded by many left-wing and right-wing Zionists, and not only by post-Zionists, as our potential allies with whom we must make peace.

The real meaning of returning to ourselves cannot be flight from the Land of Israel, from our identity, from Judaism. Returning to ourselves means returning to the land that is the historical cradle of Jewish identity, including Joseph's Tomb, Hebron, Rachel's Tomb, to our historical memory. It means returning from the Orwellian utopia of the Zionism of universalist normalization, to Jewish Zionism that strives for the national–cultural rejuvenation of the Jewish People.

An Alternative to Post-Zionism – Returning to Ourselves: A Non-Practical View

To a large extent, universalist anti-Semitism is rooted in the first universal religion that sought to replace particularist Judaism, the religion of Christianity. Yet even the cruelest Christians were no more anti-Semitic than secular anti-Semites of the enlightened modern era and of the tolerant and pluralist postmodern era, whether they are anti-Semites of the Right or the Left.[3] On the other hand, there were Christians who spoke and even acted against anti-Semitism with courage and integrity that not many Jews could muster. One of them was Sergei Bulgakov (1991), an influential Russian intellectual who emigrated from Bolshevik Russia to France in 1923 and served for twenty years (until his death in 1944) as professor of theology and dean of the Russian Christian Pravolsby Institute in Paris. This intellectual priest very sharply criticized the Jews who participated in the Bolshevik Revolution. His explanation for their utopian-messianic radicalism was that, having essentially religious souls, they found in Marxism a quasi-religious substitute for their authentic religion that they had abandoned and betrayed. He was regarded by many assimilated Jews as one of the fathers of Russian intellectual anti-Semitism. That is a gross misconception.

Bulgakov viewed the Jewish people as a special people constituting a mainstay of general human history. He devoted the last years of his life to analyzing the nature of German Nazism which he called "ontological" and "metaphysical" anti-Semitism, as he put it. In his view, this manifestation of anti-Semitism differs in purpose from the ordinary, routine kind. The anti-Semitism of the Germans, he maintained, constituted the essence of Nazi racism. It displayed the Nazis' envy of the Jews as a special people, as the people chosen by God, as a particular people with a world-universal mission. The Nazis, because of their envy of the chosen Jewish people, built their concept of their alternative chosenness on a materialist–pagan–racist basis. The notion of the German people as a people chosen on a racial basis entails negating the existence of the Jewish people.

Bulgakov saw the Nazi rebellion against the Jews as a total rebellion against the God who had chosen the people Israel to be a special people to Him. Hence, he argued, dealing with the problem of Nazi anti-Semitism was a struggle for Christendom no less than it was a problem for Jewry. As a believing Christian, Bulgakov linked the Jews' mission and their future salvation with the coming of Jesus the messiah and not with redemption in the Jewish sense. Yet his Christian messianism was less hostile toward Jews than the political messianism of the secular utopias that emerged in the modern period, of which Marxism was only one.

Bulgakov's perspectives on Nazi anti-Semitism offer a means of understanding the Muslim-Arab anti-Semitism of today, derived primarily from Muslim religious tradition and history, significantly influenced by Nazi anti-Semitism. That influence has been felt through the years since the Nazi period up to, and including, the present day. The metaphysical, ontological, and existential envy of the Jewish sense of their national election by God, as Sergei Bulgakov interpreted it in regard to the Germans of his time, is no less relevant to the national-Islamism of our time. It is evident in Islam's claim of a historical right to the Holy Land instead of the Jews, in the claim of a historical and religious right to Jerusalem instead of the Jews, and in Islam's claim of a religious right to the Temple Mount instead of the Jews.

Arab anti-Semitism is evident in the national and religious myths whose clear purpose is to totally eradicate the Jewish presence from the Land of Israel and thereby to totally eradicate the Jewish people from the world in general (Ye'or, 2002). To achieve this goal, an artificial entity known as "the Palestinian people" is being constructed here, in the Land of Israel. According to the Torah (The Five Books of Moses), The Land of Israel was given to the people of Israel as a people chosen by God. The Palestinian entity serves ascendant nationalistic Islamism as a tool for replacing and annihilating the Jewish people.

At this juncture, we must recall the important, perhaps even decisive role of the post-Zionist intellectuals, the new historians and sociologists, in building myths on behalf of an entity that constitutes a weapon aimed at destroying us by rewriting Jewish history according to the needs of the new Palestinian mythology (a rewriting of history that is called "shattering the myths of Zionism and Judaism"). In the context of this appalling trend, envy and hatred toward the Jews who remain faithful to the principle of Jewry's election in its highly moral rabbinic sense, appears to characterize not a few of the Jews themselves (Aharonson, 1997). Nor is that phenomenon new in history. Although almost one hundred years have passed since the days of the Bolshevik Revolution, Bulgakov's insights into the motives for the Jewish revolutionaries' destructive participation in Bolshevism can help to understand this phenomenon as well. Bulgakov drew a quite dismaying parallel between the "bestial racist chauvinism" of the Nazi anti-Semites and the anti-religious savagery of the Jewish commissars in the Russian Revolution. He attributed the latter to the fact that in the minds of the Jewish revolutionary intellectuals, the faith of their forefathers had been expunged under the influence of radical socialism and humanism. Yet because every Jewish person has an essentially religious soul, Bulgakov claimed, even the savage activity of the Jewish revolutionaries was a manifestation of their religiosity. This was, however, a negative and inverted religiosity in regard to the authentic Jewish religion, as reflected in the cruel war waged by these invertedly religious people against all religion and against God Himself.

Bulgakov indeed speaks of the terrible sin of the Jewish revolutionaries against the Russian people, a sin common to both the Jewish and the Russian revolutionaries. It especially took the form of deliberate and monstrous desecrations of sacred Jewish and Christian buildings and artifacts, of systematic anti-religious hooliganism driven by the goal of humiliating the believers and "occupying the temple in place of God," of anti-religious coercion that revealed "religious envy of an intensity previously unknown in history." However, the even more dreadful and appalling sin, Bulgakov emphasizes, was the one the Jewish revolutionaries committed against themselves as members of the Jewish people, "against holy Israel, the people chosen by God."

All this happened to the Jewish people, in Bulgakov's view, because "in the mystical depths of Israel there is no room for religious apathy and spiritual emptiness, so that there is a constant struggle over its soul." Thus the inverted and terrible religiosity that emerged in Russian Bolshevism does not express at all the true spirituality of Israel. Rather, it is an abominable mask that covers its true, holy face, a situation of terrible spiritual crisis in Israel, a "Jewish pogrom" that Jewish commissars perpetrated mainly against their own people, against the Jewish people as a special people. They dealt "a terrible blow...against Judaism, a blow without precedent in history...a historical suicide of Judaism, except that it involved only that part of the Jewish people that had betrayed its mission. But even in that part the holy remnant is always preserved, the eternal-immortal, because of which the entire Jewish people will be redeemed."

Of great interest is Bulgakov's direct treatment of Zionism that is surprisingly relevant to the concerns of this article. Bulgakov wrote the following passage in his article "Zion" in March 1915:

> The possibility that the powerful nations of the world will enable the Jews to establish a stable national center in Palestine and develop a full national life in it [*einen nationalen Kristallisationskern schaffen*] need not be perceived as a way of finding a solution to the "Jewish question" in the internal affairs of the countries of Europe, since even Zionists themselves do not believe they will succeed in attracting the large majority of their people to Palestine. . . . However, sooner or later Jews will realize the need to solve a much more important and essential problem than what is known today as "the Jewish question" – namely, the problem of their spiritual nature. This problem cannot be solved without a national center, and the sole sacred center of Jewry is Palestine, the land that was given to the Jews by God. The existence of such a center will help the Jews do the required soul-searching, overcome the tragic dualism, and win the spiritual struggle that has always been waged in the soul of the Jewish people. Zionism's greatest difficulty at present is its inability to restore the ancestral faith that is disappearing, so that it is forced to rely on the national–ethnic principle alone. However, on such a principle no truly great nation can be based, let alone the Jewish nation. Dostoevsky was indeed correct when he wrote: "It is not possible even to imagine the Jews without God." Yet history has furnished this holy name – Zion. There are signs that "the Jewish question" is again intensifying, that its tragic nature in the Diaspora is again being felt with great force. And just at this moment there shines a ray of light toward the future, a possibility emerges of a completely different solution to this eternal question. I pray that this great hope will not prove illusory!

As noted, when Bulgakov the Christian writes about the redemption of the Jews he does not mean redemption in the Jewish religious sense. With due repect to his Christian faith, we should not forget that Jewry has its own interpretation of our redemption in Zion. Not Christian Zionism of spirituality without matter, nor the materialist Zionism of normalization and flight from ourselves. Not anti-Semitic post-Zionism that reverts to a war by Jews against their Jewishness. Not totalitarian democracy that serves this despicable war and not postmodern relativism that erases the distinctions between truth and falsehood, between good and evil, between human and bestial, between darkness and light. Only loyalty to the truth, to clear moral discernment, only restoring to words their lost meaning, only lighting the candle that will illuminate and expel the darkness. Only a return to ourselves, to Judaism, to the Land of Israel, to true Zionism.

Notes

1   It has been suggested that a democracy has the "obligation . . . to strive for peace . . . " Kasher (1998), p. 343.

2   "For about two hundred years this faith has seethed in the hearts of millions . . . since the eighteenth century the world has been full of prophets, philosophers, flag-bearers, cliques of fighters, members of the underground, mass parties, that in one form or another anticipate and prepare themselves for the same end, for a revolution in the world order. In this camp the Jews played a huge role, and in some ways and certain situations – even a decisive one . . . [This faith] was a lifeline for those of our people who had lost or severed the link to the ancient and all-encompassing heritage of the people, and who did not succeed or were not able to attach themselves to a different culture. There were no revolutionary internationalists among the Gentiles like Karl Marx, Rosa Luxembourg, Trotsky, Karl Radek, Zinoviev, and the Jewish prophets of the New Left of our time. And one also should not overlook the fierce passion to act, to influence, to demonstrate power, and also to **rule**, which knowingly or unknowingly drove Jewish young people as such a wide, enchanting field of activity opened before them. . . . " (Talmon, 1974. Tel Aviv: Am Oved, pp. 135–6) (Hebrew).

For Rousseau, activity by a group that does not accord with the principles of majority rule does not negate that rule but it is nevertheless legitimate. Such a group claims that in a given situation, majority rule is not capable of making rational decisions, and hence it appropriates the majority's right of decision. The said group should regard itself as a tool for implementing the "real" desire of the people, assuming responsibility for the perfection of virtues and the purity of morals of the nation's institutions. Of course, such a group actually negates those virtues and empties the nation's institutions of their functions. This claim in the name of democracy ultimately destroys the democratic framework and the practice of real political rule. The Jacobin democracy of Robespierre must be understood against this background (Avineri, 1992).

3   The premise of Jacobin tyranny and theories of totalitarian demcracy is the belief that the enlightened members of society possess absolute truth and have the right to force the rest of the citizens to take one path only dictated by that truth. "The question is not, therefore, what the people desire but rather what is desirable for the people and who is qualified to make that decision. It is clear that Rousseau and his followers, and particularly Robespierre, saw that as opening the possibility of dictatorship by the individual or individuals they believed to represent moral perfection . . . and to embody what everyone would aspire to if everyone would be wise" (Avineri, 1992, 124).

References

Aharonson, Shlomo (1997) "Zionism and Post-Zionism: The historical-ideological context." In Y. Weiss (ed.), *Between Vision and Revision*. Jerusalem: Zalman Shazar Center, pp. 291–309 (Hebrew).

Avineri, Shlomo (1992) *The Rule of the Masses*. Tel Aviv: Sifriat Poalim (Hebrew).

Berger, Peter (1977) *Facing up to Modernity: Excursions in society, politics and religion*. New York: Basic Books.

Bulgakov, Sergei (1991) *Christianity and the Jewish Question*. Paris: YMGA Press (Russian).

Elbaum, Jason (1998) The decline of democracy in the global village. *Techelet 5*, pp. 11–23 (Hebrew). English edition: J. Elbaum (1998), Global pillage. *Azure* 5, pp. 118–44.

Hayek, Fredrich A. (1944) *The Road to Serfdom*. Chicago: University of Chicago Press.

Kasher, Asa (1998) The democratic imperative to strive for peaceful settlements. *Peace: Legal Aspects*. Ramat Gan: Bar-Ilan University.

Mannheim, Karl (1936) *Ideology and Utopia*. New York: Harcourt and Brace.

Orwell, George (1945) *Nineteen-Eighty-Four*. New York: Penguin Books.

Popper, Karl (1945) *The Open Society and its Enemies*. London: Routledge and Kegan Paul.

Schweid, Eliezer (1996) *Zionism in a Post-Modernistic Era*. Jerusalem: The World Zionist Organization.

Sharan, Shlomo (2001) *Zionism, the Post-Zionists and Myth: A critique*. Sha'arei Tikvah: Ariel Center for Policy Studies, policy paper 134.

Talmon, Yaacov (1974) *In the Age of Violence*. Tel Aviv: Am Oved, pp. 135–6 (Hebrew)

—— (1960) *Political Messianism: The romantic stage*. London: Secker and Warburg.

—— (1980) *The Myths of the Nation and the Vision of Revolution: The origins of ideological polarization in the 20th Century*. London: Secker and Warburg.

—— (1952) *The Origins of Totalitarian Democracy*. Harmondsworth, Middlesex: Penguin (1986 edition).

—— (1957) *Utopianism and Politics*. London: Conservative Political Centre.
Ye'or, Bat (2002) *Islam and Dhimmitude. When civilizations clash*. Teaneck, NJ: Farliegh Dickinson University Press.

7

The Future of the Ideological Civil War Within the West

JOHN FONTE

Nearly a year before the September 11 attacks on the World Trade Center and the Pentagon, wire service stories gave us a preview of the transnational politics of the future. It was reported on October 24, 2000, that in preparation for the UN Conference Against Racism, about fifty American nongovernmental organizations (NGOs) sent a formal letter to UN Human Rights Commissioner Mary Robinson calling on the UN "to hold the United States accountable for the intractable and persistent problem of discrimination" that "men and women of color face at the hands of the US criminal justice system" (Goodman, 2000).[1]

The spokesman for the NGOs, Wade Henderson, of the Leadership Conference on Civil Rights, stated that their demands "had been repeatedly raised with federal and state officials [in the United States] but to little effect. . . . In frustration we now turn to the United Nations" (Goodman, 2000). In other words, the NGOs, unable to enact the policies they favored through the normal processes of American constitutional democracy – the Congress, state governments, state courts, the federal executive branch, or even the federal courts – felt it necessary to appeal to authority outside of American democracy and beyond its Constitution.

From August 31 to September 7, 2001, the UN World Conference against Racism, Racial Discrimination, Xenophobia, and Related Intolerance was held in Durban, South Africa. The American NGOs attended the conference with financial support from the Ford, Rockefeller, MacArthur, and Charles Stewart Mott Foundations. At the conference the NGOs worked with delegates from African states that supported "reparations" from Western nations as compensation for the transatlantic slave trade of the seventeenth to nineteenth centuries. American NGOs provided research assistance and helped develop reparations resolutions that condemned only the West, without mentioning the larger traffic in African slaves that were sent to the Islamic lands of the Middle East and conducted, in large part, by Arabs. In addition, the NGOs endorsed a series of demands, including:

- US acknowledgment of "the breadth and pervasiveness of institutional racism" that "permeates every institution at every level."
- A declaration that "racial bias corrupts every stage of the [US] criminal justice process, from suspicion to investigation, arrest, prosecution, trial, and sentencing."
- Support and expansion of federal and state hate crimes legislation.
- Condemnation of opposition to affirmative action measures.
- US recognition of an adequate standard of living as a "right, not privilege."
- A statement deploring "denial of economic rights" in the United States.
- Promotion of multilingualism instead of "discriminatory" English-language acquisition emphasis in US schools.
- Denunciation of free market capitalism as a fundamentally flawed system" (International Human Rights Group, 2001).

Most importantly, the NGOs insisted that the United States ratify all major UN human rights treaties and drop legal reservations to treaties already ratified. For example, in 1994 the United States ratified the UN Convention on the Elimination of Racial Discrimination (CERD), but attached reservations declaring that it did not accept treaty requirements "incompatible with the Constitution." The official State Department reservations memorandum specifically notes that the CERD's restrictions on free speech and freedom of assembly are incompatible with the First Amendment. Yet leading NGOs including the HRW and Amnesty International USA (AI–USA) demanded that the United States drop all reservations and "comply" with the CERD treaty (Iley, 2001).

An NGO representative from the Center for Constitutional Rights reportedly said that "Almost every member of the UN committee raised the question of why there are vast racial disparities . . . in every aspect of American life-education, housing, health, welfare, criminal justice." A representative from HRW declared that the United States offered "no remedies" for these disparities, but "simply restated" its position by supporting equality of opportunity and indicating "no willingness to comply" with CERD (Iley, 2001). This would presumably mean the enactment of policies resulting in statistical equality of condition for racial and ethnic minorities in education, housing, health, welfare, criminal justice and the like. Indeed, to comply with the NGO interpretation of the CERD treaty, the United States would have to turn its political and economic system, together with their underlying principles, upside down-abandoning the free speech guarantees of the Constitution, bypassing federalism, and ignoring the very concept of majority rule, since practically nothing in the NGO agenda is supported by the American electorate.

The NGOs at the Durban conference exemplify a new challenge to liberal democracy and its traditional home, the liberal democratic nation-state. These have always been self-governing representative systems comprised of individual citizens who enjoy freedom and equality under law and together form a people within a democratic nation-state. Thus, liberal democracy means individual rights, democratic representation (with some form of majority rule) and national citizenship. Yet, as the Durban conference demonstrated, all of these principles, along with the very idea of the liberal democratic nation-state, are contested today in the West. Obviously, we are far from the ideological "end of history" delineated by Francis Fukuyama (1989).

Post-September 11

Three weeks after the September 11 attacks, Fukuyama stated that his "end of history" thesis remained valid twelve years after he first presented it, shortly before the fall of the Berlin Wall (Fukuyama, 2001). Fukuyama's core argument was that after the defeat of communism and national socialism, no serious ideological competitor to Western-style liberal democracy was likely to emerge in the future. Thus, in terms of political philosophy, liberal democracy is the end of the evolutionary process. To be sure, there will be wars and terrorism, but no alternative ideology with a universal appeal will seriously challenge the ideas and values of Western liberal democracy as the "dominant organizing principles" around the world.

Fukuyama correctly points out that non-democratic rival ideologies such as radical Islam and "Asian values" have little appeal outside their own cultural areas, but these areas are themselves vulnerable to penetration by Western democratic ideas. The September 11 attacks notwithstanding, "we remain at the end of history," Fukuyama insists, "because there is only one system that will continue to dominate world politics, that of the liberal-democratic West." There is nothing beyond liberal democracy "towards which we could expect to evolve." Fukuyama concludes by stating that there will be challenges from those who resist progress, "but time and resources are on the side of modernity" (Fukuyama, 2001).

Indeed, but is "modernity" on the side of liberal democracy? Fukuyama is probably right that the current crisis with the forces of radical Islam will be overcome, and that, at the end of the day, there will be no serious ideological challenge originating outside of Western civilization. However, the activities of the NGOs suggest that there already is an alternative ideology to liberal democracy within the West that for decades has been steadily, and almost imperceptibly, evolving.

Thus, it is entirely possible that modernity – thirty or forty years hence – will witness not the final triumph of liberal democracy, but a new challenge to it in the form of a new transnational hybrid regime that is post-liberal democratic, and in the context of the American republic, post-Constitutional and post-American. I will call this alternative ideology "transnational progressivism." This ideology constitutes a universal and modern worldview that challenges in theory and practice both the liberal democratic nation-state in general and the American regime in particular.

Transnational Progressivism

The key concepts of transnational progressivism could be described as follows:

(1) *The ascribed group takes precedence over the individual citizen.* The key political unit is not the individual citizen, who forms voluntary associations and works with fellow citizens regardless of race, sex, or national origin, but the ascriptive group (racial, ethnic, or gender) into which one is born. This emphasis on race, ethnicity, and gender leads to group consciousness and a deemphasis of the individual's capacity for choice and for transcendence of ascriptive categories, joining with others beyond the confines of social class, tribe, and gender to create a cohesive nation.

(2) *A dichotomy of groups: Oppressor vs. victim groups, with immigrant groups designated as victims.* Influenced (however indirectly) by the Hegelian Marxist thinking associated with the Italian writer Antonio Gramsci (1891–1937) and the Central European theorists known as the Frankfurt School, global progressives posit that throughout human history there are essentially two types of groups: the oppressor and the

oppressed, the privileged and the marginalized. In the United States, oppressor groups would variously include white males, heterosexuals, and Anglos, whereas victim groups would include blacks, gays, Latinos (including obviously many immigrants), and women.

Multicultural ideologists have incorporated this essentially Hegelian Marxist "privileged vs. marginalized" dichotomy into their theoretical framework. As political philosopher James Ceaser puts it, multiculturalism is not "multi" or concerned with many groups, but "binary," concerned with two groups, the hegemon (bad) and "the Other" (good) or the oppressor and the oppressed. Thus, in global progressive ideology, "equity" and "social justice" mean strengthening the position of the victim groups and weakening the position of oppressors-hence preferences for certain groups are justified. Accordingly, equality under law is replaced by legal preferences for traditionally victimized groups. In 1999, the US Equal Employment Opportunity Commission extended antidiscrimination protection under Title VII of the 1964 Civil Rights Act to illegal immigrants.

(3) **Group proportionalism as the goal of "fairness."** Transnational progressivism assumes that "victim" groups should be represented in all professions roughly proportionate to their percentage of the population or, at least, of the local work force. Thus, if women make up 52 percent and Latinos make up 10 percent of the population, then 52 percent of all corporate executives, physicians, and insurance salesmen should be women and 10 percent should be Latinos. If not, there is a problem of "underrepresentation" or imbalance that must be rectified by government and civil society. Thomas Sowell has repeatedly emphasized that many Western intellectuals perpetually promote some version of "cosmic justice" or form of equality of result (Sowell, 1999).

(4) **The values of all dominant institutions to be changed to reflect the perspectives of the victim groups.** Transnational progressives insist that it is not enough to have proportional representation of minorities (including immigrants, legal and illegal) at all levels in major institutions of society (corporations, places of worship, universities, armed forces) if these institutions continue to reflect a "white Anglo male culture and world view." Ethnic and linguistic minorities have different ways of viewing the world, they say, and these minorities' values and cultures must be respected and represented within these institutions. At a 1998 US Department of Education conference promoting bilingual education, SUNY professor Joel Spring declared, "We must use multiculturalism and multilingualism to change the dominant culture of the United States."

(5) **The demographic imperative.** The demographic imperative tells us

that major demographic changes are occurring in the United States as millions of new immigrants from non-Western cultures and their children enter the United States. At the same time, the global interdependence of the world's peoples and the transnational connections among them will increase. All of these changes render the traditional paradigm of American nationhood obsolete. That traditional paradigm based on individual rights, majority rule, national sovereignty, citizenship, and the assimilation of immigrants into an existing American civic culture is too narrow and must be changed into a system that promotes "diversity," defined as group proportionalism.

(6) *The redefinition of democracy and "democratic ideals."* Since Fukayama's treatise, transnational progressives have been altering the definition of "democracy," from that of a system of majority rule among equal citizens to one of power sharing among ethnic groups composed of both citizens and non-citizens. Former Immigration and Naturalization Service (INS) general counsel Alexander Aleinikoff, declared that "[we] live in a post-assimilationist age." He asserted that majority preferences simply "reflect the norms and cultures of dominant groups,"as opposed to the norms and cultures of "feminists and people of color"(Aleinikoff, 1990). James Banks, one of American education's leading textbook writers noted that "to create an authentic democratic Unum with moral authority and perceived legitimacy, the Pluribus (diverse peoples) must negotiate and share power" (Banks, 1994). In effect, Banks said, existing American liberal democracy is not quite authentic; real democracy is yet to be created. It will come when the different "peoples" or groups that live within America "share power" as groups.

(7) *Deconstruction of national narratives and national symbols.* Transnational progressives have focused on traditional narratives and national symbols of Western democratic nation-states, questioning union and nationhood itself. In October 2000, the British government-sponsored Commission on the Future of Multi-Ethnic Britain issued a report that denounced the concept of "Britishness" as having "systemic . . . racist connotations." The Commission, chaired by Labour life peer Lord Parekh, declared that instead of defining itself as a nation, the UK should be considered a "community of communities." One member of the Commission explained that the members found the concepts of "Britain" and "nation" troubling. The purpose of the Commission's report, according to the chairman Professor Parekh, was to "shape and restructure the consciousness of our citizens." The report declared that Britain should be formally "recognized as a multi-cultural society" whose history needed to be "revised, rethought, or jettisoned" (Johnston, 2000).

In the United States in the mid-1990s, the proposed "National History

Standards," reflecting the marked influence of multiculturalism among historians in the nation's universities, recommended altering the traditional narrative of the United States. Instead of emphasizing the story of European settlers, American civilization would be redefined as a "convergence" of three civilizations: Amer-indian, West African, and European that formed the bases of a hybrid American multiculture. The National History Standards were ultimately rejected, but this core multicultural concept that the United States is not primarily the creation of Western civilization but the result of a "Great Convergence" of "three worlds" has become the dominant paradigm in American public schools.

In Israel, adversary intellectuals have attacked the Zionist narrative. A "post-Zionist" intelligentsia (Hazony, 1996, 1997) has proposed that Israel consider itself multicultural and deconstruct its identity as a Jewish state. Tom Bethell (1997) has pointed out that in the mid-1990s the official appointed to revise Israel's history curriculum used media interviews to compare the Israeli armed forces to the SS and Orthodox Jewish youth to the Hitler Youth. A new code of ethics for the Israel Defense Forces prepared by a professor of philosophy at Tel Aviv University eliminated all references to the "land of Israel," the "Jewish state," and the "Jewish people," and, instead, referred only to "democracy." Even Israeli foreign minister from the opposition Labor party Simon Peres sounded the post-Zionist trumpet in his book, *The New Middle East* (Peres, 1993) where he wrote that "we do not need to reinforce sovereignty, but rather to strengthen the position of humankind." He called for an "ultranational identity," saying that "particularist nationalism is fading and the idea of a 'citizen of the world' is taking hold. . . . Our ultimate goal is the creation of a regional community of nations, with a common market and elected centralized bodies," a type of Middle Eastern EU.

(8) *Promotion of the concept of postnational citizenship.* "Can advocates of postnational citizenship ultimately succeed in decoupling the concept of citizenship from the nation-state in prevailing political thought?" asks Rutgers Law Professor Linda Bosniak (2000). An increasing number of international law professors throughout the West are arguing that citizenship should be denationalized. Invoking concepts such as inclusion, social justice, democratic engagement, and human rights, they argue for transnational citizenship, postnational citizenship, or sometimes global citizenship embedded in international human rights accords and "evolving" forms of transnational arrangements.

These theorists insist that national citizenship should not be "privileged" at the expense of postnational, multiple, and pluralized forms of citizenship identities. For example, the Carnegie Endowment for International Peace, under the leadership of its president, Jessica Tuchman

Mathews, has published a series of books in the past few years "challenging traditional understandings of belonging and membership" in nation-states and "rethinking the meaning of citizenship" (Aleinikoff and Klusmeyer, 2000, 2001). Although couched in the ostensibly neutral language of social science, these essays by scholars from Germany, Britain, Canada, and France, as well as the United States, argue for new, transnational forms of citizenship as a normative good.

(9) *The idea of transnationalism as a major conceptual tool.* The theory of transnationalism promises to be for the first decade of the twenty-first century what multiculturalism was for the last decade of the twentieth century. In a certain sense, transnationalism is the next stage of multicultural ideology- it is multiculturalism with a global face. Like multiculturalism, transnationalism is a concept that provides elites with both an empirical tool (a plausible analysis of what is) and an ideological framework (a vision of what should be). Transnational advocates argue that globalization requires some form of transnational "global governance" because they believe that the nation-state and the idea of national citizenship are ill suited to deal with the global problems of the future. Academic and public policy conferences today are filled with discussions of "transnational organizations," "transnational actors," "transnational migrants," "transnational jurisprudence," and "transnational citizenship," just as in the 1990s they were replete with references to multiculturalism in education, citizenship, literature, and law.

Many of the same scholars who touted multiculturalism now herald the coming transnational age. Thus, at its August 1999 annual conference, "Transitions in World Societies," the American Sociological Association (ASA) that promoted multiculturalism from the late 1980s to the mid-1990s featured transnationalism. Indeed, the ASA's then-president, Professor Alejandro Portes of Princeton University, argued that transnationalism is the wave of the future. He insisted that transnationalism, combined with large-scale immigration, would redefine the meaning of American citizenship. University of Chicago anthropologist Arjun Appadurai has suggested that the United States is in transition from being a "land of immigrants" to "one node in a postnational network of diasporas"(quoted in Kerber, 1997).

The promotion of transnationalism as both an empirical and normative concept is an attempt to shape this crucial intellectual struggle over globalization. The adherents of transnationalism create a dichotomy. They imply that one is either in step with globalization, and thus with transnationalism and forward-looking thinking, or one is a backward antiglobalist. Liberal democrats (who are internationalists and support free trade and market economics) must reply that this is a false dichotomy, that the critical argument is not between globalists and antiglobalists, but instead over the form Western global engagement should take in the coming decades: will it be transnationalist or internationalist?

Transnational Progressivism's Social Base: A Post-National Intelligentsia

The social base of transnational progressivism could be labeled a rising postnational intelligentsia, the leaders of which include many international law professors at prestigious Western universities, NGO activists, foundation officers, UN bureaucrats, EU administrators, corporation executives, and practicing politicians throughout the West.

- British "third way" theorist Anthony Giddens declared that he is "in favor of pioneering some quasi-utopian transnational forms of democracy" and "is strongly opposed to the idea that social justice is just equality of opportunity" (Giddens, 1991). Giddens wrote that "the shortcomings of liberal democracy suggest the need to further more radical forms of democratization." Instead of liberal democracy, Giddens, using the language of Jürgen Habermas, posits a "dialogic democracy" with an emphasis on "life politics," especially "new social movements, such as those concerned with feminism, ecology, peace, or human rights."
- Italian Marxist theorist Toni Negri (a jailed former associate of the terrorist Italian Red Brigades) and Duke University Literature Professor Michael Hardt, use Marxist concepts such as the "multitudes" i.e., "the masses" vs. the Empire, to attack the power of global corporations and, without being overly specific, call for a new form of "global" or transnational democracy (Negri and Hardt,).
- University of Chicago philosophy professor Martha Nussbaum, who called for reinvigorating the concept of "global citizenship" and denounced patriotism as "indistinguishable from jingoism" in a debate several years back that set off a wide ranging discussion among American academics on the meaning of patriotism, citizenship, and the nation-state (Nussbaum, 1994).
- Strobe Talbot, former undersecretary of state, who wrote when he was an editor of *Time* magazine in the early 1990s that he was optimistic that by the end of the twenty-first century "nationhood as we know it will be obsolete: all states will recognize a single global authority. . . All countries are basically social arrangements, accommodations to changing circumstances. No matter how permanent and

even sacred they may seem at any one time, in fact they are all artificial and temporary" (Talbot, 1992). He characterizes the devolution of national sovereignty "upward toward supranational bodies" and "downward toward" autonomous units is a "basically positive phenomenon."

Complementary to this general (and diffuse) sentiment for new transnational forms of governance is the concrete day-to-day practical work of the NGOs that seek to bring the transnational vision to fruition. When social movements such as the ideologies of "transnationalism" and "global governance" are depicted as the result of "social forces" or the "movement of history," a certain impersonal inevitability is implied. However, in the twentieth century the Bolshevik Revolution, the National Socialist Revolution, the New Deal, the Reagan Revolution, the Gaullist national reconstruction in France, and the creation of the EU and its predecessor organizations were not inevitable, but were the result of the exercise of political will by elites who mobilized their strength and defeated opponents.

Similarly, "transnationalism," "multiculturalism," and "global governance," like "diversity," are ideological tools championed by activist elites, not "forces of history." The success or failure of these values-loaded concepts will ultimately depend upon the political will and effectiveness of these elites.

Facing popular resistance on issue after issue, a wide range of American NGOs seek to bypass the normal democratic process to achieve their political ends by extra- or post-constitutional means, demanding that the United States:

- join the International Criminal Court;
- ratify the UN Convention on Women's Rights;
- drop reservations to the UN treaty against racial discrimination;
- reduce border policing;
- implement affirmative action legislation;
- follow international norms on capital punishment;
- accept the Kyoto Treaty on global warming;
- expand the legal rights of non-citizens in constitutional regimes.

Human Rights Activists

The main legal conflict between traditional American liberal democrats and transnational progressives is ultimately the question of whether the

US Constitution trumps international law or vice versa. "International law" here refers to what experts including John Bolton, Jeremy Rabkin, Jack Goldsmith, Lee Casey, and David Rivkin have called the "new international law," which differs from traditional concepts of the "Law of Nations" *(Chicago Journal of International Law*, 2000).

Before the mid-twentieth century, traditional international law usually referred to relations among nation-states as "international" in the real sense of the term. Since that time the "new international law" has increasingly penetrated the sovereignty of democratic nation-states. It is, therefore, in reality, "transnational law." Human rights activists work to establish norms for this "new international (i.e. transnational) law," and then attempt to bring the United States into conformity with a legal regime whose reach often extends beyond democratic politics and the guarantees of the US Constitution.

Transnational progressives (including American and non-American NGOs and UN officials) excoriate American political, legal, and administrative practices in virulent language, as if the American liberal democratic nation-state was an illegitimate authoritarian regime. Thus, AI–USA charged the United States in a 1998 report with "a persistent and widespread pattern of human rights violations," stating that "racism and discrimination contribute to the denial of the fundamental rights of countless men, women, and children" in the United States. Moreover, police brutality is "entrenched and nation-wide"; the United States is the "world leader in high tech repression"; and it is time for the United States to face up to its "hypocrisy." The report discussed "a national background of economic and racial injustice, a rising tide of anti-immigrant sentiments" and stated that "human rights violations in the US occur in rural communities and urban communities from coast to coast." The United States had long "abdicated its duty" to lead the world in promoting human rights (Amnesty International, 1998). Therefore, avowed William Schultz, the executive director of AI–USA, "it was no wonder the United States was ousted from the [UN] Human Rights Commission" (Schultz, 2001). Overall, HRW affirmed that the United States was guilty of "serious human rights violations" including "rampant" police brutality and "harassment of gay adults in the military paralleled by the harassment of students perceived to be gay, lesbian, bisexual, and transgendered" in public schools. These students "experienced" school "as a place that accepted intolerance, hatred, ostracization, and violence against youth who were perceived as different."

UN special investigators examined US "human rights violations" in 1990s. The first thing these investigators did was meet with an array of American NGOs. In their reports, the UN officials quoted freely from

American NGO documents. UN investigator Maurice Glélé of Benin wrote that, "racism existed in the US with sociological inertia, structural obstacles, and individual resistance." Glélé visited the U.S. State Department and found that discrimination complaints by African American State Department employees "had dragged on since 1986." Meanwhile, the report stated, the "State Department remains a very white institution." The UN investigator further wrote that "the fate of the majority of Blacks is one of poverty, sickness, illiteracy, drugs, and crime in response to the social cul-de-sac in which they find themselves." Rahhika Coomaraswamy of Sri Lanka, the UN Special Rapporteur on Violence Against Women found that the United States is "criminalizing" a large segment of its population, a group that is "composed of poor persons of color and increasingly female" (Maran, 1999). Bacre Waly Ndiaye, UN Special Rapporteur on Extra-judical, Summary, or Arbitrary Executions, "a significant degree of unfairness and arbitrariness" in the application of the death penalty," based on racial data showing that 41 percent of death penalty inmates in the US are African-American, 47 percent white, 7 percent Hispanic, and 1.5 percent American Indian (Maran, 1999).

Anti-Assimilation on the Home Front

The Durban conference in 2001 on Racism and Xenophobia represents a classic case of how American NGOs promote transnational progressivism. It is revealing that the language of almost all the UN treaties that ignore the guarantees of the US Constitution (including the International Criminal Court (ICC), the Convention on Women's Rights, the Convention on Children's Rights) were written by American and other Western NGOs. In other words, the documents were written by a Western postnational intelligentsia aided by a "Westernized" coterie of Third World intellectuals, including Kofi Annan.

Hardly noticed is the fact that many of the same NGOs (HRW, AI–USA.) and international law professors who have advocated transnational legal concepts at UN meetings and in international forums, are active in US immigration and naturalization law. On this front the transnational progressives have pursued two objectives: (1) eliminating all distinctions between citizens and non-citizens and (2) vigorously opposing attempts to assimilate immigrants into the "dominant" Anglo culture. When discussing immigration/assimilation issues, Louis Henkin, one of the most prominent scholars of international law, attacks "archaic notions of sovereignty" and calls for largely eliminating "the difference between a citizen and a non-citizen permanent resident" in all federal laws (Henkin, 1994). Stephen Legomsky argues that dual nationals who are American citizens should not be required to give "greater weight to US interests, in the event of a conflict" between the United States and the other country in which the American citizen is also a national (quoted in Schuck, 1998).

Two leading law professors questioned the requirement that immigrants seeking American citizenship "renounce 'all allegiance and fidelity' to their old nations." In an op-ed in the *Wall Street Journal* (Schuck and Spiro, 1998) they suggested dropping this "renunciation clause" from the Oath of Renunciation and Allegiance. They also question the concept of the hyphenated American, offering the model of "ampersand" American. They do not object to immigrants (or migrants) who retain "loyalties" to their "original homeland" and vote in both countries. Robert Bach authored a major Ford Foundation report on new and "established residents" (the word "citizen" was assiduously avoided) that advocated the "maintenance" of ethnic immigrant identities, supported "non-citizen voting," and attacked assimilation suggesting that homogeneity, not diversity, "may" be the "problem in America" (Bach, 1993). Bach later became deputy director for policy at the INS in the Clinton administration, where he joined forces with then INS general counsel Alexander Alienikoff to promote a pro-multicultural, anti-assimilation federal policy. Alienikoff, an immigration law professor, has openly and vigorously advocated a "politics" that "moves us beyond assimilation" (Alienikoff, 1998).

Congressional investigations and investigative reporting established conclusively that the financial backing for this anti-assimilationist campaign has come primarily from the Ford Foundation, which in the 1970s made a conscious decision to fund a Latino rights movement based on advocacy-litigation and group rights (Geyer, 1996). The global progressives have been aided by a "transnational right." It was a determined group of transnational and libertarian-leaning conservative senators and congressmen that prevented the Immigration Reform legislation of 1996 from limiting unskilled immigration. The same group worked with progressives in the late 1990s to successfully block the implementation of a computerized plan to track the movement of foreign nationals in and out of the United States, thereby, in George Will's apt phrase putting "commerce over country."

The EU as a Stronghold of Transnational Progressivism

Whereas ideologically driven NGOs represent a subnational challenge to the values and policies of the liberal-democratic nation-state, the EU is a large supranational macro-organization that to a considerable extent embodies transnational progressivism, both in governmental form and in substantive policies. The governmental structure of the EU is post-democratic. Power in the EU principally resides in the European Commission (EC) and to a lesser extent the European Court of Justice (ECJ). The EC is the EU's executive body. It also initiates legislative action, implements common policy, and controls a large bureaucracy. The EC is composed of a rotating presidency and nineteen commissioners chosen by the member-states and approved by the European Parliament. It is unelected and, for the most part, unaccountable.

A white paper issued by the EC suggests that this unaccountability is one of the reasons for its success: "The original and essential source of the success of European Integration is that the EU's executive body, the Commission, is supranational and independent from national, sectoral, or other influences." This "democracy deficit" is constantly lamented, particularly by the Germans, who have proposed greater power to the European Parliament, but, at this stage, the issue remains and represents a moral challenge to EU legitimacy (Casey and Rivkin, 2001).

The substantive polices advanced by EU leaders both in the Commission and the ECJ are based on the global progressive ideology of group rights discussed earlier that promotes victim groups over "privileged" groups and eschews the liberal principle of treating citizens equally as individuals. Thus, statutes on "hate speech," "hate crimes," "comparable worth" for women's pay, and group preferences are considerably more "progressive" in the EU than in the United States. At the same time, European courts have overruled national parliaments and public opinion in nation-states by compelling the British to incorporate gays and the Germans to incorporate women in combat units in their respective military services. The ECJ even struck down a British law on corporal punishment, declaring that parental spanking is internationally recognized as an abuse of human rights

A group of what Undersecretary of State John Bolton has referred to as "Americanist" (as opposed to "Globalist") thinkers has emphasized the divergence of America's liberal philosophy from the EU's. Lee Casey and David Rivkin (2001) argued this position forcefully:

> From the perspective of US philosophical and constitutional traditions, the key question in determining whether any particular model of government is

a democracy is whether the governed choose their governors . . . Unfortunately, the reemergence [in Europe] of a pre-Enlightenment pan-European ideology that denies the ultimate authority of the nation-state, as well as the transfer of policymaking authority from the governed and their elected representatives to a professional bureaucracy, as is evident in the EU's leading institutions, suggests a dramatic divergence from the basic principle of popular sovereignty once shared both by Europe's democracies and the United States.

In the world of practical international politics, in the period immediately prior to the events of September 11, the EU clearly stood in opposition to the United States on some of the most important strategic global issues, including the ICC, the Comprehensive Test Ban Treaty, the Land Mine Treaty, the Kyoto Global Warming Treaty, and policy towards missile defense, Iran, Iraq, Israel, China, Cuba, North Korea, and the death penalty. On most of these issues, transnational progressives in the United States, including many practicing politicians, supported the EU position and attempted to leverage this transnational influence in the domestic debate. At the same time, the position of the Bush administration on many of these issues has support from elements in Europe, certainly from members of the British political class and public, and undoubtedly from some segments of the Continental European populace as well (on the death penalty, for example).

Even since the September 11 attacks, many Europeans have continued to snipe at American policies and place themselves in opposition to American interests in the war on terrorism. Within a month of September 11, Spanish judge Baltasar Garzon called the planned military tribunals "simply illegal" (Taranto, 2001). In December 2001 the European Parliament condemned the US Patriot Act (the bipartisan antiterrorist legislation that passed the US Congress overwhelmingly) as "contrary to the principles" of human rights because the legislation "discriminates" against noncitizens (Opinion Journal, 2001). Time and again, leading European politicians have made a point of insisting that they oppose extraditing terrorist suspects to the United States if those terrorists would be subjected to the death penalty.

Interestingly, both conservative realists and neoconservative pro-democracy advocates have argued that some EU, UN, and NGO thinking threatens to limit both American democracy

at home and American power overseas. As Jeanne Kirkpatrick put it, "foreign governments and their leaders, and more than a few activists here at home, seek to constrain and control American power by means of elaborate multi-lateral processes, global arrangements, and UN treaties that limit both our capacity to govern ourselves and act abroad" (Commentary, 2000).

Conclusion

Scholars, publicists, and many others in the Western world-and especially in the United States, original home of constitutional democracy-have for the past several decades been arguing furiously over the most fundamental political ideas. Talk of a "culture war," however, is somewhat misleading, because the arguments over transnational vs. national citizenship, multiculturalism vs. assimilation, and global governance vs. national sovereignty are not simply cultural, but ideological and philosophical, in that they pose such Aristotelian questions as "What kind of government is best?" and "What is citizenship?"

In America, there is an elemental argument about whether to preserve, improve, and transmit the American regime to future generations or to transform it into a new and different type of polity. In the terms of contemporary political science we are arguing about "regime maintenance" vs. "regime transformation."

In the final analysis, the challenge from transnational progressivism to traditional American concepts of citizenship, patriotism, assimilation, and at the most basic level, to the meaning of democracy itself, is fundamental. It is a challenge to American liberal democracy. If our system is based not on individual rights, but on group consciousness; not on equality of citizenship, but on group preferences for non-citizens (including illegal immigrants) and for certain categories of citizens; not on majority rule within constitutional limits, but on power-sharing by different ethnic, racial, gender, and linguistic groups; not on constitutional law, but on transnational law; not on immigrants becoming Americans, but on migrants linked between transnational communities; then the regime will cease to be "constitutional," "liberal," "democratic," and "American," in the understood sense of those terms, but will become in reality a new hybrid system that is "post-constitutional," "post-liberal," "post-democratic," and "post-American."

This intracivilizational Western conflict between liberal democracy and transnational progressivism began in the mid to late twentieth century; it accelerated after the Cold War and should continue well into the twenty-first century. Indeed, from the fall of the Berlin Wall in November 1989 until the attacks on the heart of the American republic on September 11, 2001, the transnational progressives were on the offensive.

Since September 11, however, the forces supporting the liberal-democratic nation state have rallied. Clearly, in the post-September 11 milieu there is a window of opportunity for those who favor a reaffirmation of the traditional norms of liberal-democratic patriotism. The political will to seize this opportunity is unclear. Key areas to watch include official government policy statements for the use of force and the conduct of war; the use and non-use of international law; assimilation-immigration policy; border control; civic education in the public schools; and the state of the patriotic narrative in popular culture.

Fourth Dimension?

I suggest that we add a fourth dimension to a conceptual framework of international politics. Three dimensions are currently recognizable. First, there is traditional realpolitik, the competition and conflict among nation-states (and supranational states such as the EU). Second is the competition of civilizations conceptualized by Samuel Huntington (1998). Third, there is the conflict between the democratic world and the non-democratic world. I am suggesting a fourth dimension, the conflict within the democratic zone (and particularly within the West) between the forces of liberal democracy and the forces of transnational progressivism, between democrats and post-democrats.

At one level, the fourth dimension amounts to a struggle between the American/Anglo-American and the continental European models of governance about what Western civilization ought to be. The latter travels the road to a form of bureaucratic collectivism, the former emphasizes the sometimes conflicting values of civic republicanism and the liberal values of openness and individuality within a market-driven milieu. But not to be overlooked is the fact that there are Europeans who support an entrepreneurial, liberal, Anglo-American style regime, and there are many Americans (particularly among elites) who favor a more collectivist continental European approach.

The conflicts and tensions within each of these four dimensions of international politics are unfolding simultaneously and affected by each other, and so they all belong in a comprehensive understanding of the world of the twenty-first century. In hindsight, Fukuyama may have been wrong to suggest that liberal democracy is inevitably the final form of political governance, the evolutionary endpoint of political philosophy, because it has become unclear that liberal democracy can withstand its present internal challenges. Despite military and ideological triumphs over national socialism and communism, powerful antidemocratic forces that were in a sense Western ideological heresies remain. Western liberal democracy will continue to face an ideological-metaphysical challenge from powerful post-liberal democratic forces, whose origins are Western, but, which could, in James Kurth's word, be described as "post-Western" (Kurth and Petras, 1993).

Note

1   The NGOs included the Leadership Conference on Civil Rights, Amnesty International–USA (AI–USA.), Human Rights Watch (HRW), the Arab-American Institute, National Council of Churches, American Friends Service Committee, the National Association for the Advancement of Colored People, the American Civil Liberties Union, the Mexican-American Legal Defense and Educational Fund, the International Human Rights Law Group, the Lawyers Committee for Civil Rights under Law, and others.

References

Alienikoff, T. Alexander, Citizens, aliens, membership and the constitution. *Constitutional Commentary* 7, 1990, pp. 30.
——, A multicultural nationalism? *American Prospect*, January–February 1998.
——, and Klusmeyer, D. (Eds.), *From Migrants to Citizens: Membership in a changing world*. Washington, D.C.: Carnegie Endowment for International Peace., 2000.
——, and Klusmeyer, D. (Eds.) *Citizenship today: Global perspectives and practices*. Washington, D.C.: Carnegie Endowment for International Peace, 2001.
Amnesty International, Rights for all: Human rights concerns in the USA. October 1998.
Bach, Robert, *Changing Relations, Newcomers and Established Residents in US Communities*. New York: The Ford Foundation, April, 1993.
Banks, James, Transforming the mainstream curriculum. *Educational Leadership*, May 1994, p. 4.
Bethell, Tom, The cultural wars in Israel. Paper prepared for the Institute for Advanced Strategic and Political Studies conference on "Israel: The Advanced Case of Western Afflictions," Washington, D.C., December 15, 1997.
Casy, Lee and Rivkin, David Europe, In the balance: The alarmingly undemocratic drift of the European Union. *Policy Review*, June/July 2001, pp. 41–53. A later version of the EU position is: *European Governance*. White paper, Commission of the European Community, Brussels, July 25, 2001.
Chicago Journal of International Law, AEI confernece: Trends in global governamce: Do they threaten American sovereignty? Fall 2000.
Commentary, American power – for what? A symposium. January 2000.
Goodman, Anthony, *United Nations*. Reuters, October 24, 2000.
Fukuyama, Francis, The end of history. *National Interest*, Summer 1989.
——, History is still going our way. *The Wall Street Journal*, October 5, 2001.
Geyer, Georgie Anne, *Americans No More: The death of citizenship*. New York: The Atlantic Monthly Press, 1996, pp. 190–230.
Giddens, Anthony, *The Consequences of Modrnity*. Cambridge: Polity Press, 1991.
Hazony, Yoram, The end of Zionism? *Azure*, Summer 1996
Hazony, Yoram, *The Jewish State: The struggle for Israel's soul*. New York: Basic Books, 2000.

Henkin, Louis Immigration and the constitution: A clean slate. *Virginia Journal of International Law,* Fall 1994.

Huntington, Samuel, *The Clash of Civilizations and the Remaking of World Order.* New York: Touchstone, 1997.

Iley, Karen, *New York Times,* Agust 6, 2001 (Reuters, AP: Yahoo News).

International Human Rights Group, *Report on the US Leadership Meetings on the World Conference against Racism* (convened by Gay McDougall).

Johnston, Philip, Straw wants to rewrite our history. *Electronic Telegraph,* October 10, 2000.

Kerber, Linda, *Revolutionary Generation: Ideology, politics and culture in the early republic.* Washington, D.C.: American Historical Association, 1997.

Kurth, James and Petras, James, *Mediterranean Paradoxes: Politics and social structure in southern Europe.* Providence, RI: Berg, 1993.

Maran, Rita, International human rights in the USA: A critique. *Social Justice,* Spring 1999, pp. 61–3.

Negri, Antonio and Hardt, Michael, *Empire.* Cambridge, MA: Harvard University Press, 2000.

Nussbaum, Martha, Patriotism and cosmopolitanism. *Boston Review,* October–November, 1994.

Opinion Journal, Welcome to Europe, Mr. Ashcroft. December 14, 2001.

Peres, Shimon, *The New Middle East.* New York: Henry Holt,1993.

Schuck, Peter, "Plural citizenship." In Noah Pickus (ed.), *Immigration and Citizenship in the 21st Century.* Lanham, MA: Rowman and Littlefield, 1998.

Schuck, Peter and Spiro, Peter, Dual citizens, good Americans. *Wall Street Journal,* March 18, 1998.

Schultz, William, Amnesty criticizes US record on rights. *Washington Post,* May 31, 2001.

Sowell, Thomas, *The Quest for Cosmic Justice.* New York: The Free Press, 1999.

Taranto, James, No justice, no peace: Why it's fatuous to regard September 11 as a "crime." *Opinion Journal,* October 8, 2001.

8

The West and Yasser Arafat

NORMAN DOIDGE

How is it that the Bush administration, which is deadly serious in opposing terrorists and those who harbor them, could let Colin Powell declare (2002) – on the same day that senior terrorist Yasser Arafat was caught funding the *al-Aqsa* suicide bombers – that Arafat is no terrorist at all? On April 4, President Bush asked Israel to halt its attacks on Arafat's terrorist infrastructure. What must be going on in their minds? Are they serious or aren't they?

Actually, they are serious about fighting terror. But they are also caught in a psychological bind that they do not understand. Letting Arafat go is part of a pattern that has recurred so often it cannot simply be described as a mistake. It is the same pattern that caused George Bush senior to refrain from finishing off Saddam Hussein when he had overwhelmed him. Europe, the Arab world, and the Bush administration are hoping to see a diplomatic initiative develop that will ensure that Israel makes the same mistake George Bush senior did in Iraq, forbidding it from destroying Arafat and his regime.

No one survives as long as Yasser Arafat – forty years as a terrorist – unless he knows something important about the weak spots in Western psychology. Israeli foreign minister Abba Eban once quipped that the Palestinians, under Arafat's leadership, "never miss an opportunity to miss an opportunity." The remark hasn't aged well. Closer to the truth is that the West has, mysteriously, never missed an opportunity to revive Arafat. Arafat has been able to keep up his spirits because he understands how the Western psyche works in these near-death confrontations. This is because he, as a terrorist who lacks a conscience, can see things that those who have a conscience cannot. It is these insights that have preserved Yasser Arafat.

It would be easy to attribute Arafat's endless second chances –that predictably will continue to be offered to him and his associate terrorists in the future as well - simply to a deluded Left, since the Left, and the European Union, favors dealing with Arafat not as a criminal but as an equal. But now, the Right and not the Left holds power in Israel and the United States. Besides, historically, those who have revived Arafat have not all been Leftists or ideological enemies of Israel. Many of them have known that Arafat is a liar and a terrorist. Arafat's psychological magic is most evident when he casts his spell on such men.

But first, to make the case. The list of distinguished fighters of terrorism and tyranny who nonetheless have found themselves overriding their principles to let Arafat go rather than ringing him to justice is remarkable. Ronald Reagan brooked no compromise with the "evil empire," and bombed Muammar Qaddafi's home, nearly killing him. Yet in the 1980s, President Reagan pressured Menachem Begin to let Arafat and his fighters go free when the Israeli army had them cornered in West Beirut. Begin, who had made a career of resisting liberal democracies when they offered Israel bad advice, succumbed. Yitzhak Rabin, after fighting Arafat much of his adult life, decriminalized and rearmed him through the Oslo agreements, precisely when Arafat was at his weakest, fresh from endorsing the defeated Saddam Hussein. Ehud Barak had an extraordinary career fighting terrorists before Arafat proved his political undoing. The current President Bush came into office refusing to talk to Arafat or treat him like a normal head of state. Bush's position was reinforced when Palestinians celebrated in the streets on September 11; and he appeared to be viscerally revolted by Palestinian and Fatah suicide bombings in Israel this past December (2001).

But when such men are dealing with Arafat, there is eventually an about-face, and President Bush did his in March. When Israel sent troops into a terrorist nerve center in Ramallah to prevent further attacks on civilians – when it did, in essence, what the United States is doing in Afghanistan – President Bush said Israel's action was "not helpful." When dealing with Arafat, even the foes of terror become inconsistent and incoherent.

The archetypal releaser of Arafat is a leader who has criticized him many times, has shown himself capable of the assertive use of deadly force in other situations, and, like Reagan, Bush, Begin, Sharon, Rabin, and Barak, has criticized others for letting terrorists go free. The typical, last-minute liberator is a reluctant and soon-to-be-regretful redeemer, who has often battled terror. Usually, he is utterly disquieted as he finds himself letting Arafat off, but he feels trapped by some force larger than himself. Something always seems to happen so that the knowledge that it is dangerous to let such men go unpunished is not translated into effective action. It is as though these leaders come under a spell.

This "spell" is part of a dynamic that operates when the evil being confronted is brazen and relentless, and it occurred when the first President Bush let Saddam Hussein off at the end of the Gulf War. The fact that Bush allowed Saddam to escape a just defeat when he was all but conquered is crucial: The person who decides on the ill-advised release does not act from a position of relative weakness. Neville Chamberlain and the others who released Hitler – another representative of brazen evil – at Munich did so before the Fuhrer perfected his war machine. It is as though there were an unwritten psychological law that evil at its most shameless – the most barbaric murder of children and civilians, the most outrageous claims and lies – is somehow, in the minute before midnight, to be treated as an exception worthy of reprieve.

In each historical instance, there is of course a political imperative that is cited to justify snatching defeat from the jaws of victory. In Arafat's case, the political imperative has turned out each time to be based on a flawed calculus. In March, US pressure on Israel to loosen its hold on Arafat was justified in the name of shoring up Arab support for Washington's new effort to topple Saddam. That Arab support did not materialize, any more than Oslo's promise had. In fact, Washington's Arab "friends" declared at the Beirut Arab summit that any attack on Iraq was an attack on them. To which Secretary of State Powell replied that Arafat, a man who had boasted of killing the American ambassador and his assistant in Khartoum, was no terrorist.

The student of human nature who seems best to have recognized the importance of this bizarre dynamic, in which a conscientious hero proves unable to finish off a foe he knows to be evil, was none other than Shakespeare. Indeed, the Bard was obsessed with understanding the phenomenon. Hamlet hesitated to bring Claudius to justice, and he paid with his life and the lives of those he loved. But it is in "Richard III" that one can learn most from characters who see evil, yet freeze at the key moment. The principal characters are fully aware of Richard's undeniable evil, yet they let him have his way despite themselves. Richard is the most systematically evil character in all of Shakespeare's plays. "I can smile, and murder while I smile," he says, swearing that he will outdo all the villains of history "and set the murderous Machiavel to school." The most important thing Richard knows is that while conscience allows us to understand ordinary crimes, it actually blinds us before the most extraordinary ones.

The idea that conscience blinds us, making us less able to oppose evil's most brazen forms, is deeply disturbing, for conscience is the sine qua non of civil society. Conscience is supposed to be the faculty that helps us become aware of our effects on others and our motives towards them, notably our baser motives. In Elizabethan English, "conscience" is an equivocal word that can mean either that faculty that allows us to feel guilt or "awareness," as in "consciousness." When Hamlet says, "Conscience does make cowards of us all," he means consciousness, by making us aware of the possibility of death, makes us cowardly.

But conscience, designed to ferret out evil within, can also actually narrow our awareness of evil. This happens, according to Freud, because the person with a conscience learns to repress automatically his own most destructive inclinations so as not to act on them. He becomes ignorant, for example, of the thrill of evil that a sadist like Richard III feels when he plays God and exercises the freedom to kill whomever he pleases. But the cost of repressing one's most destructive feelings is an inability to understand, without significant effort, those who give these feelings free rein.

This is seen over and over in "Richard III," especially in Richard's seduction of Lady Anne, whose husband he has murdered, and it is seen over and over in our dealings with terrorists. Richard actually gets Anne to drop her sword when she's about to kill him. Anne, although she knows Richard is evil, cannot see that he has no conscience. She tells him he should hang himself for what he has done. She keeps missing the point. He feels no guilt. Eventually, she marries him, and he murders her.

Conscience, when it is functioning well – automatically and without the intervention of reason, so that we do the right thing without thinking – is not simply rational. It is a force, a blunt instrument before which the conscientious person is guilty until proven innocent. As the preventive agency of the mind, conscience blocks first, thinks later. Men like Arafat and Richard know this. That is why both men constantly charge others with crimes – to paralyze them. Both know it doesn't matter whether the charges are false. Richard brazenly accuses Anne of inspiring the murder of her husband, as Arafat accuses the West of causing terrorism.

It is this force inside the psyche of his enemies that the person without a conscience can so effectively enlist as a fifth column. Having himself no such inner force always second-guessing him, he can see it clearly in others – far more clearly than do those who are in its thrall and take each of its charges seriously. Arafat gets endless second chances because the conscience of the West is doing what a conscience does: second-guessing the West's own actions. That is why Arafat is always playing upon the conscience of the West, especially by his endless recourse to "international law" and invocation of "human rights," an utterly brazen ploy coming from a terrorist.

Law, in the democracies, is like a civic conscience, and like conscience, it is the bluntest of instruments. Because in democracies law is made by the people, it has their respect. Democratic citizens are prone to the illusory hope that the law can be applied successfully in international affairs between regimes regardless of whether they are democracies or tyrannies, strong or weak. The name for this hope is "international law." But because the law in tyrannies is ultimately the product of one man's whim, a mere vehicle of preeminent will and power, it cannot restrain the preeminent will and power. Conscientiousness in no way attaches to the law in tyrannies. International agreements with tyrants are meaningless, yet pursuit of such agreements is precisely what the State Department is now endorsing by trying to get Israel to sit at the table with Arafat. "What is the law?" Saddam Hussein once asked. Then he answered his own question. "The two lines above my signature."

When a terrorist such as Arafat or bin Laden uses bombs as well as language, his goal is to weaken the society he targets by manipulating not just fear but also conscience. He seeks to create a fifth column within each individual, sympathetic to his ideals, and a fifth column within the society, an anti-self-defense movement that will righteously lobby the government to open the gates, so that the terrorist can destroy his target with ease. But the mechanism by which societies succumb must be in large part unconscious. After all, few can face themselves if they say, "I am succumbing to fear."

The terrorist therefore must persuade his victims that they are "doing the right thing" by submitting to fear. To do so, the terrorist needs to recruit or take over each victim's conscience and change it. This happens in stages.

Terror does not work simply by killing: It is malignantly theatrical. Terror aims not only to maim its immediate victims but also to induce a second-hand trauma in its audience, to change them against their will. The core tactic of terrorism is the use of random violence on the target population's home turf. This instills a sense that one can never leave the field of battle, because the field of battle is one's home. The genius of terrorism is that it uses infrequent, random violence to create a sense that terror is omnipresent (chapter 5).

During the 1970s, when planes were frequently hijacked and people kidnapped, a bizarre phenomenon occurred. Consciences were hijacked too. People who had been held at gunpoint and forced to beg for their lives, dependent on their captors for their next breath, emerged to describe those captors as just people who treated them well. Former hostages right-eously lectured their own governments on the need to support the terrorists' demands. Unremitting terror gave rise to an almost psychotic wishful thinking, which recast the terrorists as good people, nay, even deliverers.

The psychological mechanism involved is called "identification with the aggressor" and was first described by Anna Freud. When this identifica-tion occurs, it is as though the terrorist implants his own ideals and moral code inside his victim's conscience.

The paradigmatic example of this occurred in Stockholm in 1973, when four tellers were held at gunpoint for 131 hours in a bank vault. Soon the captives were expressing more fear of the police who were trying to rescue them than of their captors. One prisoner, in a phone call to the Swedish prime minister, Olaf Palme, said, "The robbers are protecting us from the police." After the tellers were released, they expressed no hatred for their captors, and even said they were emotionally indebted to them. Throughout the seventies, the Stockholm Syndrome was demonstrated over and over. Americans captured by terrorists in Lebanon emerged from captivity praising the same Arab terrorists who had murdered their fellows. Patty Hearst, kidnapped in California by the Symbionese Liberation Army, did the same.

The Stockholm Syndrome is not a conscious attempt to ingratiate oneself with one's captors, but an automatic emotional response, seen in many, though not all, captives. With the help of TV, terrorism creates what one might call a "Second-hand Stockholm Syndrome" in the body politic. The goal is to make the target population fall back on wishful thinking, and say, "Maybe if we listen to their demands, they will stop. Maybe the problem is how we are handling the crisis. Maybe we are being too forceful. Maybe they can be reasoned with. Maybe we should hold our fire and give peace a chance." The citizenry becomes progressively more passive and confused and willing to appease. This confusion is mani-fest whenever pundits who are apologists for terror speak of terrorist violence as caused not by the perpetrators, but by some abstract "cycle of violence," suggesting a moral equivalence between the terrorist and his victims and blotting out the reality of barbarism and human psychopathy. How much nicer to live in a world of abstractions than of Richards, Arafats, Saddams, and bin Ladens.

Like Richard, the terrorist is brazen and relentless. America is new to terror on its home soil, and has yet to see relentlessness in action. It is societies such as Israel, targets of sustained terror campaigns, that are most susceptible to the Second-hand Stockholm Syndrome.

Israel clearly had a bad case throughout Oslo. This is the period when the Israeli Left rewrote Israeli textbooks, dropping most references to the Holocaust and its role in the creation of the state, to the Arab armies' attacks of 1948, 1967, and 1973, to the utter failure of Western liberal democracies such as France to help save their Jews (which became a major justification for Zionism), and placing a Palestinianocentric view of events before Israeli teenagers who would soon have to serve in the army. While Shimon Peres was arguing in "The New Middle East" (a place which would have no anti-Semitism) that there would be no need for a Jewish state, Israeli intellectuals like the novelist David Grossman were accepting the aggressor's notion of Jewish self-defense as evil:

> The Jews living in Israel are now being asked not only to give up on geographical territories. We must also implement a "redeployment" – or even a complete withdrawal – from entire regions in our soul. . . . Slowly, over long years, we will discover that we are beginning to give them up: . . . Giving up on power as a value. On the army itself as a value. . . . On "It is good to die for one's country," on "The best to the air force," . . . and on "After me" [the doctrine that commanding officers lead their troops into dangerous situations].

The repeated message of that short incantational passage? Israel, drop your sword!

Terrorists can work through language, as did Richard until he had access to violence, or through violence alone. What makes Arafat's career in terror so remarkable is that when he has had limited access to violence, he has been able to use the very means Richard did to convince his enemies not to run him through. Arafat has been able to paint himself and the Palestinian people as victims because, lacking a conscience, he could glibly encourage Palestinian children to stand as human shields for his snipers. Fighting such an enemy so pricked the conscience of Israel that many Israelis felt they could not live with themselves – even though they knew that Arafat was manipulating them. This was another reason the Israelis ignored common sense, and decided to give in to the Oslo illusion that Arafat could be trusted.

It is interesting that the person who finally defeats Richard III in Shakespeare's play, Richmond, is the one key character who never talks to Richard or gives him a hearing, and thus never comes under his spell. To talk to Arafat, which is what all pundits say must be done to bring peace to the Middle East, is precisely the wrong move, for there is no dialogue with a man without a conscience. Another wrong move is the game of decriminalizing Arafat. By refusing to punish him for horrendous crimes, as a serious nation would, Israel leaves the world, the Arabs, and itself with the sense that maybe his crimes can be justified, and its own attempts to restrain him from further criminal acts are criminal excesses in themselves. Israel would do better to relentlessly show the world pictures of Arafat's victims, including the American ambassador he assassinated.

Not all criminals are equally brazen. Arafat seems to have the power to neutralize the very foes who see him as most evil, perhaps because they, by virtue of seeing him as virtually the devil incarnate, attribute to him a kind supernatural indestructibility. Such superstition has made many who are far more powerful than Arafat hesitate to end his career. He has effectively used his own brazenness to convince the world that bringing him to justice would be a catastrophe, creating more Arafats by making him a martyr (as though the Middle East lacked for martyrs now).

Spooked, America is unwilling to allow Israel to end Arafat's reign of terror. Washington has retreated into approaching him with a kind of primitive behavior-therapy that says, "If he renounces terror" or "If he controls terror," then we will talk to him. It is as though all that matters is to get him to say the right words, never mind his intentions; as if no distinction need be drawn between his strategic goal – the destruction of Israel – and a tactical willingness to say he opposes terror.

Arafat has discovered, as Shakespeare understood, that the more brazen and relentless one's acts of brutality, the more likely it is that one will be allowed a second chance, and find even powerful men of conscience coming to one's door offering to forget, to forgive, and to give forgiveness a bad name.

9 Israeli Anti-Semitism

ARIEH STAV

"If for 2,000 years they keep telling you that you have a long and crooked nose, then you have a long and a crooked nose . . . "   *Jean Amery*

"Black ants . . . dogs tied up in the yard . . . dogs barking Psalms all night long . . . a humming collection of locust . . . .a death causing plague . . . rude baboons . . . bloodsuckers . . . a terrible evil . . . a black genie . . . armed groups of gangsters, criminals against humanity, sadists, pogromists and murderers." These are all quotations from the Israeli press or from comments made in the Knesset, written or spoken by Israeli journalists, professors, members of Knesset, well-know novelists, and former diplomats. The people being referred to are, of course, the *Haredim* (in Hebrew) or ultra-Orthodox Jews, as they are known in English.

The authors of these statements would recoil from publishing them about some other group of people anywhere in the world. But this loathsome abuse is reserved for members of their own people. Even the most vicious anti-Semites in a democratic nation anywhere would not have the unmitigated audacity to utter in public any expression equaling the hatred for Jews as regularly expressed by certain Israelis in their own country. In the United States, Louis Farrakhan of the black Nation of Islam, called Judaism "a gutter religion." After being bombarded by an outcry of revulsion at his comments he felt obligated to stammer out an apology of sorts. Patrick Buchanan says that he opposes the "destructive influence of the Jews in the media" but his rejection of any charge of anti-Semitism has not convinced anyone.

The Jewish Parasite

One of the most vicious of Israeli anti-Semitic expressions that replicates Nazi propaganda is the comparison of *Haredim* to blood-suckers of the secular population. When Uri Avnery wrote that "tens of thousands of Yeshiva students are parasites, sucking the blood of the country,"[1] or the writer Haim Be'er stated that "they [the *Haredim*] grew up as do-nothing parasites"[2] one could conceivably consider the phrase as allegorical. But when Shulamit Aloni, former Minister of Education, member of the Knesset and former head of the Meretz political party, says that "the *Haredim* are leeches . . . sitting on us like parasites, drinking our blood literally . . . actually shedding our blood . . . ,"[3] her statement is plainly a blood-libel even in her own perception, which is why she feels compelled to add "literally" and "actually" to her statement. Perhaps Aloni really doesn't believe what she is saying, but she nevertheless employs language reminiscent of the "Black Hundreds" and Julius Streicher.

Professor Yitzhak Ginzburg is a "researcher...of the inter-related links existing between parasites and their carriers insofar as diseases are concerned." He found an "amazing similarity" between the behavior of parasites and "what occurs in the Knesset's hallways and its committees."[4]

> The parasite . . . is a living organism that has lost its ability to produce... its food and therefore it makes efforts to obtain (it) ...from the carrier. The parasite, which makes no contribution to the well-being, benefit or defense of the carrier, is not interested in destroying its carrier. At times, though... it may go beyond its normal patterns and will deplete its carrier of resources and even destroy it.
>
> The course of parasitism . . . depends on the complacency of the carrier which does not adequately respond to the parasite at the first stages of the connection. The carrier, finally recognizing the parasite's existence, attempts to apply its defense mechanism but in many instances, it is already too late.

In order to strangle the "development of the infectious disease" in its infancy, Ginzburg suggests that "every caring person in our state, that is, the carriers, should oppose . . . the parasites . . . who suck the bone-marrow of our country and push it to the edge of the precipice."

Ze'ev Fabian wrote in *Ha'aretz* newspaper how his eyes were opened: "to understand that the Israeli Jews are in the midst . . . of a war for existence . . . the take-over of the country by religion . . . is becoming an ugly wave threatening to sink all of us in a new catastrophe...They [the *Haredim*] do not need a country but a carrier that will feed their parasitism, and when the carrier is enfeebled, or ceases to exist, they will transfer to a new carrier [and this is the essence of] the unholy covenant between extreme nationalism and fanatic orthodoxy."[5]

Fabian's article appeared on the day following the mass terrorist attack in Jerusalem's Ben-Yehuda Mall and a month after the slaughter in the city's Mahaneh Yehuda market where twenty people were killed and hundreds injured. One might have expected him, or the editors of the newspaper, to relate to this act of Arab barbarism that is part of the campaign to annihilate the Jewish state. *Ha'aretz* did not. At the very moment that volunteers belonging to the *Haredi* organization, *Hesed shel Emet* [Grace of Truth], were carrying the shattered bodies of the "victims of peace" to burial, this Israeli anti-Semite quoted *Mein Kampf*. The editor of *Ha'aretz* newspaper decided that the most appropriate time to publish an anti-Semitic onslaught was when Jews were burying the dead killed by Arab terrorists.

The comparison of any group to parasites accused of causing infectious diseases, *à la* Ginzburg, is brutish racism and a caricature of science.[6] In a normal democracy, Ginzburg (assuming that is his true name) would be dismissed for expressing such ideas, the academic institution where he teaches/does research would repudiate him and his academic degree would have been invalidated. Most likely, he would have been put on trial. It is improbable that any self-respecting newspaper in a democracy would publish such a grotesque piece of racism, and had it done so, the editors would have been charged with libel, the executive editor would have been fired and penalized with a substantial fine. In Israel, however, racist remarks by Ginzburg and his ilk are a daily phenomenon, and anti-Semitic expressions are standard features of the media. All this takes place without protest from any source.

The Nazis conducted a campaign to compare Jews to parasites. "The Jew leech sucking the country's blood" was a party slogan that was as widespread as "the Jews are our misfortune." But even the Germans treated the slogan of Jewish parasitism as a metaphor. Among the Nazi elite, only Hitler explicitly spoke of the Jews in the terms used by Ginzburg.[7] When the Hungarian Regent Admiral Horthy visited Berlin in August 1943, Hitler insisted to him that Jews were like germs that cause infectious diseases and damage the immunization system of the body. One must, therefore, strike before danger takes effect and destroys them.

> The Jews . . . were always parasites in the body of other nations . . . their Diaspora is a typical phenomenon of all parasites; they always seek out new sources of nutrition for the race . . . Wherever it appears, the carrier-nation dies sooner or later.[8]

"A Light Unto the Nations," Shlomo Cohen, *Al HaPanim*, Keter, 1988 (first appeared in the newspaper *Hadashot*)

Judaism, according to Cohen, in his sarcastic use of the Biblical phrase "Light Unto the Nations," is the absolute and ultimate evil. Judaism is the devil attired in *tallit* casting a dark shadow of dread over Israel, and with a little graphic imagination, over all the Middle East and from there – over the whole world.

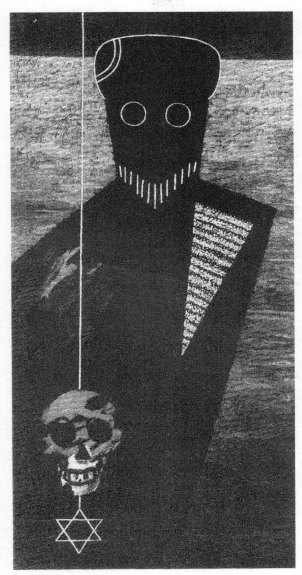

"Bandalolo," Dan Kedar, Association of Israeli Painters and Sculptors, 1997

Bandalolo, explains Kedar, is the bad man children are warned of if they do not eat their cereal ("Bandalolo will come and get you"). The devil, dressed in the style of Rabbi Ovadia Yosef, former Sefardi Chief Rabbi, with a turban and robe, also possesses a beard in the shape of shark's teeth. He holds a human skull, reminiscent of the S.S. Totenkopf symbol. The Magen David, attached to the skull, completes the equation between Nazism and Judaism.

Rahel Shavit, the Tel Aviv branch chairperson of the Artists' Association, in the notes for the exhibition, describes Kedar's work as "a personal reaction to the gloomy darkness of the black Middle Ages in which we are living."

A Haredi teaches his son to steal. From the (now defunct) *Monitin* magazine, Winter 1994

This is a recurrent motif in Nazi children's literature which showed Jewish schools as places to learn crime. Hitler, in his Mein Kampf, termed them colleges for the learning of crime. Professor Michael Har-Segor, a historian at Tel Aviv University called Yeshivot "schools of darkness." In such institutions, it would appear, "Hitler Youth" are being educated, according to Professor Moshe Zimmerman who referred to the Jewish youth of Hebron by that term.

Who is A Jew?, Danny Kerman and Aharon Shemi, Kivunim, 1989

This booklet displays 32 caricatures of the traits of the religious community. The booklet contains replicas of classic anti-Semitic portrayals, mostly Nazi-inspired. In a broadstroked fashion, these characteristics include: pornography, violence, avarice, fanaticism, shrewd behavior, racism, crime, exploitation and xenophobia. One main difference from other anti-Semitic literature, aside from the contents of the pictures, is the fact that the "Jew" is awarded a normal nose, unlike the usual crooked beak.

"Help!" *Yediot Ahronot*, March 9, 1987

Yeshiva students and settlers, sitting upon a pile of money at the expense of a (war) invalid in a wheelchair. This is a fixed topic of anti-Semitic cartoons, developed especially in *Der Sturmer* in the aftermath of the First World War.

Now, as then, anti-Semitism feeds off the Big Lie. The Haredi section of the population is amongst the poorest in the country. The settlement in Judea and Samaria is the cheapest in the history of Zionism, not costing the public a sheqel more than infrastructure development in any settlement on the "correct" side of the Green Line.

"The Settler", *Ha'Ir*, September 10, 1993

This drawing appeared on the frontispiece of a Tel Aviv weekly published by the prestigious Schocken chain. The demonization of the Jew was intended to cast him out of human society. The demonization of the settler (as Dan Tadmor wrote: "a loudmouth, stammering idiot . . . portions of spit and food leftovers caught up in his unkempt beard . . . a fool, simpleton, hotheaded, ignorant and cruel," *Iton Yerushalayim*, May 28, 1993) works in the same vein, presumably towards the day when, "There will be a bloodbath and civil war here in order, once and for all, to really fight the just war", *HaKibbutz*, August 17, 1995.

The Jewish Parasite: The Marxist View

The Socialist–Zionist ethos propogated the "vision" of the "new Jew" through the notion of "the Religion of Labor." This concept soon metamorphosed from the Tolstoyan naïvéte of A. D. Gordon, grandfather of the Jewish pioneers, to the doctrinaire harshness of Marxian historical materialism and the class struggle ideology. The basic claim was that anti-Semitism arose from the skewed social structure of *Galut* Jewry. This was the "inverted pyramid" concept preached by Ber Borokhov, one of the founding fathers of Socialist Zionism. He asserted that in a normal society, the productive section of the population made up the wide base of the pyramid whereas at the top were found the "parasitical elements." Among the Jews, he claimed, the top was wider than the base. The curse of the Jewish inverted pyramid was, therefore, the cause of anti-Semitism. Socialist Zionism sought to turn the pyramid over, to set it on its base. By changing the Jews' occupational structure, Zionist socialism expected to terminate Western anti-Semitism. Of course, viewing Jews as "non-productive" parasites, as did Zionist-Socialism, was an anti-Semitic notion entirely adopted from Karl Marx. In his own words Marx asserted:

> The chimerical nationality of the Jew is the nationality of the merchant, of the moneyed man generally . . . What is the secular base of Judaism? Practical need, self-interest. What is the worldly cult of the Jew? Huckstering. What is his worldly god? Money . . . Out of its entrails bourgeois society continually creates Jews…Emancipation from huckstering and from money, and consequently from practical, real Judaism, would be the self-emancipation of our era.[9]

This definition was given a broad interpretation by Hitler in his *Mein Kampf,* even if the author understandably did not choose to identify his source.[10] Indeed, Hitler dealt with Marx and his theory at length, treating Marx as the linchpin of Jewish evil. Hitler simply copied Marx's own anti-Semitism. Hitler's basic position, that "the Jew never produces but always appears as the go-between"[11] and that Jewish greed was the basis for the hatred of Jews by the masses, was part of the socialist tradition that preceded Hitler. Ironically, the Socialist Zionists adopted the ideas of the greatest anti-Semites of modern times as part of their "Zionist" theory.

This notion shaped the image of the "New Jew" who lived from the work of his own hands, who had to build and fight simultaneously, with spade in one hand and a gun in the other, to paraphrase the book of Nehemiah. This figure was held up by Labor Zionists as the antithesis to the middleman of the Exile, to the *luftmensch* who made a living out of nothing, as told by Sholom Aleikhem in Yiddish, or to the "filthy

Yiddelakh" written about by the Hebrew author, Yosef Haim Brenner. Even if some justification could be found for the use that Socialist Zionism made of this anti-Semitic element in its bitter struggle with the effects of the Exile on the Jew, it had little or nothing to do with historical reality. The great twentieth-century scholar and thinker of Judaism and Zionism, Yehezkel Kaufmann, repeatedly demonstrated[12] that the socioeconomic stratification of Diaspora Jewry in Europe in the early twentieth century was no different from that of the non-Jewish society of their environment. If the percentage of Jews in commercial enterprises and finance was greater than their numerical representation in the general society, it stemmed from objective reasons. In any case Jews made a major contribution to the economies of the countries they lived in, and their economic history bears no relation whatsoever to the Marxian notion of parasites.

The Marxian variety of anti-Semitic propaganda took root among socialist Jews in Palestine. Eventually, hatred for the "filthy Jew" of East European anti-Semitism, for Brenner's "dirty Jews," was revived amongst Israel's Leftists of the "Peace Now" era.

The Zionist Failure

"Israel is a ghetto, albeit better armed than the Warsaw ghetto and in a better economic condition than the Lodz ghetto, but there ends the difference." This remark is attributed to the late General (Res.) Benny Peled, former commander of Israel's Air Force. Israel is compared to an East European *shtetl* (Jewish town) and its leaders to members of the community synagogue board. Peled unwittingly revealed still another, more serious truth to the effect that Zionism failed to bring about the end of anti-Semitism. Theodore Herzl asserted in *The Jewish State* (1896) that "immediately upon the preparations for the establishment of the Jewish state . . . anti-Semitism will cease at once, everywhere." Also, Herzl devoted only two lines to the matter of a Jewish army: "the Jewish state is intended to be neutral. It needs but a standing professional army . . . to keep public order both externally and internally." Herzl perceived Jewry's miserable condition in the world as the tragic consequences of Exile. He and the other founding fathers of Zionism perceived political sovereignty as the solution to the problem of anti-Semitism. This faith became a categorical principle of Zionism and the credo of the pre-state Jewish community in Palestine, and after the Holocaust, of the State of Israel. From Ze'ev Jabotinsky to Ber Borokhov, from David Ben-Gurion to Menahem Begin, Zionist leaders and visionaries took pains to highlight the axiom that "the entrance of the Jewish people into history" would rid the Jews of the curse of anti-Semitism.

Regrettably, not only did anti-Semitism not "disappear immediately" but the State of Israel became the focus for Jew-hatred. During Israel's short history, it has fought five major wars and has had to maintain the largest army in the world relative to the size of its population. Israel has referred to the intervals between these conflagrations, marked by vicious Arab terrorist attacks from within and wars of attrition from without, as "peacetime."

The Arab nations' acquisition of weapons of mass destruction evokes nightmares of gas chambers. This factor, combined with the Nazi character of Arab Islam that parades its preparations for Israel's annihilation, turns the basic principles of Zionism on their head, and adds to them a macabre dimension. Abba Eban, certainly not a hawk, more than adequately defined this dimension when he referred to Israel's 1967 frontiers as resembling "Auschwitz borders."[13]

After 54 years of independence, Israel remains the most dangerous place in the world for Jews, and the difficult choice she faces is to live by the sword or not live at all. This cruel alternative demands powers from the depths of one's being, a demand the Israeli Left cannot meet. With the double collapse of socialism and its Zionism, the Left must face the collapse of its ideology and *raison d'être*. It desperately needs a new messianic challenge or it will soon find itself on the trash heap of history, a process that began several years ago.

The comprehensive de-Zionization that started among Israel's elites was enhanced by the 1975 UN resolution equating Zionism with racism. That pronouncement granted legitimacy to the radical and "Zionist Left," for identifying with that accusation. Israeli historical revisionism as published in the writings of the "new historians," such as Benny Morris, Avi Shlaim, and particularly Ilan Pappe, presents Zionism in the spirit of that UN resolution.

One ought to bear in mind that Zionism is Jewish nationalism whose essential features are known throughout the world. To deride Zionism is equivalent to negating Jewish nationalism and tantamount to committing national suicide. The lethal mockery called the "peace process," whereby Zionism is programmed to relinquish its physical and spiritual existence, is the default option of Jewish radicalism that seeks a way to resuscitate itself.

Israel's Left maintains intellectual hegemony over the elites that shape the mental world of the secular population. The public is bombarded incessantly by the slogans of peace. They nurture Jewry's ability for pathological self-deception after centuries of being in the role of victim. The term "peace process" is a euphemism for the destruction of the Jewish nation, but the Left clings to it because it has not found any ideological substitute. No wonder the Left perceives the Arab enemy as its ally, and Jews who "obstruct" this so-called "peace process" as threatening the Left's existence. First and foremost is the threat from the Jewish religious community in Israel of all gradations (i.e. knitted skullcaps and black ones).

The Knitted Skullcap

The Gush Emunim movement is identified by the Israeli public with the settlement of Judea and Samaria. Along with Jerusalem, Judea and Samaria are the cradle of the Hebrew nation, part of the historical foundation of Zionism. Any link to this territory represents a threat to the trend of alienation of the Left from both Zionism and Judaism. A thriving Jewish presence in Judea and Samaria casts doubt on the establishment of a Palestinian Arab state, which is the core belief of the Israeli allies of Yassir Arafat (witness Shulamit Aloni's –among others- demonstratively cordial visit with Arafat during the recent Arab uprising). The combination of these factors is called by the Left an "obstacle to peace." This phrase is now an anti-Semitic epithet employed primarily (though not exclusively) in the European Union and adopted by Israel's Left as a fundamental political principle.

Jews who wear knitted skullcaps have been substituted for the Nazis in the fantasy world of the radical Left. The journalist Amnon Abramovitz called them "*Einsatzgruppen*" (in his column in the *Ma'ariv* newspaper*)*. A professor of German Studies at the Hebrew University, Moshe Zimmerman, called the Jewish children of Hebron "*Hitlerjugend*" (in an interview with the Jerusalem weekly *Kol Ha'Ir*). General (res.) Shlomo Gazit, former head of military intelligence who is certainly not identified with the radical Left, compared the soldiers serving in the Israeli army who wear knitted skullcaps to "those who wore the swastika in the Wehrmacht" (Gazit, a senior researcher at the Jaffee Center for Strategic Studies, Tel Aviv University, wrote a position paper published by the Center in which he suggested that Israel compensate the Palestinian Arab refugees with $10 billion dollars, the sum that Israel was supposed to receive but has not yet, received from unified Germany after 1989 as East Germany's share in German reparations to Israel). According to the original agreement, that sum was to be paid after German reunification, since Communist East Germany refused to recognize a debt to the Jews. In Gazit's opinion, this would be a fitting token of Israeli recognition of the suffering of another people. Gratitude on the part of the Palestinian Arabs for this noble gesture by Israel would pave the way to true peace, in Gazit's view.

The anti-Semitic statements emanating from such journalists as Orit Shohat and Haim Hefer, Philosophy Professor Asa Kasher, (former) MK Dedi Zucker and others against Gush Emunim,[14] could fill a large volume. But it was the writer Amos Oz who more than anyone else gave vent to the Left's venomous hatred for Gush Emunim. In an article published on June 8, 1989 in the *Yediot Aharonot* daily titled "In the Name of Life and Peace," Oz wrote:

> [Gush Emunim is] a messianic junta, insular and cruel, a bunch of armed gangsters, criminals against humanity, sadists, pogromists and murderers, that burst forth from some dark corner of Judaism . . . from out of the cellars of bestiality and defilement . . . in order to bring about the rule of a thirsty, mad worship of blood.[15]

Oz's words are probably the worst example of Jewish anti-Semitism to be found in print They surpass those of Yigal Tumarkin, an Israeli sculptor, who frequently makes provocative headlines to assure his position as the *enfant terrible* of Israeli art. Tumarkin and his pronouncements can be disregarded, but Amos Oz is a different matter altogether. He is a novelist with an international reputation whose career does not depend on diatribes in a Tel Aviv local weekly.

His comments contain the two classic elements of pathological anti-Semitism typical of *Der Sturmer*, namely, hate and fear. Everything is here: gangsters, criminals against humanity, sadists, pogromists and murderers. The long list of synonyms is intended to stamp the mark of structural wickedness upon their foreheads so that they lose their humanity. Oz (Klausner) after all, was born in Israel, the grand-nephew of the famous Zionist, historian and scholar Yosef Klausner, and he knows well that there is no connection between such poppycock and the truth. His statements about Gush Emunim are an unequivocal falsehood intended to create the Big Lie (a term shrewdly used by Goebbels who knew that the more a big lie is repeated the more people will believe it). Moreover, he knows full well that he will not have to stand trial for his libel.[16]

Nevertheless, public expressions of hatred towards Gush Emunim have been limited to the political echelons. Gush Emunim is the offspring of the National Religious Party, once an ally of the Labor Party. The Gush has benefited from remnants of the Zionist ethos still found in broad circles of the public, where settlement and military service in elite units remain respectable. Removal of Jewish communities from Judea and Samaria, or their abandonment, are still acts opposed to the national consensus (even if this attitude is rapidly dwindling).

The Black Skullcap

The remnants of the Left's self-restraint regarding Gush Emunim does not apply when the issue is *Haredi* Judaism.[17] The hatred displayed toward them receives general acclamation, for the secularist community contains a latent anti-Semitic element, something the Left skillfully plays upon. In addition, vicious statements like those quoted at the beginning of this chapter avoid punishment, since the *Haredi* community is incapable of fighting back. The mass media are closed to them. And even if the media were opened to them, they prefer not to involve themselves. The *Haredi* press, such as *Yated Neeman* and *Yoman HaShavua*, is completely foreign to the secularist community, who are generally unaware of its existence.

The traditionally insular nature of the *Haredi* neighborhoods of Bnei Braq and Meah Shearim in Jerusalem, has elicited for some time the atavistic feelings of hatred for the stranger and fear of the unknown within the secularist camp, essentially no different from expressions of classic xenophobia. However, despite the first steps of relative openness taken by the *Haredi* community toward becoming part of the political system of the "Zionist state," no parallel change has taken place among the secular public. Indeed, the very opposite has occurred. Hatred of the *Haredim* has increased and has assumed an anti-Semitic character.

The explanation for increased animosity toward the *Haredim* is directly linked, paradoxically, with the budding openness of the *Haredi* community. This openness has taken the form of a sharp increase in the power of the *Haredi* political parties and their representation in the Knesset and, consequently, their growing participation in government coalitions. That means involvement in fateful national decisions. But this transition has been sensed as a threat to the secularist community on the everyday level. The *Haredi* Jew, thus far segregated within the walls of his ghetto, has suddenly become a flesh and blood person, no longer a derided, despised, yet innocuous, curiosity. And this is what released the slumbering anti-Semitic genie from the bottle.[18]

Israel's Left-wing racism has achieved legitimacy even among many of those who do not accept Leftist ideology or its political manifestations. An example of this is the center-right Tzomet Party. It echoes Meretz in besmirching the *Haredim* even though there is a major ideological/political cleavage between these two parties.

Tumarkin's Tragic Error

"When I see the *Haredim*, I understand the Nazis."[19] The core of the Nazi racism that Tumarkin "understands," and thereby "accepts" (and later on suggests ways to apply), seemed to him to derive from the hatred aroused in the Nazis by the attributes and clothing of the *Haredi* Jew.[20] "When you look at them, you understand why there was a Holocaust . . . ."[21] A recurring motif in the sculptor's remarks was his disgust with the external appearance of the *Haredi* Jew, and the connection between that appearance and the built-in wickedness within the person. This motif is central to Israeli anti-Semites. It also recalls the classic anti-Semitic loathing that Hitler repeated so many times in describing his horror when observing Jews in Vienna: "at times, I felt a deep feeling of revulsion at the smell emanating from these caftan-wearing Jews."[22]

The repugnance over the *Haredi* mode of dress crosses political camps. Yael Lotan, a radical left-winger, wrote in the Marxist daily *Al HaMishmar*, "we are disgusted by their black garb, the alien wigs on the heads of the women, the mikvehs [ritual baths], the necrophilia, the obsessive interest in people's bowels."[23] Ora Shem-Or, identified with what is called the Right, wrote: "It is disgusting to see the shiny, oily years-old caftans, the fur hats, walking through the city streets . . ."[24]

The physical appearance of the *Haredim* does not conform to the accepted aesthetic code and hence partakes of moral baseness. "The black clothes represent a black flag over elementary morality and our very existence . . . pardon me but visual art is my specialty."[25] Tumarkin says that, as an artist, he is more conscious of external appearances than the average Israeli anti-Semite.

In the view of the Peace Camp, the war against the *Haredim* is a condition that determines the existence, welfare and prosperity of the entire State of Israel, because "the *Haredim* are undermining our existence and are ruining our future."[26] Furthermore, "in Israel, the secularists do not jump into the abyss; they are thrown in by the religious."[27]

Naomi Hazan articulated this line of hatred for *Haredim* as a condition for Israel's existence. As a member of the Knesset for the Meretz party, she spoke at the convention of the Federation for Humanistic Judaism, saying: "Only if we succeed in getting rid of this terrible evil, of the taking over of our lives by the black demon, can we nurture all that is good in the state."[28] The demonization and moral negation of Orthodox Judaism in Hazan's statement was appropriate for her audience who call themselves "humanists." Her term "black," the semantic opposite of humanism, depicts Orthodox Judaism as inhuman and criminal.

Tommy Lapid, ironically identified with the Right, is another MK who claims to understand the anti-Semites: "We shouldn't complain about the *Haredim*. They are, after all, simply faithfully acting out the role assigned to them by anti-Semitic literature. They exploit the non-Jew, trade in his blood, and laugh at him behind his back. Only this time, the '*Goy*' is us."[29] Lapid reiterates the fact that he is a Holocaust survivor, but he does not perceive the anti-Semitic paradox in his own words. Yigal Elam, a historian, also echoes the secularist Jews' empathic understanding of the anti-Semites: "The suspicion was aroused long ago that historical Judaism has been the greatest collaborator with historical anti-Semitism. I have no qualms anymore about openly stating my well-founded suspicion."[30] Needless to say, "historical Judaism" is, according to Elam, the hated *Haredi* public. Yigal Tumarkin adds: "Traditional Judaism fashioned wondrous techniques of parasitism . . . the fanatic self-enclosure of the Jews [who] laid a solid layer of bricks for anti-Semitism."[31] In Naomi Hazan's words, the "black demon" that takes over our lives, "imbibes its mendacity from the poison of the Jewish religion which poisons people,"[32] and from "the *Haredi* beard that now threatens to cover the earth."[33]

The Phase of Application

The parasitic demon must be dealt with to prevent the "development of the infectious disease" while in its incipient stage, as Ginzburg phrased it (quoted above). Another professor at the Hebrew university suggested that "the *Haredim* should be hanged from the lamp-posts,[34] . . because they are religiously observant, (and) they should receive the death penalty," he wrote in *Yediot Aharonot*.[35] "The time has come to bury them," advises Uri Avnery,[36] "Meah Shearim should be entered with half-tracks and 50-caliber machine-guns, and they should be crushed," a listener remarked in a radio debate.[37] Tumarkin followed in the footsteps of Professor Ze'ev Sternhell and called for a civil war.[38] "My true contribution would be if I grabbed a sub-machine-gun, instead of a pen and pencil, and killed them."[39] This is Tumarkin's variation on the opening lines of the *Horst Wessel Lied*:

> "*Und wenn das Judenblut von dem Messer sprizt, dan geht noch mal so gut*" ("and when the Jewish blood spurts from the knife, then it would be even better").

At the root of Israeli anti-Semitism lies the claim that the *Haredim* are the source for all the calamities that have fallen upon Jewry throughout history and they are the basis for all that is wrong in Israel. These notions express Jewish assimilationists' auto-anti-Semitism, especially in Germany, as repeated incessantly over the past two centuries or more. They are as dangerous and disastrous now as they always have been. Today as in the past they are an outlet for the anxiety the Jewish radical feels as he faces the wall of Arab hatred and the anti-Semitism of the Christian West. Jewry's historic role of "a nation that dwells alone" (Numbers 22:9) is clearly damaging to secularist messianism and a shattering of the cosmopolitan self image of the radical Jew. Channeling one's frustration and hatred towards the *Haredi* community is a convenient way to rationalize one's condition.

The assumption of Tumarkin, Sternhell, Shem-Or, Lotan, Ginzburg and others, that the source of anti-Semitism lies in the *caftan*, the *shtreimel*, the *sidelocks* and the beard of the *Haredi*. This view emphasizes the short or selective historical memory of the Left, as well as an astounding and misleading superficiality. Of course the Nazis ridiculed *Haredi* Jews for their strange attire, but the source of German hatred of Jews was elsewhere. In addition, the aesthetic features of *Haredi* attire had a positive folkloristic attraction at the end of the nineteenth century and the beginning of the twentieth. Ironically, the target of Nazi anti-Semitism was not the *Haredi* Jew but the Jewish assimilationists. The assimilationist Jew at that time deflected (in his own mind) Nazi hatred onto the *Ost Juden*. In this sense, Tumarkin is a direct descendant of the German Jewish heritage.[40] The Nazis adopted the slogan coined by Heinrich Von Treitschke's: "The Jews are our misfortune" ("*Die Juden sind unser Ungluck*"). German Jewish assimilationists latched on to this phrase with one small change: "*Die (Ost) Juden sind unser Ungluck.*"

How terrible must have been the Jewish assimilationist's awakening in Germany when he was dragged at dawn to the collection point and sent east to a concentration camp. His identity card was imprinted with the despised letter J with his new name alongside. No longer Max, Franz or Hans but *Israel*. No more Greta, Lenni or Hilda but *Sarah*. With historical irony, so typical of Goebbels' macabre sense of humor, the Nazis "restored" Jewish identiry to assimilated Jews. They were murdered in concentration camps as Jews, not as partial apostates.

The Nazis understood assimilation as a mask that hid the Jewish devil in his authentic garb: "The appearance and style of the liberal European Jews are but a thin external veneer," Eichmann wrote in a set of SS orders. The Nazis warned their countrymen of this deception. The threat to the Nazis and Germans was not the *Haredi* Jew who kept to his own circumscribed world. Hitler could tolerate them. He could put them in cages as a folklore show when necessary.[41]

The mask had to be ripped off the Jew's face so as to remove the almost human visage from this devil. The main theme of two famous films from the Nazi period called *The Eternal Jew* (Der Ewige Jude) and *The Jew Suss* (Jud Suss) was the need to reveal the muderous enemy of the Reich beneath the Jew's mask. The *Eternal Jew* was filmed in Polish ghettos immediately after the Nazi conquest in 1939 and displayed the "authentic Jew in his native habitat." The filth, ugliness, miserable living conditions, of the Jews described as bloodsucking leeches, cunning, greedy, lazy and xenophobic, were presented to the viewer in the guise of a "documentary film" which drew its force from the purported objectivity of the camera which records the "truth." The motif repeated often in these films was the total identification of the subhuman Jew from the Polish ghetto with the Jew from Germany who was known to the viewer in the guise of "the cultured German."

The announcer read the following text at the beginning of the film:

> The cultured Jew whom we know in Germany, knows well how to cunningly disguise his race. This film presents actual photos from the Polish ghettos. It shows the Jews as they truly are prior to their success in hiding behind the mask of the cultured European.

To prove the point, a group of Jews was filmed "before" and "after." A young man, cleanly shaven, smiling, head uncovered, in a tie and suit, could be an innocent and pleasant neighbor. But this is a veil for the truth revealed in his authentic image and clothing when he is seen with a bearded face, wearing a hat and caftan. The main character in *The Jew Suss* is an eighteenth-century Jewish moneychanger from Frankfurt, dressed in a large skullcap, with sidelocks, who speaks in an unpleasant accent, waves his hands about, and who assumes the character of the perfect courtier in the best rococo style. In this latter guise the Jewish devil in him is discovered.[42]

In sum, Tumarkin, Hazzan, Avnery, Lapid and company would be surprised to learn that most of the caricatures published in *Der Sturmer* did not portray the *Haredi* Jew but Jews similar to themselves, that is, the assimilationist attempting to flee his identity and pretending to be a cultured European. Clearly, groveling before criminals, anti-Semites and Jew-haters of the ilk of Arafat, Assad, Chomsky or even Nobel prize-winning Portuguese writers will not help Israel's *Haredi*-hating Leftists in the least. The same was true for Germany's Jews at that time when they uttered sycophantic praise of "our Chancellor."[43] Israeli assimilationists do not comprehend Nazism, even if they would have us think that they want to.

The Aesthetic Aspect

The black caftan and shtreimel that stand out as elements of male *Haredi* apparel derive from the fashion of the late Middle Ages in Eastern Europe.

They recall the long coat and fur hat that were worn in a broad geographic region stretching from the Carpathian Mountains in the south to Lithuania in the north; from Poland's Vistula River in the west to the banks of the Volga River in the east. The *Haredi* has clung to this attire for two hundred years or more. That costume became the symbol of Jews in anti-Semitic caricatures since the nineteenth century.

This conservative, frozen-in-time wardrobe has appeared in the climate and landscape of Israel vastly different from its place of origin. The long coat and the fur hat contrast far more blatantly with the Mediterranean environment than in Europe. One should not dismiss the antagonism that may be aroused in us when we see a yeshiva student in Israel's summer heat wrapped from head to toe in black garments while we peal off from our bodies every unnecessary article of clothing. It's as if he were still walking in the autumn along the banks of the Dnieper at the end of the Middle Ages.

The *Haredi* garb is an authentic, if stubborn, conservatism, which challenges the world. In defiance of the sweltering sun, of the widespread western ritual of bodily exposure and exhibitionism, of the worship of youth and of the commercially dictated rapid changes in fashion, the *Haredi* remains clothed in his caftan, indifferent to change, sure of himself and at peace with his Maker.

This phenomenon bespeaks a certain integrity that flies in the face of our local Leftist who is searching for his own identity but finds little more than a caricature of an American sub-culture. The "religious Jew," and the *Haredi* even more so, becomes a cruel mirror, which reflects the Israeli secularist's failure to escape his Jewish heritage that weighs heavily upon him. The collapse of kibbutz utopianism, the cultural and political brainwashing practiced by "the media" and the recent bitter and tragic joke called the "peace process" strewn with Jewish bodies - these and more contrast with the image of the *Galut* Jew dressed in caftan, black hat or shtreimel. To hate the *Haredim* appears to be an "existential imperative," in Sartre's term, for the Israeli Leftist who is propelled by a demoniac compulsion to fight against the *Haredim* in a lamentable struggle for his own identity. Its own Jewish roots are so shrivelled that it can think of no alternatives available in 3,000 years of Judaic culture to nourish its soul.

Evading Military Service

The average Israeli male spends between five to six years in uniform during his adulthood. He has gone through three or four wars, and if he was lucky, he emerged from this experience live and whole. The release of Yeshiva students from military service is an offense to the principle of the existence of the Jewish state, forced to live by the sword. The yeshiva student who studies Talmud for many years has become the object of enormous animosity on the part of the secular Israeli, as could be at least partially expected. The explanation that the study of Torah contributes to the preservation of the Jewish people is seen as a despicable attempt to exploit religion for expedient self-interest.

In recent years, nihilistic trends among Israeli youth have long ceased to be problematic for the extreme Left. Over the years, fringe groups have organized and published pamphlets that sought legitimacy for radical nihilism, hatred and frustration. On occasion these youngsters direct their hatred towards the IDF that they view as the backbone of the national consensus they oppose and wish to destroy.

For example, *Milhemet HaMilim* (The War of Words) is the publication of a group calling itself "Isra-Hell Collective"[44]. An entire issue of that periodical was devoted to a discussion of methods to avoid military service. One article is called "21 Tips to Get Out of the Army through the Psychologist."[45] The issue, which consists of 27 pages crammed with articles and cartoons (including one anti-Semitic caricature reproduced from an Egyptian magazine, which the group claims as its own), relentlessly defames the army and the nation of Israel.

A youngster who soldiers by-passed when standing in line at a hitch-hiking station at the side of a road wrote as follows:

> 'Only for soldiers'. Screw 'em. How many times have I heard these words 'only for soldiers'. Only death for soldiers. You son of a bitch! You and your car should overturn and you and all the f*cking soldiers in this stinking f*cking country should die with you! I would like to see your picture in the paper under the headline: "Terrible Accident," with your children crying, you jerk, and your smashed body and those of the Judeo-Nazi soldiers squashed next to Neot Mordekhai, you stinking dog, and your reading glasses and your ugly tie soaked in dark red blood, thick and dried . . . (p. 7)

On page 9 of the same issue, a kibbutznik from the northern part of the country describes his feelings when observing a group of soldiers:

> They have come from Lebanon to eat lunch in the dining hall of my kibbutz where I work, in my kibbutz . . . I want to reiterate again that I hate the IDF, yes, hate. I am not 'critical' nor am I 'ambivalent' nor do 'I reserve my opinion' but I hate it. (emphasis in original)

The aim of this trash is to provide "ideological" support for their hatred. Important here is to note the seething, spontaneous hatred that easily can be diagnosed by professionals as rooted in self-hatred.

These excerpts are culled from the bulletin of a fringe group. However, the weekly *Ma'ariv LaNoar* is the most widely circulated youth periodical in Israel; it represents the broad consensus of the 14 to 18 year-old age group. Aviv Gefen, an Israeli pop protest singer who exploited his refusal to serve in the army to his own advantage, was selected by the paper as one of three young men designated as "Man of the Year" in 1996. The second was Shimon Peres, who also never served in uniform, and the third was a male model and actor in an Israeli soap opera. In an interview, Gefen preached emigration from Israel. What we see, then, in Gefen, is the crisis in Zionism, the flight from the battle. He is held up as a model to be imitated by Israeli youngster who voted for him because of what he is.

The youth who avoid military service by not returning to Israel from trips abroad number approximately 13,200[46] per annum and they are all from the secularist public. That number equals the manpower needed to staff an armored division and is approximately the same as the figure for Yeshiva students who are excused from enlistment during a given year. To these 13,200 draft dodgers we must add an equal number who are excused because of mental/emotional problems. The total number of secular evaders/rejects is therefore more than twice that of Yeshiva students who are excused from military service.

Yet, it is true that in proportion to their numbers in the general population, the percentage of draft dodgers among the *Haredim* is greater than among the secular population. Nevertheless, the fuss made over the issue is out of proportion to reality. Much worse is the phenomenon of draft evasion and demoralization within the IDF, which is a dangerous trend that has emerged over the past decade. Public attitudes toward these trends are silence and coming to terms with them after the fact.

Towards a Definition of Self-Hatred

Sandor Gilman asserts that self-hatred is a product of the frustration experienced by a minority group (such as Jews, Blacks, homosexuals) in its attempt to assimilate and blend into the predominant social group.[47] This "melting" process is definitely not possible for a person with a different skin color than the majority group. Except for rare circumstances, a Jew cannot stop being a Jew. Consequently, to vent his frustration the assimilationist must direct his anger toward his own group, toward persons of his own kind because they are the people who are responsible for his inability to assimilate.

In our view, Gilman's thesis is marred by two major errors:

There is a basic difference between Jews and other minority groups.

Blacks and homosexuals have already achieved social legitimacy. Jews, though, and especially the Jews of Israel, remain as they have been throughout the centuries, a pariah nation.

The vote in the United Nations General Assembly on July 1997 is typical. One hundred and thirty-one states, representing the majority of mankind (95 percent to be exact), denounced the Jewish state for daring to prepare land for housing construction within the municipal boundaries of its capital. For the sake of comparison, consider the Arab-Islamic regime in Sudan that has been engaged in genocide for four decades. According to recent conservative estimates, more than two million Southern Sudanese Blacks, both Christians and animists, were killed during 17 years of war and slaughter. The General Assembly does not castigate Sudan.[48]

Gilman's second mistake is more serious in that it touches the very root of the uniqueness of Jewish self-hatred. The beliefs and symbols of the *Haredi* community represent, in the eyes of the secular Jews, an expression of traditional Judaism: hatred for this community derives from its very authenticity. It reflects the failure of the secularist to shrug off his Jewishness. This is not the case with homosexuals and blacks whose defining characteristics – in the case of both groups – have been largely accepted and they are regarded as equals to the majority population. Moreover, these two minorities aspire to remain a part of their reference group as a moral and aesthetic priority, whereas the Jewish Left seeks to turn its back on their Jewish roots and identity, and cultivate a racist anti-Semitism. The fact that the Israeli racist simultaneously prides himself on his social liberalism and his campaign for the rights of Arabs, blacks and homosexuals, is one of the paradoxes that characterize the pathology of Jewish radicalism. In this sense as well, Gilman has erred.

Jewish anti-Semitism possesses traits of Catholic anti-Semitism, also a form of self-hatred with the common object of hate being Judaism. What distinguishes the two, though, exceeds what they share. The heart of Christian anti-Semitism was expressed in the Eucharist Sacrament, whereby the Church breaks off from Judaism, i.e. from the Old Testament. The Eucharist is the most sacred of Christian ceremonies shared by all denominations. Without it, Christianity is not Christianity. In the course of the ceremony called, without a trace of macabre irony, the Lord's Feast (namely, a meal in which the main course is Jesus' body and blood), the Christian eats the flesh of the Jewish God/Messiah and drinks his blood. Christian doctrine asserts that this is not just a symbol but literally true. It is a miracle known as transubstantiation which is a process of physical conversion that takes place where union, or Holy Communion, occurs between the participant in the ceremony and God.[49]

The psychological price of this mystical ceremony was paid by the Jewish scapegoat in the form of the notorious blood libel. The deep link between the Eucharist and the blood libel against the Jews is painful and glaring, accurately expressed in Freud's concept of projection.[50] Unlike the Church, the radical Jew in his Israeli guise has no lethal ceremony of expiation such as the Eucharist Sacrament. But in the blood libel he spreads about his own people, he parallels his mentors in the New Testament.

Thus far we mentioned the similarity between Christian anti-Semitism and that of Israel's radical Left. However, as previously noted, what is shared is much less than what divides them. Christian anti-Semitism, in general and the Catholic version in particular, does not suffer any of the Jewish pathological consequences of anti-Semitism due to the comprehensive spiritual power of Western culture that affords the average European anti-Semite a firm national and cultural identity. By contrast, our own Jewish anti-Semite lacks identity, and is a cast off of Western civilization. He finds consolation for himself, at best, in American subculture on the one hand, and in anti-Semitic activity on the other.

It is widely acknowledged that a people's denial of its national heritage leads to spiritual decay and cultural prostitution. Thus, for example, what there is of "Israeli cinema," that film critic Aharon Dolev calls, "corrupt celluloid," is a pale imitation of the fringes of European radicalism. The primary purpose of this cinema is to raise the savage but noble Palestinian to the level of the divine versus the Judeo-Nazi storm trooper. The theater in Israel that was once a celebration of the Hebrew language and a cultural shrine for the Hebrew-speaking public, is dominated by a revolting wave of anti-Semitism, pornography and coarse jabber.

Jewish self-hatred is a singular phenomenon with no counterpart. The Jewish anti-Semite will not rest until he tears the "parasites sucking our blood" off of his body and soul. But what our radical does not, has not and probably never will understand is that he cannot cut the "parasites" out of his heart without removing the heart as well.

Notes

1. *HaOlam HaZeh*, November 10, 1988.
2. *Ha'aretz* Weekend Magazine, March 2, 1984.
3. *Proceedings of the Knesset*, July 3, 1991.
4. "Isn't It Enough For Us?," *Kol Ha'Ir*, January 3, 1992.
5. *Ha'aretz*, September 7, 1997.
6. The life sciences in universities would not ordinarily spew forth such pseudo-scientific claptrap. Hence, I surmise that one of the reporters assumed the false identity of an imagined "Ginzburg" to lend his article authenticity.

7   And, of course, *Der Sturmer*. The Nazi higher echelon despised Julius Streicher and his paper. Streicher was kept on only because of his, however problematic, friendship with Hitler, a comrade-in-arms from the early days.

8   Adolf Hitler, *Mein Kampf*. Translated from the German by Ralph Manheim. Boston 1943, p. 150 and pp. 304–5.

9   Karl Marx in his article "On the Jewish Question," and in *Capital*.

10 Hitler, *Mein Kampf*, pp. 308–24.

11 Ibid., p. 309.

12 Y. Kaufman, "Umma uMa'amad." In *B'hevlei HaZman*. Dvir: 1936.

13 Lately, Eban has sought to escape this comparison by claiming that his words were taken out of context and that he never uttered them. Nevertheless, those are his exact words in an interview granted to the German weekly, *Der Spiegel*, June 13, 1968.

14 The term "Gush Emunim" has become an empty label to a great extent. The movement that began in the wake of the Yom Kippur War no longer exists as such, although several of its leaders are still active, such as Rabbi Moshe Levinger, Benny Katzover and others. Gush Emunim is a symbol for the Jewish settlement presence across the Green Line.

15 Remarks that he had delivered the previous night before a large crowd of Peace Now demonstrators in Kings of Israel Square, now called Yitzhak Rabin Square.

16 Oz was awarded the Israel Prize for Literature for 1998. The Israel Prize is the most prestigious of all prizes awarded in Israel. The award was made by by Minister of Education Yitzhak Levy, a leader of the National Religious Party.

17 The sweeping generalization contained in the term *Haredi* is problematic. The term covers a wide range of observant Jews, from anti-Zionists to Habad. Many who earlier negated the Jewish state, now share in governmental power and should be considered no less Zionist than the Meretz party, for example.

18 A similar process has taken place in the wake of the "peace process" with the Arabs. When the Israeli became a real flesh-and-blood person rather than some abstract threat, Arab anti-Semitism took a quantum leap.

19 Y. Tumarkin, "The Soweto of the Religious," *Tel Aviv* (local newspaper), April 1986. In a conversation with the author, Tumarkin claimed his words had been taken out of context.

20 Said during a conversation with the author.

21 Y. Tumarkin, *Tel Aviv* (newspaper), April 1988.

22 Hitler, *Mein Kampf*, p. 57. Hitler's adoption of the Medieval claim of a *Foetor Iudaicus*, a Jewish stench, was repeated by the Israeli anti-Semite Tumarkin according to whom "The *Haredim* spread a stench," see *Yediot Aharonot*, December 20, 1992.

23 Words Can Murder (1996). *Manof*. Jerusalem: Center for Jewish Information, p. 46

24 *Yediot Aharonot*, Seven Days Magazine, September 26, 1984.

25 *Yediot Aharonot*, October 21, 1992.

26 Motke Yehezkeli, *Davar*, July 4, 1987.

27 Amos Kenan, *Yediot Aharonot*, December 20, 1985.
28 *Hadashot*, October 30, 1992.
29 Words Can Murder (1996). *Manof*. Jerusalem: Center for Jewish Information, p. 29
30 *Hetz, Journal for Thought and Education*, Issue 1, p. 9.
31 *Politika*, September 1985.
32 Uzi Ornan, *Kol Ha'Ir*, December 30, 1983.
33 *Ma'ariv*, November 9, 1988.
34 *Kol Ha'Ir*, December 30, 1983. See also *Hadashot*, October 30, 1992.
35 Words Can Murder (1996). *Manof*. Jerusalem: Center for Jewish Information, p. 49
36 *HaOlam HaZeh*, November 10, 1988.
37 In a televised interview on the *Erev Hadash* program on December 22, 1985.
38 When he called for tanks to overrun the community of Ofra in Samaria, *Ma'ariv*, 1988.
39 *Hadashot*, September 28, 1988.
40 He is part of this heritage together with other *landschaftmen* such as Moshe Zimmerman, Yeshayahu Leibovitz, Ilana Hammerman, Yitz'hak Laor, Natan Zakh, Uri Avnery, Tom Segev, Ilan Pappe and others.
41 This idea, which the Nazis toyed with (as with the Lublin reservation), found favor with Israeli anti-Semites: "If we had locked them up in reservations, and had tourists view them for pay." See Motke Yehezkeli, *Davar*, July 4, 1987.
42 See Arieh Stav,"Ripping the Human Mask Off the Jewish Devil." In *Peace: The Arabian caricature: A study of anti-Semitic imagery*. Jeruslaem and New York: Gefen Publishing, 1999.
43 For further references to the flattery German Jews applied to Hitler, see J. Trachtenberg (ed.), *Greuelpropaganda*: Berlin, 1934, with a preface by Hermann Goering. For a concise excerpt, see *Nativ* 5, 95, p. 67.
44 P.O. Box 6579, Tel Aviv. Other journals include *Necrophilia for Youth* and *They're All Lies*.
45 Number 21 is the category for mental health problems in the pre-induction army medical profile.
46 *Ma'ariv*, September 18, 1997.
47 Sander Gilman, *Jewish Self-Hatred*, Baltimore: Johns Hopkins, 1986.
48 See the article by Eliyahu Green, "Four Decades of Forgotten Genocide in the Sudan," *Nativ* 4, 97, p. 37. The estimate of those killed is from the respected reference work, *New Columbia Encyclopedia* (New York, 1975).
49 For additional treatment, see Robert Wolf's article, "'The Lord's Feast' – Sources of Jew Hatred in the Christian Ceremony of Cannibalism," *Nativ* 4, 91, p. 44.
50 See Arieh Stav,"The Blood Libel and the Sacrament of the Eucharist." In *Peace: The Arabian caricature: A study of anti-Semitic imagery*. Jerusalem and New York: Gefen Publishing, 1999.

Post-Zionism and Anti-Zionism in Israeli Literature

10

YOSEF OREN

In a speech to the 25th Zionist Congress held in Jerusalem in 1961, Haim Hazaz, among the great Hebrew writers of the twentiethth century, commented on the unique features of Hebrew literature.

> Literature in general deals with the person, the individual and everything that is within him and stems from him – Love, desire, secrets of the heart, joy, sorrow, regret, lust, heroism, weaknesses, failures and the like . . . Hebrew literature is distinct from all or most of the literary attributes listed here, in that . . . its only hero is the Jewish people, the Jewish collective. The pathos found in Modern Hebrew literature and the allegories that burst forth and emerge from it stems from this. It goes without saying that it never amused itself with literary schools and trends, it didn't take pleasure in didactic, sterile and narrow Jewish intellectualism, nor with the illusions of mysticism and the other condiments of art and refinement . . . Hebrew literature was completely constructive and purposeful, totally directed inward, completely suffused with a sense of responsibility, concern and anxiety regarding the fate and future of the nation and was full of introspection and gravity – especially gravity. (Hazaz, 1977, pp. 113–14)

Hazaz was not trying to present a new perspective on Hebrew literature because throughout Jewish history writers always expressed "concern and anxiety regarding the fate and future of the nation." He wished to call attention to the transformation that already had begun to overtake Israeli literature. By the time of his premature death in March 1973, he witnessed what he had feared, the visionary impoverishment of the literature produced by writers living in the relatively young nation of

Israel and their alienation from Zionism or from "the redemption" as he referred to it in his works.

Over the first 50 years of Israeli's existence, Hebrew literature expressed a bitter and unyielding attitude toward Zionism. At first, the approach was critical. Later it turned genuinely hostile. This "dialogue" can be characterized as consisting of two main themes. The first theme focused on the *content* of the claims which various writers raised against Zionism both as an ideology and as a movement directed at implementing in the real world the Biblical prophets' vision of Jewry's redemption from Exile and its restoration to the Land of Israel. The claims made by some authors emphasized four failures for which Zionism was allegedly responsible.

1 **The Failure in Vision** – To correctly predict the manner in which renewed Jewish sovereignty would be established.
2 **The Moral Failure** – Zionism played a role in defiling its own vision due to moral injustices committed during the process of establishing the Jewish state. These injustices referred primarily to the dispossession of Arabs and to acts of violence against them.
3 **The Genetic Failure** – Zionism is responsible for the progressive deterioration in the behavior of the founders' descendants and in their ability to adhere to the vision.
4 **The Failure of Continuity** – Zionism failed to maintain Jewry's motivation to sustain the implementation of the Zionist vision by future generations.

The second theme traces the historical events that exerted major influence on Hebrew literature's attitude towards Zionism. This approach underscores the decisive influence of the recurrent wars fought between Israel and its Arab neighbors since its inception (Oren, 1998, pp. 123–8).

The first 50 years of Israel's statehood has witnessed a distinct deterioration of many, but not all, Hebrew writers' attitudes toward toward Zionism. We shall examine here works of three authors, members of three of the four literary cohorts active at present in Israeli prose. Zionism plays a central role in their works and constitutes a theme that appears with considerable frequency. In the scheme employed here, the three generations or cohorts are represented by the following writers:

• S. Yizhar: one of the more outstanding members of the first literary cohort of Israeli-born writers ("The Generation in the Land"),
• A. B. Yehoshua, among the central figures in the second generation ("The New Wave"),

- Meir Shalev, one of the more well-known figures of the third generation ("The Disillusioned Wave").

The Stage of Disappointment: *S. Yizhar*

In reaction to the War of Independence in 1948, Yizhar's early work portrayed Zionism as the cause of the Arabs' dispossession and misery. In his story "Hirbat Hiz'a", for example, Yizhar bases his indictment of Zionism on an analogy between the injustice done to the Jews throughout their long history and in the Holocaust and the fate of the Arabs in Israel.

> Exile. It played on all of my heartstrings. Our people's complaint against the world: *Exile!* And that apparently became part of me, with my mother's milk. What essentially have we done here today?

Yizhar also refers obliquely to the Bible that expresses the eternal moral doctrine of the Jewish people. If you take your neighbor's garment as a pledge, you must return it to him before the sun sets; it is his only clothing, the sole covering for his skin. In what else shall he sleep? (Exodus 22: 25–26)

In his story "The Captive", written less than a year before "Hirbat Hiz'a", Israeli soldiers are portrayed as a violent gang of aggressors who invade an idyllic scene and violate its natural harmony and tranquility. Yizhar's stories about the War of Independence represent the first stage in the dialogue of the nascent Israeli literature with Zionism – the stage of disappointment. His works paved the way for later expressions in Israeli prose of disappointment with Zionism by emphasizing the first two of the four failures listed above: The visionary failure and the moral failure. Literary critics soon revealed the expressions of disappointment in Yizhar's texts and those written by others who followed in his path.

To date no satisfactory explanation has been offered about the enigmatic connection in Israeli literature between the War of Independence and the authors' disappointment with Zionism. In our view, Hebrew literature in Israel ignored the 1948 war's political and military reality. Instead of depicting the magnitude of the victory and the historical significance of what it accomplished in terms of Zionism's efforts to establish an independent nation for the Jewish people in Zion, the authors preferred to offer a searing critique of Zionism that did not reflect the historical substance of the 1948 war but concentrated instead on the spiritual anguish which affected the soldiers in that war. One must remember that the Jewish population of Israel in 1948 was very small and the soldiers constituted a fairly large sector of the population compared to almost every other country in the world. Writers active during and after the War of Independence, absorbed Zionism's innocent and naïve assumption that the Jewish state would be achieved in a peaceful and conciliatory fashion, at home, in school, in youth groups and in the community. Even though different Zionist ideologies disagreed as to which road such conciliation and peaceful transition would take, they shared the common assumption that Zionism would not require military conflict in order to establish an independent Jewish nation. Disappointment developed among the soldiers when it became clear that Zionism had not prepared them for their generation's central challenge: the experience of war. It is possible that had the Jewish people possessed practical political experience and a military tradition, people of the 1948 generation in Israel would not have been so easily surprised by what the establishment of Israel would demand of them and, they in turn, would not have subjected Zionism to such scathing criticism.

Disappointment with Zionism and even the desire for revenge was expressed by the authors of the 1948 generation in a number of ways. First, they shifted the focus from the concrete events of the war to its moral implications. However, since they recounted the story of the War of Independence in a realistic style, later readers who were unfamiliar with the events could get the impression that they were reading an accurate description of the 1948 war, which is patently not the case. Second, they enclosed the word Zionism with quotation marks in order to mock it. No sooner had Zionism achieved its greatest accomplishment when the literature of "The 1948 Cohort" already employed the word Zionism as a synonym for prattle, for a pompous speech composed of words that have no real substance. S. Yizhar's heroes *Days of Ziklag* (1958) speak of Zionism like a "speech". In an earlier novel, the heroine, Erella, of Yehudit Hendel's book *Street of Steps* (1955) thinks in similar terms about her grandfather, Yeshayahu Dagan. "He has a great love for fancy words and enthusiastic speeches . . . and what are those phrases or speeches? They call it Zionism" (p. 144, 1998 edition). A mere ten years after Israel was established, Israeli literature completely abandoned the theme of the War of Independence, another expression of its discontent with Zionism. The appearance of Yizhar's huge novel *The Days of Ziklag*, for all intents and purposes, marked the end of the literary treatment of the most significant historical event in modern Jewish history.

Yizhar did not change his outlook on Zionism after he returned to writing almost 30 years later. In the five books that he published during the course of the 1990s, he continued to attack its nationalist aspirations. In each of them, Yizhar identifies "The Land of Israel" in ironic terms such as "Square," "Field," and "Land" to express the view presented

most explicitly in *Lovely Malcomia* (1998): "There was never any homeland here for any one nation . . . and it always was a *land* and there were
always nations living here. Each nation had its turn" (p. 105). In *Zalhavim*
(1993), Yizhar mentioned all of the rulers of the country throughout
history in one breath, without ascribing an advantage to any of them:
"Our ancestors and the Philistines, the Byzantines, the Arabs and
everyone". However, our "ancestors'" invasion in this generation was the
most destructive of all because they came to "develop the backward deso-
lation with sophisticated Zionist blossoming". Yizhar concealed his
resolute conclusion regarding the renewed presence of the Jewish people
in the Land of Israel behind ironic phrasing. In *Lovely Malcomia*, Yizhar
puts it this way:

> We are really strangers here. Look how they don't want us in this land. The
> land itself doesn't want us. We are nothing more than another group of
> invaders who recently insinuated themselves here, after the interminable
> series of invaders, sons of invaders, throughout the generations who
> constantly came and went in turn, wave after wave, to inherit a land not
> theirs. (p. 177)

Of course the Jews can wait in vain for the first Palestinian author who
will negate in this way, directly or through some polished irony, past or
present Arab "rights" to Palestine.

The Rejection Stage: *A. B. Yehoshua*

Writers of "The New Wave" follow the period of Yizhar Smilansky and
his contemporaries. Initially they did not challenge the position appearing
in the works of authors of the earlier "Generation in the Land" who
expressed "disappointment with Zionism". The New-Wave writers
sought to make their imprint on the Hebrew literature of the time by
choosing existential topics and by composing prose in less realistic forms,
such as symbolism, allegory, absurdity and irony. The Six Day War forced
the authors of that group to relate intensively to Zionism. The leading
authors did not wait for signs of decline in the public's pride over the
restoration to Israel sovereignty of large parts of its historical national soil
in Judea and Samaria. They quickly accused Israeli society of primitive
bestiality and of additional dispossession of Arabs from the "occupied
territories".

Some well-known authors of the 1948 cohort took a position against
the critical stance of the "New Wave" writers. The former expressed their

belief in "The Entire Land of Israel" in the pages of the paper called *This is the Land*. The debate over the future of the territory to the east of the ceasefire line ("the Green line") between Israel and the Jordan River (the so-called "West Bank") began in the period between the Six Day War and the Yom Kippur War. However, in those days it still did not assail the role of Zionism in the national culture of Israel. The claim that Zionism failed and had therefore forfeited its right to influence Israel's national policy and was proffered only in the wake of the Yom Kippur War. This conceptual position was advocated in the 1970s and 1980s by Yehoshua who at that point abandoned a symbolic, absurd and ironic style of writing in short stories, and adopted an allegorical–conceptual–political approach in the form of the novel.

After the Yom Kippur War, literature in Israel undertook to react to current events. Most prominent in this posture were authors from the two younger literary cohorts known as "The New Wave" (Yoram Kaniuk, Amos Oz, and Yehoshua) and "The Disillusioned Wave" (Yitzhak ben-Ner, David Grossman, and Meir Shalev). Since then, the political novel has thrived in Israeli prose. The main message in most political novels written during the past two decades is transmitted by means of a multi-generational story line involving three generations in the life of a family. This mechanism is the primary tactic employed to describe the ultimate failure of the Zionist vision to which the founding father had dedicated his life. Novella-length stories like *Requiem to Na'aman* (1978) and *Minotaur* (1980), both written by Binyamin Tammuz, sufficed to achieve the conceptual purpose for which they were intended. The first political novels of Amos Oz, *A Perfect Peace* (1982) and *Black Box* (1987), emphasized Zionism's responsibility for the genetic failure. These stories, also of novella dimensions, employ the very same model.

A. B. Yehoshua emphasized the failure of historical continuity of the generations. He departed from the multi-generational novel, and preferred to adopt the more limited family saga model. His stories portray couples whose married life ran into trouble because of the disparities between them. The disparity that Yehoshua stressed time and again in the couples' lives, was between one member of the couple who entertained some spiritual vision and the other earthy figure who had a more concrete and practical orientation toward life. The plots of the four novels he wrote during the past two decades describe attempts to dissolve the marriage and separate the two people who are incapable of peaceful coexistence. In *The Lover* (1977), Adam (the couple's realistic member) attempts to separate from Assia (the more visionary of the two) by searching for a lover who would accept her and thereby free himself from the torments of his conscience. His pangs of conscience derived from a distressing incident that occurred during the War of Independence. Adam was able to consummate his love for Assia because her lover was killed in the war. Another man's death was the source of his erotic fulfillment. The rather shallow symbolism conveys the obvious message that the Jews acquired the Land of Israel at the expense of the Arabs who fell in the war. Adam abandons his plan when he is surprised to discover that someone is prepared to enter a love relationship with her. That person is none other than the Arab boy, Na'im, who became the lover of Dafi, Adam's daughter who closely resembles his wife, Assia. The story ends with the hurried return of Na'im to his village in order to escape the anticipated danger. This entire incident takes place at the periphery of the dramatic story-line. As expected, Zionism is depicted in this allegory as an elderly woman named Veduca who was born the same year that Zionism was founded.

In *Late Divorce* (1982), the separation between the mates is more successful than in *The Lover*. Kaminka (the couple's visionary member who henceforth will be represented in the series by a hero of Ashkenazi–European origin) brings a group of rabbis to the hospital in which Naomi (the earthly character who will be portrayed in later stories as being of Sephardic background) is hospitalized. The rabbis' presence is required by Jewish law in order to divorce a wife who is mentally ill. Naomi's dementia is manifest in an intense desire to horde food as a result of the upheaval in Israeli society that resulted from the economic boom that swept the country after the Six Day War and the significant extension of the territory under Israel's control.

Yehoshua's novel ends strangely. After Kaminka finalizes the divorce he does not leave the gates of the hospital to fly into the arms of his new lover waiting for him in America. Instead, he attempts to leave the hospital grounds through a gap in the fence and gets stuck there. The strange end to the novel seems to express a state of partial limbo: To refrain from a complete rupture between the Zionist vision and its earth-bound expression in the national entity of Israel. By contrast with the author's treatment of Adam in the earlier novel discussed above, in the novel *Late Divorce*, Yehoshua has his main character Kaminka complete the legal separation from his first wife, but he does not implement his divorce from Naomi. Instead, he remains caught with her in the mental hospital which, of course, is Israel itself.

Only in the third in the series of allegoric, ideational, and political novels called *Molcho* has a fatal illness that represents the terminal condition of Zionism. The novel's story begins with the death of Molcho's wife (the couple's visionary member). Molcho (the realistic member of the couple) finds it difficult to part from his deceased wife and she continues to influence his behavior even after her death. This novel presents a new phase in the severing of ties between Israeli literature and the Zionist vision of Israel. His wife's death completed Molcho's separation from her *de jure* and *de facto*. Nevertheless, he must still overcome the emotional ties that continue to bind him to her. Molcho has erotic relationships with three women during his first year as a widower. Each of the three bears some resemblance, in appearance or personality, to his dead wife, and each one assists Molcho to regain the ability to accept separation from his dead wife. The process of separation is completed only when Molcho falls in love with a girl who lives in the remote moshav called Zerua. She possesses the leadership qualities that fit in with Molcho's practical Sephardic mentality. Molcho knows that he must wait until she matures, but for the first time, thanks to her, he experiences the sense of freedom for which he longed. He feels that he finally succeeded in liberating himself from his dead wife and he prepares himself for his new love. However, he too, knows that the previous connection with the wife who died exacted a huge price from him. He lost valuable time by succumbing to the temptation of the ideology that enchanted him in his youth. It had squeezed his personality from him and almost destroyed his masculinity.

After writing about the separation between Zionism and the State of Israel in *Molcho*, Yehoshua proceeded to the fourth novel in the series. In this work, entitled *Mr. Mani*, Yehoshua suggests a different Zionism conceived by Sephardic Jews as an alternative to the Zionism developed by Ashkenazi (Western) Jews, which, in his estimation, prevented Israel from resolving the Arab–Israeli conflict. Through the Mani family lineage, the novel points to a Sephardic Jewish solution. It might be superfluous to add that a solution of that kind never existed. It is solely the product of the author's imagination, despite Yehoshua's efforts to ascribe to it a dynastic character. In contrast to Ashkenazi Zionism that ignored the national aspirations of the Arabs when conceiving the establishment of the Jewish state, each generation of the Mani family in Yehoshua's novel attempts to establish the Jewish hold in the Land of Israel by means of a compromise with the Arabs. In the three previous novels, Yehoshua first gradually severed the State's ties with classic Ashkenazi-Western Zionism, and thereby laid the groundwork in "Mr. Mani" for the solution he wanted to suggest for the Arab-Israel conflict, namely *that the ideology of compromise with the Arabs in the Land of Israel should be called Zionism*. In this way, Yehoshua moved Israeli literature from the disappointment stage led by S. Yizhar, to the stage of rejecting Herzl's political Zionism, which he portrayed as unfit to direct the country's policy. His demand to separate the Zionist vision from the State was raised in the four novels so that, at long last, Israel could be led in accordance with the realistic possibilities that prevailed in the Middle East in the late twentieth century.

The Abandonment Stage: *Meir Shalev*

A. B. Yehoshua's solution of separation between Zionism and the nation of Israel apparently was not sufficiently radical for some writers after the Lebanon War and the *Intifada*. A decree of "Post-Zionism" as the next stage in Zionism's development was announced by Meir Shalev. In his four novels, Shalev tells of the deterioration of the Zionist village from a period of brief success to that of continuous failure, thus preparing the way for the conclusion that it is necessary to abandon Zionism immediately and be liberated from the death rites which developed to preserve its memory. One must begin Meir Shalev's fictional story about the Zionist village with the novel, *Esau* (1991) that opens with "the family" departure from Jerusalem. There it is told that the great-grandmother, Sarah, the convert, despised Jerusalem. She stole the Patriarch's carriage, and loaded on it the twins and her spineless husband. He is an exemplary descendant of the parasitical life led in the city that trained its children to passively await messianic salvation. The carriage brought the family to the village.

The entire Zionist story is encapsulated in the move from Jerusalem to the village that symbolizes taking fate into one's own hands and bringing about salvation by means of auto-emancipation. Sarah hopes to initiate the new Jewish dynasty supported by manual labor or the "inverted pyramid" of the socialists, by settling in the village and baking bread in the bakery. The significance of the departure from "Jerusalem" to the village is illuminated by Pines, the teacher in *A Russian Novel* (1988), the first novel in the series. He explained to generations of students that at the village settlement, Zionism is changing the history of our people. In this revolution, Zionism is annulling the Land of Israel's traditional role over the past 2000 years as a place where Jews come from the *Galut* to die and be buried. Thanks to Zionism, Israel was to become a national homeland where Jewry would renew its temporal-national lives. The failure of Zionism is illustrated in the request one of the village's founders, Mirkin, makes to his grandson, Baruch Shinhar, to uproot the orchard and turn the land into a "pioneers' cemetery".

In the novel, *Esau*, the reason for the failure of the family's settlement in the village is articulated. The temporal-Zionist salvation initiated by the great-grandmother by taking the "family" out of "Jerusalem", led to a dispute between her two twins over the inheritance. At the conclusion of the first round of their struggle, which takes place around the year 1948, Ya'akov gets the woman and the bakery and the ability to produce children and bake bread, while his brother, who adopts the nickname "Esau", is forced into exile.

Ya'akov's acquisition of the inheritance transferred his fate to his competitor. The novel, *As a Few Days* (1994) also tells about how an attempt to settle in the village failed. The struggle for a woman's heart appears in this novel as in others, but this time there are three competitors for her: Globerman, Rabinowitz and Sheinfeld. In this novel, the failure of the Zionist village is manifest in the group of eccentrics who find refuge there. They encounter the confusion of Zeide (the mythical Grandfather Israel), who is the grandson of the village founders. Who of the three men who courted his mother, Yehudit, should he emulate? The dilemma Zeide confronts is whether to pursue the destiny of Sheinfeld who is the "tent-dweller" *à la* Jacob, or to follow the path of Rabinowitz, the "man of the furrows". Like all of the grandchildren telling the story of Zionism in Shalev's novel, Zeide, too, will not produce a new generation for his nation's dynasty and will wait for the end of his life watching the crows and reconstructing his enigmatic past and undetermined future.

The village was not identified in his first three novels. In the novel, *In His House in the Wilderness* (1998), the village is identified as Kinneret, a historically significant site in Zionist history located on the shores of the Sea of Galilee. Pioneers of the "second aliyah" founded Kinneret in 1909.

The story begins with the "family's" abandonment of the settlement, when their expectations to support themselves through agriculture proved futile. The survivors of the ill-fated Zionist adventure in Kinneret took refuge in Jerusalem described as a city with three institutions for refugees from Zionism: a house for the blind, an orphanage and an insane asylum. In this way, Jerusalem, too, assumes its symbolic significance in the story as a city representing the stage before the secular-Zionist redemption, the stage of passive waiting for the religious-messianic redemption. The retreat from the "village" to "Jerusalem" commemorates Zionism's failure. The grandson, Raphael, who narrates the story of "the family" in this novel, describes the death rites customary in the house whose widows raised him as well as the rites he acquired from their neighbor Avraham, the stonemason. They were the women who survived the premature deaths of their men in various catastrophes.

Raphael's education is completed when he realizes that his destiny is to end the failed Zionist adventure with a post-Zionist solution: to perform for Zionism the ultimate act of kindness and bury it in the most appropriate place, the desert, a cemetery for visions of that sort, which were corrupted during their realization. After claiming the lives of those who implemented them, the departed visions continue to depress the survivors due to the rituals they must perform in memory of the deceased. This last novel is the most decisive of all. In it, the suggestion is not only to bury Zionism in the desert, but also to bear the consequences of having been enticed by its vision. Raphael accepts the edict and awaits his death in the desert. He does not want to father any children to perpetuate the existence of the dynasty, even though the continuity of "the family" is totally contingent on his offspring since all the men died and their widows refused to marry. And indeed, Raphael relocates to the desert, but also to bear the consequences of having been enticed by its vision. Raphael accepts the edict and awaits his death in the desert as the last descendant of a dynasty, a descendant who bears the responsibility to bury Zionism in the primeval desert so that ultimately it may be engulfed by the Dead Sea.

The Buds of Return

Thus far we have related to the deepening rejection of Zionism displayed by three influential Israeli writers whose works represent the conceptual position of most of their literary contemporaries. The few who strayed from the majority position in their literary generation paid, and continue to pay, a heavy price. Their different assessment of Zionism and its appropriate role in Hebrew literature and in Israel remains largely unknown because the printed or electronic media systematically squash presentation of their views and works. Only a handful of writers in the halls of Hebrew literature remain faithful to the redemptive message and goal of Zionism. These numbered few stood up to the perverse post-Zionist philosophy and to their demoralized and demoralizing proponents. The pro-Zionist authors alerted readers to the danger of abandoning Zionism. That act threatens the very existence of Israel as the sovereign nation of the Jewish People. Their steadfast faith and devotion to Jewry's national rejuvenation has produced the beginning of an attitudinal change towards Zionism in the final decade of the twentieth century.

The renaissance of the Zionist novel displays four characteristics that took form in the Hebrew prose written in Palestine during the period of the *aliyot* to Israel during the first half of the twentieth century, up to the time Israel became an independent nation. These four characteristics are:

1 *An Expansive Story Line*: The plot extends over the entire length of Zionist history in the life of the Jewish people.
2 *The Re-emergence of the Hero*: The figure of the hero is the opposite of the image of the anti-hero so common in Israeli prose for years. The renewed hero of Israel Jewry provides an image of leadership who fights to realize the vision of national redemption of the Jewish people in their homeland.

3 **Ideology as Motivator:** The heroes' motives in the Zionist novel are grounded in Zionist ideology, in conjunction with the psychological, social and economic motives that generally propel literary characters.

4 **Allusions to pro-Zionist Literature:** References to phrases and images from literary sources on which Zionist philosophy is based.

The renaissance of the Zionist novel was led by Moshe Shamir in his trilogy, *Far Greater than Pearls*. Installments of these novels were published over the course of twenty years (1973, 1984, 1991). In this epic wide-ranging work, Shamir continued to develop the central idea, which he raised in *My Life with Ishmael* (1968), that the Six Day War prepared Zionism for its finest hour. Through the wondrous image of Leah Berman, Shamir tells of the history of the "mini-revolution" and its success in the shadow of the class-related and cosmopolitan "great revolution" that so many people believed would be victorious. They contemptuously rejected Zionism as hopeless. The crowning achievement of Moshe Shamir's Zionist literature is his extensive historical novel Yair (2002) about the unusual life and ideas of the heroic figure of Yair Stern, the leader of LECHI (Freedom Fighters of Israel) until his assassination by the British secret police in mandate Palestine. Natan Shaham also compared the two revolutions in his ironic novel, *Bone to Its Bone* (1981), but continued to describe people's blindness regarding Zionism in his *Rosendorf Quartet* (1987). In the novel called *The Heart of Tel Aviv* (1996), he chose to recount Zionism's success through the nondescript residents of one house in Palestine's first Hebrew city. Shaham sought to explain Zionism's success as a movement that encompassed all segments of the nation.

Aharon Megged chose the satirical path to battle post-Zionism in the novel, *Iniquity* (1996). He relates the tale of a poet named Levinstein who discovered after the Six Day War that a Zionist poem, similar to the one which he published after the War of Independence and for which he was widely acclaimed, was rejected by all editors because "love of the land, its expanses, its skies, its contiguity, is forbidden love! It is sinful! It is permissible to talk about such subjects only with cynicism and irony". In his next novel, *Love-Flowers from the Holy Land* (1998), Megged reacted to the blindness of the post-Zionists towards the success of Zionism with the image of an English pilgrim, Beatrice Campbell-Bennett, who arrived in Palestine for a visit at the turn of the century. Despite her difficult personal problems, she discerns that an unusually daring enterprise is developing in the Holy Land by Jews the likes of whom she never encountered in England and whom her anti-Semitic father never imagined existed anywhere. These were Jews whose life in the Diaspora did not cause them to forget their love of Zion. The influence of Zionism on a native-born Israeli manifested in his simple love for his homeland was told by Hanoch Bartov in the novel, *Halfway Out* (1994).

The renaissance of the Zionist novel in the writings of the authors who belong to the first cohort of literary figures is the most conspicuous phenomenon in the return to Zionism trend, though the phenomenon appears as well in the works of the second literary generation such as *A Thousand Hearts* by Dan Tzalka (1991), in two novels by Eli Amir, the more successful, *Farewell, Baghdad* (1992) and the less successful *Saul's Love* (1998).

The Moral Choice

In addition to their literary significance, these novels can be appreciated for their contribution to a reassessment of two accusations previously leveled against Zionism: The first is rethinking the assessment of Zionism's morality, thereby challenging the doubts raised by S. Yizhar. The second is the revaluation of Zionism's success as the movement for the redemption of the Jewish people, thereby challenging Yehoshua's resolute rejection of Israel's ability to derive any benefit from its continued affiliation with Zionism. It seems clear that the day is not far off when the egregious errors committed in Israeli prose about Zionism, some rashly and some intentionally, will be corrected by means of a third revision that will perpetuate the Zionist view of Jewry's national and cultural redemption. By so doing, Hebrew literature will completely reject Shalev's message that Zionism has completed its role in the life of the Jewish nation.

The attitude that Israeli literature has displayed toward Zionism can be summed up in a number of conclusions:

(1) This attitude demarcates the literature written since the establishment of Israel as a new literary period in the history of Hebrew literature, the *Israeli period*, as distinct from the three previous periods of "Modern Hebrew literature" (the Enlightenment period, the Renaissance period and the period of mass immigration). During those three periods, Hebrew literature related constantly to Judaism and Judaic historical-literary sources. Since the establishment of Israel, literature's relation to Judaism ended and the ever-growing attack on Zionism began. As we have seen, this attitude emerged in 1948 with the literature of disappointed though still legitimate criticism of Zionism, and by the time of Israel's 50th year, literature's attitude had deteriorated to an anti-Zionist, so-called post-Zionist position.

(2) The attitude toward Zionism in Israeli literature was not latent or

static. It developed gradually, as was depicted here by an examination of several central works of three authors from the first three literary generations of Israeli literature. Three stages were discerned: Disappointment, Negation and Abandonment.

(3) The deterioration in Israeli literature's attitude towards Zionism during the first 50 years of Jewish national sovereignty in Israel was influenced by fluctuations in the national mood. This latter factor replaced any consideration by writers of Zionism's objective accomplishments, either ideologically or as a social–political movement that strove to implement the transition in reality of a large part of Jewry from its state of exile to existence under conditions of national redemption and political independence.

(4) Fluctuations in Israel's national mood were influenced by events that were truly decisive in terms of its collective survival, namely the wars that Israel was forced to wage with its neighbors, from the 1948 war through the latest *Intifada*.

(5) Each war's influence on the national mood did not necessarily correspond with its military outcome. On the contrary, it almost always deviated from the military result due to the political influence possessed by those who dictated the national mood at the time. The deviation from the historical truth had serious ramifications for the power of the State of Israel, which continues its existential battle with its neighbors.

(6) The role of Hebrew literature in the State of Israel at this time is to rehabilitate Jewry's trust in Zionism which is not only the twentieth century's singularly most successful revolution, but it is also the only prospect capable of ensuring continued Jewish existence in the future. One cannot rule out the self-mobilization of Hebrew literature in Zionism's favor, any more than mobilization against it. As all great literature is mobilized for some purpose – artistic or principled – the choice to side with the Zionist vision is a moral choice, and in and of itself, it will not impede the literary career of authors who possesses proven literary talent despite current discrimination by the media, in and outside of Israel, against Zionism. It will only add depth and meaning and almost certainly longevity to the works of writers with that sort of talent. Estrangement from the Zionist vision and its ultimate abandonment provided a "bandwagon" on which less talented writers could attract attention with their provocative, cynical and banal pronouncements or stories. Those ideas cannot serve any nation and certainly not the Jewish nation in its long struggle for survival and cultural rejuvenation.

References

(All books were published in Tel Aviv by Am Oved publishers, unless indicated otherwise)

Amir, Eli (1992) *Farewell, Baghdad.*
—— (1998) *Saul's Love.*
Bartov, Chanoch (1994) *Halfway Out.*
Hazaz, Haim (1977) *The Right of Redemption.*
Hendel, Yehudit (1995) *Street of Steps.*
Meged, Aharon (1996) *Iniquity.*
Meged, Aharon (1998) *Love Flowers from the Holy Land.*
Oren, Yosef (1981) *Splinters.* Rishon L'Tsion: Yahad.
—— (1983) *Disillusionment in Israeli Fiction.*
—— (1987) *The Israeli Short Story.*
—— (1990) *Zionism and Sabraism in the Israeli Novel.*
—— (1991) *A Salute to Israeli Literature.*
—— (1992) *The Pen as a Political Trumpet.*
—— (1994) *Identities in Israeli Prose.*
—— (1995) *Trends in Israeli Prose.*
—— (1997) *New Voices in Israeli Prose.*
—— (1998) *Israeli Literature – Where To?*
—— (2000) *Best Sellers and Quality Books in Israeli Prose.*
—— (2001) *The Feminine Voice in Israeli Prose.*
—— (1974) The fear of impulsive Zionism. *Moznaiyim* (September).
—— (1988) Language in bad shape. *Ma'ariv Literary Supplement* (October 28).
Oz, Amos (1982) *A Perfect Peace.*
—— (1987) *Black Box.*
Shalev, Meir (1991) *Esau.*
—— (1994) *As a Few Days.*
—— (1998) *A Russian Novel.*
—— (1998) *In His House in the Wilderness.*
Shamir, Moshe (1973) *From a Different Yard.*
—— (1984) *The Bridal Veil.*
—— (1991) *To the End.*
—— (2001) *Ya'ir.* Tel Aviv: Zmora-Bitan.
Shapira, Anita (1992) *The Sword of the Dove.*
Shaham, Natan (1981) *Bone to its Bone.*
—— (1996) *The Heart of Tel Aviv.*
Tammuz, Binyamin (1978) *Requiem for Na'aman.* Tel Aviv: Zmora-Bitan.
—— (1980) *Minotaur.* Tel Aviv: Ha-kibbutz Hameuchad.
Tzalka, Dan (1991) *A Thousand Hearts.*
Yehoshua, A. B. (1977) *The Lover.* Tel Aviv: Schocken Publishing House.
—— *Late Divorce.* Tel Aviv: Hakibbutz Hameuchad.
—— (1987) *Molcho.* Tel Aviv: Hakibbutz Hameuchad.
—— (1990) *Mr. Mani.* Tel Aviv: Hakibbutz Hameuchad.
Yizhar, S. (1958) *The Days of Ziklag.*

—— (1962) *Four Stories*. Tel Aviv: Hakibbutz Hameuchad.
—— (1993) *Zalhavim*. Tel Aviv: Zmora-Bitan.
—— (1998) *Lovely Malcolmia*. Tel Aviv: Zmora-Bitan.

11

The Messianic Theme in the Works of A. B. Yehoshua and Amos Oz

HILLEL WEISS

Post-Zionism is a continuation of Jewish assimilation and renunciation of Judaism whose initial manifestations date back to the Enlightenment. Paradoxically, post-Zionism facilitated the birth of secular Zionism as the liberation from authentic Judaism. The notion of "be a person (i.e. a non-Jew) when you leave your house" transformed much of Zionism into a flight from the center of Judaism out into assimilation into the prevailing norms of Western societies, for good and bad. In part these norms prove the inhumanity of modern man and validate the fear of collective destruction in the future.

Some post-Zionists assert that only a Jew who eradicates the Covenant of Abraham and conceals his Judaism can gain respect in the universal academic community while the fundamental concepts of collective existence, such as land, language, religion and commitment, confirm the Jew's distinction as an arrogant racist – overt or covert. Commitment to the sovereign right of Jewry to self-determination in the Land of Israel is totally illegitimate. George Steiner (quoted by Sagiv, 2002) and others recommended that Jewry abandon the State of Israel and Judaism completely. Collective baptism was once considered by Theodore Herzl. The State of Israel, with the aid of the post-Zionists, can realize Herzl's initial position, which was the assimilation of Jewry's scattered remnants. Whether or not assimilation involves conversion to another religion, it reflects post-Zionist impulses. Perhaps this notion resulted from existential anxieties.

The postmodern branch of post-Zionism automatically grants legitimacy to the illegitimate. Once moral relativism gained sway, the enemy is recognized as having his own narrative that justifies behavior. In other words there are no righteous or wicked, no truth or falsehood.

Hebrew Literature is the outstanding conscious process that signifies liberation from the effects of the *Galut* (Exile) that were automatically identified with Jewishness. The process of liberation from the Exile reached its apex in the doctrines of the Young Hebrews (Canaanites) and was supposed to point to the fact that a secular Hebrew – Israeli – nationalism was feasible.

The critic of modern Hebrew literature, Baruch Kurzweil, showed that Hebrew Literature is essentially a revolutionary phenomenon. The revolution included some anti-Biblical effects, but, paradoxically, it also preserved linguistic and conceptual traditions and the potential for consciousness that could bring the Jew back from the road of total escape.

Were it not for its latent existential danger to Jewish life, post-Zionism could be justifiably ignored. The danger is that death at the hands of our enemies has already begun to bore the Jews due to its daily appearance in our streets and homes. A sense of despair has penetrated the country. Therefore, morally, it is important once again to examine the post-Zionist story. Perhaps we can make another crack in the wall of public submission to the creeping despair that undermines our power to resist. The pathology of post-Zionism has implanted itself as an institution in Jewish Israel in a multitude of dimensions – historical, political, cultural, anthropological and existential – and has decisively influenced the Jewish–Zionist ethical perception. Treatment of the topic remains on the public agenda even if it is not identified as such. It has become a code word for Israeli anti-Semitism and self-hatred as a consistent Jewish phenomenon. Every edition of the news carries some post-Zionist perception that has archetypal representation, along with the submission to the processes of transnationalism that renders all ethnic matters extraneous **(chapters 6 and 7)**. The most conspicuous problem is the media that promulgates the post-Zionist political lexicon and its agenda. The same is true regarding the topics preferred in literature and the arts and in the lexicon of contemporary Hebrew Literature whose orientation is post-Zionist. A limited vocabulary or compendium of concepts is adequate to represent an ideology.

For example, Yonatan Ratosh created an anti-Jewish Hebrew dictionary. For decades his brother has proposed lexicographical ideas and issues relating to spelling in order to eliminate Jewishness from the Hebrew Language. However, more threatening than the issues of language and literature are the latest inventions of the extreme Left that renounce any genuine faithfulness to the Jewish People. The most recent examples are the information gathering about, and acts of violence against, military personnel and their condemnation by Leftist "activists" as war criminals. This was preceded by a well-publicized wave of refusal to serve in the army, and the burial of legislation regarding the right of Jews to establish communities that excluded Arabs. Note that Arab communities in Israel, not to speak of the communities in the few Arab countries where a small number of Jews still reside, would not tolerate Jews. The "right-wing" government talks about the need to dismantle Jewish communities that are located in allegedly Arab territory that must be *judenrein* to satisfy the Arabs! The Israel government lacks awareness of its obligations and rights as the government of the Jewish people in the Jewish state and has internalized the concept of Israel as a country of "all of its citizens," i.e. the country belongs to the Arabs as well as to the Jews, even if that kind of society does not actually exist. The Muslim suicide bomber enterprise has partially opened the eyes of more than a few Jews and forced them to re-adopt basic Zionist positions. Perhaps Israel stands on the verge of a partial awakening from the domination of the post-Zionist elites and a return to its historic Jewish positions.

Post-Zionism is motivated by the fear that the Jews, perhaps even unwillingly, will gain control over the Land of Israel in its entirety. They will thereby complete the process of their national self-determination. That is not only a juridical act but also an identification of the full extent of Jewish authenticity. Because if "God forbid", the Jew again trounces his enemies as he did in the Six Day War, he will no longer be able to escape his destiny.

Meanwhile, the post-Zionists continue to affect events alongside philosophical processes underway around the world. These philosophies are part of the postmodernist context, such as the claim regarding the disappearance of meaning that stems from particular languages and cultures (Huntington, 1996). One issue is at the heart of the matter: Judaism versus non-Judaism. Our patriarch "Abraham stands on one side while the rest of the world is on the other," as formulated by Jewry's sages. It is the belief in the *nihilo* contrasted with the belief in nothingness. The *nihilo* is the belief that the world was created by the will of God "ex-nihilo" as opposed to the belief that all is naught, absolute or latent nihilism. In short, the conflict is between "essence versus nothingness," to paraphrase one of the more widely published nihilists of the twentieth century (Sartre, 1946).

There is a relationship between the matter of the "territories" and the philosophy of language based on the notion that language is arbitrary. The post-Zionist position expresses a malicious disavowal of essence, existence, the uniqueness of time and place in history. Therefore, theoretically, it precludes the writing of durable literary works. The doctrines of internal annihilation of meaning negate the validity of the word as representing any sort of stable reality. Consequently, there is no meaning to a creative imagination that replicates itself infinitely for no discernible purpose, like a virus that inundates a computer's memory. Terms absorbed into the postmodern society are the simulacrum and the pastiche (Yaniv, 2001). Therefore, literary works are doomed to oblivion even before they are written, and in the course of their actual writing they self-destruct, not only in theory but in practice as well.

Man is trapped. He wants to express the truth, but political correctness prohibits him from doing so. As a result, truth seemingly, but only seemingly, does not exist as far as he is concerned. These steps involve a lie, which is almost self-aware. In other words, all means are legitimate to put a stop to history, which is striving towards its resolution. However man who continues to seek meaning knows that despair is itself only a façade (Yaniv, 2001).

Hebrew Literature today, for all intents and purposes, presents a multitude of variations on justifying the enemy and negating the Jewish state and everything that transpires in it. These anti-Zionist and anti-Israel views appear almost anywhere in the published works of writers like Meir Shalev, Ronit Matalon, Itamar Levy, David Grossman and many others. Post-Zionism actually negates the concept of the subject (Inbari, 1996; Weiss, 2000) while identifying with evil as an ideal (Sagiv, 2001). Fundamentally, it is a manifestation of a severe mental illness whose only justification is the requirement that the normative Jew put on a mask of tribal worship designed to distance his enemies from him. For example, Amos Oz's book, *A Panther in the Basement* (Oz, 1995) negates the very concept of treason. The child, the hero of many of his works, is incapable of knowing which side he is on – the mother, the father, the Right, the Left, the British, the Jews, the intellectuals, the wise men of the university or the simple hooligans.

Post-Zionism took control of the public mind, including that segment of the public which considers itself nationalist. Since the first Camp David in 1979, it became apparent that the Jews' denial of their selves, their land, their religion and their God is a fundamental component of contemporary Israeli identity and behavior. All essentials should be relinquished in order to make peace with the enemy. Jews decided that in the external dimension of their personality and world, they want to be liberated from the existential, meta-historic burden, which subjects them to one Holocaust after another. Jews hate victory. They consider themselves responsible for the death and destruction engendered by war. The latter sense is echoed in the statement attributed to Golda Meir following the 1967 war: "We can forgive you for having killed our children, but we cannot forgive you for forcing us to kill your children." These ideas are given stark expression in books such as *Soldiers' Discussions* (Shapira, 1967) after the Six Day War and *Just Between Us Youngsters* (Shapira, 1969).

That mentality ultimately leads to the notion that Jewry's identity and *raison d'être* arise not from being a potential victim but rather from being a victim in practice - destruction by the enemy. According to this concept, as soon as the Jew ceases to be a victim, he ceases to be a Jew. He deserves being a victim as a punishment and his martyrdom serves to eliminate an eternal anomaly, as if the Jew has internalized Christian theology. For veteran condemners of the covenant, aficionados of the Greek culture or of the overseers who collaborated with the enemy during the Egyptian exile in Biblical times, this is a normal phenomenon of persecutors and victims, of majority and minority (Morgenstern, 2002; Sharan, 1995), in addition to the Patricia Hearst complex or the Stockholm syndrome **(see chapter 8)**.

Why are the Jews constantly being killed? Is it only because of the behavior pattern typical of a minority? Or is it due to the victim's identification with the criminal, as known from victimology? Or perhaps it is due primarily to the fact that the Jewish minority group poses a perpetual threat to the legitimacy of the ruler, whoever he may be? Do Jews pose a challenge to others due to a vision of justice and expectations from human beings to render human pretenses as ridiculous and temporary. These perceptions underscore the Jews' alienation in the world. Our very existence seems to negate the non-Jewish world because, since antiquity, Jewry affirms the sanctity of the world and life as opposed to the affirmation of success as primarily material in nature (Berkowitz, 1987).

The roots of the anti-Zionist illness have always been present in Jewry (Sadan-Lowenstein, 1991). While our current condition exemplifies the problem clearly, Israel's political and intellectual climate provides it with new instruments of expression. However, anti-Zionism, which is the nucleus of post-Zionism, dates back to the Israelites in the desert after the Exodus apparent in their very refusal to enter the land as told in the episode of the spies (Numbers: chapters 13 and 14).

Post-Zionism is a far more immediate and lethal form of Jewish pathology than the story of the Israelites in the desert. It is a form of self-negation that demands national suicide. Moreover, it has adopted intellectual instruments to justify the phenomenon. The primary instrument operates according to Marshal McLuhan's statement that "the medium is the message." In other words the tool is the content and the content is the tool, that is to say that the media constitute the tool that determines the fate of the message **(see chapter 5)**. Television, the Internet, cellular phones and so forth have gained control of the public arena and of "enlightened" institutions of higher learning that allegedly provide the environment for contemplation.

Negating the Hero: Negating the Person

The term post-Zionist appeared in a book called *Portrait of a Warrior* (Weiss, 1975, p. 231). The book diagnosis the negation of heroes and heroism in Israeli fiction from the sixties until the eve of the Yom Kippur War. Negation of heroes and heroism in Israeli literature does not deal exclusively with combat soldiers. Nor is it only a struggle against the legitimacy of the army and of the Israel's wars: "There is nothing in this world for which it is worthwhile to sacrifice anyone" (Yizhar, 1992). In literature it is the negation of the concept of the persona, of a person, a process that developed into a philosophical orientation typical of many postmodernist theories (Rabinowitz, 1967). In Israel the negation of the hero is a struggle against the legitimacy of self-defense for the Jewish–Zionist–Israeli entity and its Jewish individuals, just as it negates the distinction between attacker and aggressor in every place and throughout history.

This implicit perception laid the groundwork for the later emergence of post-Zionist principles based, among other things, on the idea of "imaginary communities." Titles like *"To Invest a Nation, to Invent a Land"* (Berlowitz, 1996) or *"Captive of Her Dream"* (Graetz, 1995) became fashionable. Books by intellectuals and sociologists also appeared, such as the books by Almog (1997) or the French writer Musse, who attempted to explain nationalism as a manipulative organization undertaken by the power elite, an oligarchy that specializes in political ceremonies and establishing military cemeteries. The negation of nationalism and the undermining of the legitimacy of the concept of the nation-state by radical theoreticians were manifestations of an anarchistic struggle, similar to the communist struggle against the legitimacy of countries, laws and apparatuses that do not obey the rules of the revolution. This is a step that engendered or at least contributed to the contempt in Western countries for self-defense, and to stretching of so-called "democratic principles" to absurd lengths **(see chapter 7)**.

These ideas became transparently dangerous in wake of the attack on the Twin Towers. Legitimacy, in the eyes of the post-Zionists, exists only in entities and apparatuses capable of destroying the Jews. In other words, the only legitimate, not imaginary, community is the Palestinian community or the European Union that has mobilized to further the Arab cause

(Ye'or, 2002). The EU finances the academic conferences and publications of those who seek to erase the State of Israel. It seeks to determine the world agenda in opposition to the United States.

The Yom Kippur War brought to the surface judgements and fears that always existed within the profound Zionist despair - like the sense that we live on top of a volcano. That feeling had wide currency during the early 1920s) in the works of Yosef Brenner (Anita Shapira, 1996). There was also the widespread use in Israel of the code-word "nevertheless" to characterize our general recognition of the fact that the Zionist endeavor contained an element of absurdity and is often mistakenly referred to as "messianism" or hopelessness, irresponsible or suicidal, if one invoked any rational criterion. The writer S. Yizhar asked (1992): "What kind of father places his son on a hornet's nest?"

The struggle against the Jewish–Hebrew–Israeli hero consolidated over time. Jews scattered in many nations, and many in Israel, battle against their Judaism, perhaps as compensation for their feelings of rejection. In the future, someone will investigate how Jews contributed to the deconstruction of the old world, their own and others'. First and foremost, they will document the dissolution of language consciousness in the theory of Jacques Derrida regarding the asymmetry between the marker and the marked, which is the twin to the idea of arms reduction. At first glance Derrida's notion seems to be a peaceful even prophetic one. Actually, it is a satanic idea because it transforms self-defense into an illegitimate concept. For Derrida, there is no genuine subject and no real essence. No use of violence is justifiable because there is ostensibly nothing to defend.

The same approach is applied by the post-Zionists to Zionism which is a national decision manifest in the ingathering of the Jewish exiles in the Land of Israel and the establishment of a sovereign state by the Jews many of whom who fled from the terror of anti-Semitism and pogroms. That decision was presented many times as a rational, secular and normal decision instead of an unjustified stychic decision. It is unjustified a la PZs because there is no Jewish people and no obligatory history but there is always the "other" whom the non-subject is obligated to serve.

The view of the Zionist movement as a secular movement that started during the twentieth century positions us as almost equal partners to the post-Zionist claim that Zionism was a colonialist movement. There doesn't seem to be any reply to the question of which "motherland" dispatched the Jewish colonialists in the twentieth century to a Palestine which wasn't theirs. The Jews had no Spain, Portugal, Germany, Holland, England or France on whose behalf they established colonies, as those nations did worldwide. The perception of Zionism as a colonial enterprise engaged in establishing "foreign colonies" lacks an essential ingredient.

The answer is that the Land of Israel with all its implications, namely the Torah and its sanctity and the various nationalist Jewish cultures that were already located in Palestine, are totally renounced by PZ writers, just as they renounce archeology, the Bible, or Masada (Golan, 1992; Yahav, 1994). Contemporary authors who battle against the Land of Israel and Zionism oppose Jewish legitimacy and Jewry's right to national self-determination.

Post-Zionism, justifiably, will always find an internal flaw or inherent contradiction within Zionism paraded as a secular movement with pretenses to possessing the historical inheritance of The Land of Israel as a fundamentally religious-historical value. Since post-Zionism does not wish to recognize any essence inherent in Zionism, it asserts that history is nothing more than a collection of narratives that always lacked essence and, consequently, there is no point in searching for it. According to the PZs, only the Palestinians have history. Jewry's unequivocal and age-old claim is that the source for negating our essence by groups and nations around the world stems their negation of Zion as the source of all essences. When the nucleus of Zion, that consists of an amalgam of time, place, language and being, is reduced to one isolated element, our very existence apparently decomposes and allows deceit to enter. But as the degree of deceit increases, so too does the thirst for truth, the word of God (Amos 8: 11). Reality will change diametrically.

The deep historical roots of the Jewish people and its connection to the Land of Israel were manifest in the uninterrupted immigrations of Jews to the Land of Israel. They continued throughout the centuries of Jewry's life in the Diaspora, from earliest times up to, and including, the modern period (Morgenstern, 2002). Attempts to ignore the long history of Jewish immigration to Palestine, and concentrate almost exclusively on the late nineteenth- and twentieth-century settlement by the Jews of Palestine/Israel, ultimately caused significant damage, not only to the truth, but also to the adoption of the "narrative" hobby. In other words, everyone can begin his right of precedence wherever it suits him. The post-Zionists had the groundwork laid for them by the Zionist movement itself that prepared the official history of the War of Independence, of the IDF, the Haganah or any other official group of the Zionist Organization. A more comprehensive history is needed that pays attention to the events and groups that pre-date political Zionism and continue to this day. Many Jews participated in these events who did not have any known connection to the Zionist movement. It can be demonstrated, for example, that almost all of the nationalist forces, supporters of the Hebrew language, did not believe that Zionism as a movement would develop into a sovereign state or would prevail over its many rivals in the Jewish world. Various religious and political Jewish groups considered official Zionism nonsense, while what ultimately became known as "Zionism" eventually achieved the status of a predominant majority movement by many devious paths. The essential point is that the ideas and goals of Zionism were, and are, fundamental elements of the Jewish historical–religious tradition and Jews thoughout the ages sought to carry them out in their own lives unrelated to organized Zionism that began at the end of the nineteenth century.

The Writers' Guilt

Israeli Hebrew literature, as distinct from the Hebrew literature of the Zionist immigrations that preceeded the establishment of the State of Israel, never accepted the legitimacy of Jewish sovereignty in the Land of Israel. Above all, Israeli literature was written by Jews who were born in Palestine/Israel, especially the authors included under the title of the "generation in the land" (Anita Shapira, 1997, pp. 122–54). Although the writers of the Palmah generation were, ostensibly, those who expressed the famous collective "we" (Yizhar, Shamir, Meged, Bartov, Tammuz, Shahar), they all voiced their disappointment and doubts. The entire Zionist establishment was conditional upon maintaining the ethos of the collectivity, but the dissolution of the cooperative ethos stalled Zionism "in the middle of the novel" (Bar-Tov, 1984). Specifically, the positions of the "young Hebrews" known as the "Canaanite movement" did not represent just the opinion of a small group (Kurzweil, 1961). Most of the Zionist youth movements in pre-Israel Palestine felt embarrassed by the fact that the Zionist movement represented the Diaspora generation. They preferred to consider themselves more as Israelis and less as Jews. That is how they repaid their parents for rebelling against Jewish life in the little towns (shtetl) in Eastern Europe, even though had it not been for the "parent" generation, there would have been no Hebrew literature and no Zionism.

As long as the struggle against the British and the Great Arab Revolt continued alongside the settlement efforts of the incipient state, the Zionist ethos united Jewish ranks in Palestine. However the horrors of the Holocaust dwarfed the physical and most certainly the spiritual pretensions of local Zionism in Palestine/Israel, particularly its portrayal of the sabra as a sovereign giant. After the Holocaust, the need for a total renaissance of the Jewish People was relinquished, although for some years after the Holocaust writers discontinued their criticism of the Diaspora and of Zionism. The Canaanite perspective was rendered obsolete and irrelevant.

The War of Independence and the establishment of the new nation's institutions and bureaucracy shattered the fighters' collectivist-socialist values and their expectations for the establishment of a just society. Massive immigration of Jews from European and Middle Eastern countries obfuscated the sabra identity and their sense of ownership of the land. Pioneer training, for life on the agricultural collectives (kibbutzim) and socialism itself also became obsolete. Therefore some of the post-Zionist terms can be categorized under the rubric of a post-traumatic reaction to this relatively sudden lost of their preeminent position in Israel society. The Holocaust and the establishment of the state led to the demise of the nativist personality and facilitated the incursion of postmodernism as a local multi-cultural movement. This development paralleled worldwide processes exacerbated by World War II. These processes inundated the world following the American wars in Korea and Vietnam. The dissolution of the Soviet Union generated ridiculous concepts such as "the end of history" (Fukuyama, 1991) discussions of which finally climaxed in the mid-nineties.

Hebrew literature is not dependent on the level of the books nor on their artistic achievements, but rather on its ability to come to terms with the distinctiveness of the life of the Jewish people. The book of Exodus states the words of Moses: "For how would it be known that I have gained Your favor, I and Your people, unless You go with us, that we may be distinguished, I and Your people, from every people on the face of the earth?" (Exodus 33: 16). That is especially true for this "post-Zionist" generation who many authors of Hebrew literature believe is the last generation of the great Jewish redemption, heaven forbid. Due to the authors' inability to deal with the distinctive, a-rational, historical events that occur with great intensity, they often choose the easy way out: Debasing the principles of Jewish existence. In those circumstances the writer abscondes from the world to the world of the individual, the little person who screams, "who cares about Messiah, who cares about redemption, meanwhile they are closing the sea and how can I return with the first ship without the flight of the dove."

It goes without saying that Israeli literature published after Israel's independence, is one of the branches of Hebrew literature and of the literature of the Jewish people in recent generations. Almost against its will this literature continues to deal intensively and obsessively with problems that have occupied Jewry since the Enlightenment period, despite the conscious abstention of some authors.

One main theme is Jewry's lack of psychological ability to withstand the existential stress that accompanies the very affiliation with the Jewish world; tensions which continued to be exacerbated in the twentieth

century, due both to modern and universal processes and to the strange-
ness and distinctiveness of Jewish history, which consumes allies and
adversaries alike **(see chapter 12)**.

Many authors grasped Jewish history as a total experience, generally
negative, which includes a dialectic super-system replete with contradictions and opposites. They encountered difficulty in interpreting Jewish
culture, or the "Jewish world", as a whole able to be artistically represented, conveying any sort of harmony among the extraordinary historical
adventures: Exile, immigration, settlement ("immigrant literature"),
pioneering, Holocaust, ingathering of the exiles and the relationship
between Jews and Arabs.

On this score part of a letter sent to the well-known senior figure of
Hebrew letters in Israel, Aharon Meged, is partially reproduced here:

The Writers' Guilt

Dear Aharon Meged,

*You are indeed conspicuous in your differences from your fellow
authors and you have done so consistently over many years. . . . In
"Sodom City" or "Hell Country", your voice is precious in its soli-
tude, and when the day of historic reckoning arrives, if anyone at
all survives, your voice will be remembered for its resonance and
clarity. . . .*

*At the same time, I would like to apprise you of the fundamen-
tally problematic nature of your article . . . manifest in your
consistent support for a Palestinian State. The works of S. Yizhar,
"Hirbat Hiza" [Yizhar 1948] and "The Captive" ('48–'49) became
the normative model for the Israeli author, such as your story called
"The Treasure," the story "At Bulletpoint" by Yitshak Orpaz, and
"Swim Meet" by Binyamin Tammuz. The latter works were
perceived by Rasan Kanafani, a the member of Fatah killed in a 1970
IDF operation in Beirut, as manifestations of the fact that the
Hebrew author recognizes the justice of the Palestinian cause. These
works appear in an anthology callled* Homeland of Contradictory
Yearnings *(Ben Ezer, 1992) recommended by the Israel Ministry of
Education as part of the peace curriculum.*

*These works and thousands like them cultivated Jewish self-
hatred until it reached pathological dimensions. This sense of guilt
originated during the War of Independence, due to the lack of
profound Jewish ethical norms and the resulting lack of faith in the
justice of the war. The ultimate expression of this was in the decid-
edly pornographic work "Nation, Food, Kings" (Yitzhak Laor,*

1993). An army as thoroughly rotten as that deserves to be annihilated.

Israeli literature, which is, indeed, the product of rootless sabras, is more responsible than any other cultural-spiritual factor - much more than the media or politicians - for the bloodshed in this region, because it created the perverted linguistic and mental codes that have dominated the scene since that time. Just as Hebrew literature was more responsible than any other factor for the renaissance of secular Zionism, so too it is more responsible than any other factor for the destruction of the Zionist State, and it manifests itself among other ways in the worship of the new historians who have inundated the land ... The idea of a Palestinian State is primarily an Israeli concept that had disappeared during the period of Hussein and the Gulf War. The path to its realization involves the most terrible of wars, which is drawing near in an irreversible, irrepressible process.

I have no doubt that your motives, like those of your fellow authors are pure. However, you are unwilling to admit ... that a sovereign Palestinian State alongside a decomposing Israel – and a secular, nihilistic Israel can be nothing other than decayed – will see its destiny in the total destruction of Israel. Western democratic ideas are incompatible with Arab society just as the idea of elections in Judea, Samaria and Gaza is a joke. S. Yizhar already wrote about this in his racist and accurate article regarding the Tel al-Zaatar episode (The Man Filled with Contradictions) during the Lebanese civil war in which he described the bestial Arab murderousness so well.

Therefore, your position vis-à-vis the Palestinian State fundamentally does not help the Jews, but rather is part of the same process, which is causing its destruction. It is true that the Jews, and especially the authorities in all of the governments, have not treated the Arabs properly. They humiliated them, discriminated against them for no reason and mistreated them. They were not cruel and generous geniuses and therefore they ultimately lost the war. ...

When I see the Arabs murdered by the Jibril Rajoub hooligans I know that the Left is responsible. However, I cannot demonstrate against you in the square. (Ha'aretz, January 21, 1994)

The Messianic Monster and the War against Tehilah

We would like to present the internal confrontations, the rejection-attraction relations of Hebrew writers to the Jewish issue by examining two works among the most recent, significant and famous works of literature published this year 5761–2 (2001–2). The two novels in question are *The Liberating Bride* by A. B. Yehoshua and *A Story of Love and Darkness* by Amos Oz. The two are postmodern novels but they also attempt to preserve the old Zionist by rebelling against him and in that sense they are standard, modern corrective novels, and not only those which here and there employ postmodernist techniques

Amos Oz's book *A Story of Love and Darkness* is principally a very finely crafted memorial album. Each picture has its value. In fact it is not an uninterrupted autobiography replete with links but rather it is close to a stylized memoir. The time line, or the development along the biographical line is completely mechanical. But one thing is clear in this album. Profound empathy is expressed towards the right wing, nationalist world of the Klausners and especially to Grandfather Alexander Klausner, professor Yosef Klausner's brother, while the narrator's conversion to the Left is portrayed in a childish, juvenile and unconvincing manner (Shalev, 2001–2002). The left-wing characters on the kibbutz are shallow and short. The reasoning for the departure from the Right began with "Begin's armament speech" in which he used a term now famous for its sexual connotation instead of using the common word for "arms race." That is one of the only motifs in the book that appears twice at two different memory sites. Nevertheless, it remains equally insipid and infantile. The urges of insult, inferiority, conquest, revenge, victory, Revisionist and Rightist messianic urges, are much more conspicuous in this book by Amos Oz than any portrayal of reality as peace

A. B. Yehoshua's novel *The Liberating Bride* is a fascinating book, psychological and allegorical. The code that opens the novel's meaning is extremely artificial. The book attempts to deal with the question of how to liberate ourselves from the Messiah complex, also the theme of his earlier novels *Mr. Mani*, *Molcho* and *The Journey to the End of the Millennium* (1997). The thesis is presented by means of the liberating bride, by defiling Tehilah and turning her into a witch and a despicable whore. It is Yehoshua's Tehilah against the Tehilah of Agnon, in the most provocative manner possible. Tehilah who is supposedly the archetype of the mother and bride, the most exalted angelic figure reminiscent of God's Holy Presence (Sh'chinah) and of the entire House of Israel.

The Persona-Mask in the Works of Yehoshua and Oz

Yehoshua and Oz over dozens of years unceasingly alternate between positions considered to be radical left-wing post-Zionist and those derived from normative Zionist or even Jewish positions. For example, the former Armenian Arab from Jaffa, Anton Shmas, characterized Yehoshua as a little Kahane (Shmas, 1985). The ideas of Oz and others regarding separation of Jews and Arabs are at times ideas of that sort. In order to understand the phenomenon in depth, we return to the concept of the persona mask to examine the phenomenon of messianic masks in the works of Yehoshua and Oz.

Karl Jung (1974) discussed the connection between the anima [assimilation into the mother] as the loss of persona (p. 97) and man's desire to flee from it. "Therefore man shall leave his father and mother . . . " (Genesis 2: 24). It is important to understand the apparatus by means of which a person identifies with the persona and its limitations, the dissolution of the persona and its reconstruction. Jung writes:

> Only the fact that the persona is an arbitrary or, more or less, private sector of the collective soul is liable to cause us to err and think that it is all something individual. However, as attested to by its name, it is all a mask of the collective soul – a mask, which conjures a *mistaken sense of individuality*. It arouses in a person the thought that he is an individual, and the truth is that it is only an actor's role through which the collective soul speaks . . . Fundamentally, the persona is not something "real"; it is a compromise between the individual and society over "the appearance of man". He takes a name, crafts a title, holds a job . . . The persona is only apparent, a two-dimensional reality, as it can be characterized sarcastically. (37–8)

Jung cites primitive man who conceals himself in a mask and in that way distances himself from the collective soul, which represents the anima. Yehoshua accomplishes this by use of parody while Oz employs patronage and irony. The author is successful, briefly, in creating estrangement and alienation and thus fashions an ancient prestige by means of which, in Oz's formulation, he attempts to "bind the tribal forces by oath" to follow in his path (Oz, 1979). As Jung puts it: "It would, obviously, not be difficult to claim that the motive driving this development is the intent to rule. However, by doing so, we totally ignore the fact that the existence of prestige is invariably the result of a collective compromise".

These formulae explain the perpetual conflict. Excessive distance from the collective soul renders the individual storyteller or speaker irrelevant and therefore after the distant one has taken giant steps away and has separated himself from the public, he must return to within earshot, within a relevant range of leadership.

In Israeli literature, we encounter a fascinating phenomenon of authors with dual identities. Religious or nationalist parents, especially father figures, revisionist or ethnic affiliation as well as extreme fluctuation in ethics or identity caused by different sources of influence – east and west, are only some of the components of the identity crises which infiltrate the works of these storytellers. The authors encounter a contradiction between the affiliations of their internal world which is contrary to their political world. Ostensibly, they enjoy both worlds but actually they are torn between the worlds (Weiss, 2000). Where is their collective soul? Is it located on the plane of fundamental, archetypal symbols or does it withdraw to external political representation, which manifests itself in Knesset elections? The sharp distinction between external and internal is impossible because there are reciprocal overlaps. The political aspect, too, is an echo of the reparative archetype, which resulted from an unsatisfactory dialectical process.

An additional contradiction exists between the messianic archetypes. They are at odds and in conflict. For example, the Messiah as an asocial phenomenon or as a rebellious, Prometheus-like, anti-God phenomenon like the biblical Cain or his reincarnation Tuval Cain who are declensions of the word "transaction" itself: "For I have purchased a man with God" said by Eve in Genesis as the reasoning behind the name of her first-born son Cain; the aspired legitimacy of the insane as a stimulus for the illegitimate, of the anti-nomian; the identification with the Id found in each and every human being. An example is the psychotic and yet poetic identification with the false Messiah Shabbetai Zvi who was called a true Messiah, and whom the ordinary public did not have a chance to know. There is also the example of God's choice of the archetype of Abel His chosen one, the loyal shepherd, who is obedient and offers sacrifices according to God's will, and who, because of his naievete, is himself sacrificed.

The confrontation is within the ahistorical messianic archetype, between the figure of Cain or of Abel. In general, that is what transpires in the artist's mind who presents to the external world one dimension of his messianic choice. The expectation is that the artist will choose Cain. Yehoshua chose for the title of one of his books the slogan *In Favor of Normalcy* (Yehoshua, 1984) that presumed to present the "sane" version of Zionism. This was a hollow or farcical disguise that indicated a temporary postponement of the move to disengage from the Judaism that threatened him/us. The talk in Yhoshoua's book about "sane" Zionism merely sought to conceal the destructive instincts that permeate A. B. Yehoshua's and Amos Oz's works since their inception.

The "Situation of the Third Kind" of Amos Oz

The subject of messianism appears in the works of Yehoshua and Oz in different forms depending upon whether the ego is divided into a constellation of characters vertically, as in *Mr. Mani* (Yehoshua, 1989), or horizontally, as in *Touch Water Touch Wind* (Oz, 1973). There are single-minded characters like Pima, the hero of Oz's novel *The Third Situation* (1991) who appears as a secular Messiah battling 'our Angel of Death' who is really the classic Jewish Messiah. There are also secondary characters scattered through different novels such as Guillaume de Touran or Claude Crooked Shoulder, the leaders of the crusade in the novella, *Unto Death* (1971) into which elements of the Jew or the Jewish Messiah seeped and who were split off from the figure of the author. Then there is the character from the period of the Judges, Gilead the Gileadite and his son Yiftah, the central hero in the story " On This Bad Land" (1976). These are figures of leaders, like Amos Oz's massive ambivalence toward Ben-Gurion and Eshkol who are archetypal elders. The former is the murderous father while the latter is the bereaved father, as Oz revealed partially in what he tells from behind the mask in the *Story of Love and Darkness* (2002). These are characters whose ambition is to affect total reality. The preponderance of these archetypal personalities in the works of these two and other authors, such as Yoram Kaniuk in *The Last Jew* (1981) which treats the adventures of Rabbi Joseph de la Raine, conveys the complex symbolism found in Israeli fiction.

The desire for "normalcy" was one of the Zionism's central ideas. Yehoshua's book *In Favor of Normalcy* (1980) sought to draw an analogy between Freud's concept of the Oedipus complex and the modern idea of nationalism. However in recent years, Yehoshua has begun to take exception to the very notion of Israeli normalcy. He discovered Jewishness and the Sephardic-Jewish experience as psychological forces that had to be faced. In 1998 Yehoshua spoke about the nature of our androgynous identity (Yehoshua, 1998). In a lecture and an interview that followed, he points to the eternal paradox in our national and religious identity. He draws an analogy between the Jewish people and an androgynous creature, "which contains both male and female components but is neither male nor female. It is a nation that embodies national and religious elements but is neither a nation nor a religion, but something problematic in between". Thus, the androgynous identity of the Jewish people exhibits an existential paradox that, in his opinion, arouses the considerable uneasiness found in the Jewish people. Yehoshua claims: "Religion by its very essence, especially a religion which has universal contents and pretenses, cannot be arrested by national borders, and a nationality cannot make membership conditional on beliefs and opinions."

But Yehoshua recently (after 1998) renounced that view and formulated his ideas very dramatically in his new book *The Liberating Bride* (2001). His new version is that androgyny is comprised of Jews and Arab-Palestinians who share the same feature. One of the impressive and central scenes in the book is the poetry festival in Ramallah in which the Arab student, Samahar, presents the Jewish play, "The Dybbuk" in which each of the play's major characters is possessed by one or more demons (Fish, 1994). The book's main character is Yohanan Rivlin, a petty, zealous professor, who despite all of his evil and nastiness, is ten times more responsible and ethical than the young, talented careerist, Dr. Miller, who recites the entire lexicon of post-Zionism and postmodernism interwoven with post-colonialist perceptions. The author appears to be closely identified with the main character Rivlin who despises himself. But he despises Miller's world a thousand times more. Rivlin sends him far away although he envies him and seeks legitimization from him.

During an interview after the lecture mentioned above, Yehoshua was asked how his views about the Jews and Israel had changed since the publication 15 years ago of his book *In Favor of Normalcy*. Yehoshua replied that when he wrote that book he felt that it was possible to completely separate the religious elements from the definition of Jewish identity. He said that now he was less optimistic about the possibility that nationality will conquer the religious aspects of Jewish life in Israel in any profound sense (p. 25). "My intellectual credibility would be harmed if I continue being irresponsibly optimistic . . . The Jewish religion is part of the makeup of our protein and that is something very substantial . . . "

The problem of bisexuality, which is a serious problem of unfocused identity, appears in many of Yehoshua's works ever since *Late Divorce* or *Cantata to Divorce*. The problem is even more blatant in works like *Molcho* (1987) or *Mr. Mani*. The intensification of sexual differentiation is also familiar from stories of the development of the messianic character itself. For example, the Biblical stories of Lot and his daughters, Judah and his daughter-in-law, Ruth and Boaz and David and Bathsheba, contain this theme. Of course it is important to emphasize that the Biblical stories have a religious purpose in a universal or national mythical context and not in a private one. In these and other stories, the Bible presents concepts of the world of lovingkindness, the world outside the law, as a condition for overcoming limiting differentiations or laws of taboo. The messianic stories of Yehoshua and Amos Oz portray situations of incest or family conflicts similar to incest.

Mr. Mani

Mr. Mani (Yehoshua, 1990) was characterized as "The Opposite Direction" (Ben-Dov, 1997). That metaphor refers to the possibility of making a different, opposite, choice. The hero vacilates between classic messianic redemption that the author turns into pathological incest, and normal Zionist redemption. The main character, Hagar Shiloh, goes back and forth between Jerusalem and its doppelgänger Tel Aviv. Most of the members of the house of Mani, in Yehoshua's novel *Mr. Mani*, are indeed "mani-acs" who comprise the Mani dynasty over a period of 200 years. They transmit insanity genetically from one generation to the next. The Mani pathology expresses a grotesque messianic monster who strives for self-fulfillment by means of incest, homosexuality and other sexual and psychic perversions. In Yehoshua's novel, they all become Walkyries, the mythological beasts adopted as a symbol by the Nazis.

Undoubtedly, A. B. Yehoshua and Amos Oz as intellectuals express their opinions as political trendsetters. They publish books and political articles, appear before assemblies as speakers and, occasionally issue declarations, in support of physical separation of Jews and Arabs in Judea and Samaria by a wall or some other form of separation, in support of Palestinian Arabs' "right to return" to Israel (in large numbers, perhaps millions of people), in support of fund raising to implement the dismantling of Jewish communities in Judea and Samaria, or in support of their call to join Reform Judaism. The latter idea is an attempt to undermine the orthodox hegemony in order to alter Israel's political structure, not just an expression of identification with Reform theology or concepts of Jewish life.

The Liberating Bride

Messianism is one of the radical manifestations of the translation of religious faith and religious life into historical-political action. The messianic complex and the desire to escape from it to a better, more lucid world, appears in *The Liberating Bride*. The bride's sister, Tehillah, is portrayed as a defiled witch, a degraded whore. She intentionally and provocatively stands in stark contrast to Agnon's Tehillah. Originally she was supposed to be the bride-and-mother in the archetypal sense, an exalted and angelic presence such as the Divine Spirit or the Community of Israel.

Yehoshua and Oz appear to have "signed an agreement" about a common code to guide their work. Recently, both expressed their disgust with Jews and Judaism in the public domain. Yehoshua spoke about the fact that "we have penetrated their veins" and therefore it is possible to understand the German attitude towards Jews and consequently the Arab attitude. That statement could be acceptable if the "penetrating elements" are reversed and are recognized as the opposite of what Yehoshua supposes. The reason for the Palestinian's ruthless terror against Jews and Israel is the illusion of imminent victory cultivated by the political Left, just as in Germany the "penetration of the veins" of German culture and society by assimilated Jews was singularly pronounced, while such "penetration" by religious Jews with beards (Scholem, 1975) was hardly visible. From a racist perspective, the fear of the German was that the masquerading, assimilated Jew – the journalist, the banker or the academic – would infiltrate German "blood." The Jew who educates the world to accept outsiders and battles racism was perceived as weakening national-ethnic countries just as did the pacifist movements after World War I.

It is possible that Yehoshua said "we have permeated their veins" as a commentary on one of the potentials of his new novel that haunted him as an extremely introverted thesis. On the other hand, Amos Oz every so often discharges genuinely anti-Semitic statements, such as the one made on a morning radio news program. In an interview broadcast on the radio he stated that the Bible, the Mishnah and the Talmud are objectionable works that have caused much damage to the world in contrast to fiction that beautifies the world.

Both Oz and Yehoshua express extreme contradictions in their public remarks and written works. They exemplify what can be called a split consciousness. They portray themselves as Leftist freedom-fighters. How is that kind of self image to be reconciled with their view of the Jew as afflicted with mental illness while describing the Arabs with more hatred and contempt than one can find in any other book in the Hebrew language? *The Liberating Bride* expresses considerable consciousness of Jewish mental illness that Yehoshua seeks to eliminate in a violent and crude manner.

Ideology and Literature

Just where in Yehoshua's works is the point where ideology and literature converge and the point where they diverge? In what way does a novel serve a political position and in what way does it contradict it? Here, we will restrict our discussion to two topics: jealousy of S. Y. Agnon and an attempt to overcome that jealousy through incest as justification for the understanding and removal of guilt.

Mordechai Shalev (2002) already discussed the matter of incest in Amos Oz's book *The Story of Love and Darkness*. The young Klausner is enveloped by his mother beneath a winter blanket as she tells him her seductive stories. A parallel matter, which repeats itself in this work is the jealousy Oz expresses of Agnon. Oz attempts to settle a shadowy family score over Agnon's treatment of his revered uncle, Yosef Klausner (a Jew from Russia) whom Agnon (from Galicia) did not respect, and who was not respected by Klausner. Many comments about Agnon are interspersed throughout the book, among them transparently jealous comments by these two authors who are light years away from Agnon's literary stature. The settling of scores is beyond rumormongering. It is conceived in the fundamental national and tribal models, not only in terms of Agnon's Galician roots. Another irritant is Agnon's form of messianic religiosity that both authors find disgusting. At that point their stories tie into the episode of Tehilla, who is the heroine of A. B. Yehoshua's *The Liberating Bride*, and like the heroine of one of Amos Oz's more problematic essays "The Righteous Woman's Insanity" in *The Heaven's Silence - Agnon Wonders about God* (Oz, 1993), in which he ostensibly discusses Tehilla's character in order to destroy it as a feature of the collective anima in whose vicinity one cannot survive. This is the classic struggle against the Jewish mother as in *Portnoy's Complaint*. But even more important is its struggle against the heavenly, transcendent mother, the anima that represents the Sabbath, the Torah, the soul, Jerusalem, Zion, and so forth, whose prayers and demands the secularist author cannot abide.

The image of the mother–bride–daughter in The Liberating Bride

At the end of *The Liberating Bride*, the main character Prof. Yohanan Rivlin states that he has successfully liberated himself from the ghostly figure that pursued him. That figure is the image of an old lady on the porch of the house across the way. For Rivlin, she was an incarnation of his monstrous mother who had recently died and who had dominated him and all members of her family until her dying day. The same is true for all the other old ladies in this and other stories who represent history. The mothers in Yehoshua's works, like the old woman named Vaduce in the novel "The Lover," all represent Zionism and the Land of Israel. Galia's unpredictable and astounding divorce from his son became a litany of suffering for the father, an obsession and his life's unsolved riddle. The resolution of this enigma of his daughter-in-law and the reason for the divorce, ostensibly liberates the father and the son from tyrannical subjugation to the hopeless, unrequited love of messianism that embodies a barren and insane nationalist matriarchate.

In order to resolve the riddle of his son's divorce that holds the key to the father's emancipation, the father pursues the son with relentless prying. He entangles the son with his divorcee from whom he, the father, is unable to separate himself psychologically. Galia, the beautiful divorcee has a tall, older and single sister named Tehilla, named after Agnon's famous heroine, whose house was adjacent to a lodge owned by Tehilla's father, Yehuda Handel (referring, of course, to Freidrich Handel who composed the oratorio The Messiah).

A. B. Yehoshua turns Tehilla into a tyrannical mistress who manages the lodge. This manager figure is based on Agnon's story "The Mistress and the Merchant", that provides us with Agnon's basic model of man-woman relations a la Otto Weininger. Allegorical interpretations of Agnon's story "The Mistress and the Merchant" (1943) state that Helena, the heroine of the story, represents the gentiles, anti-Semitism and Nazism, while the merchant, Yosef, represents the despised and weakling Jews. In Yehoshua's story, Tehilla, the heroic, modest Jerusalemite is transformed into the daughter who entices her father into incest. That is the secret discovered by Rivlin's son, Tehilla's brother-in-law, when he descends one day to the hotel's cellar. The shocked son tells it all to his wife, Galia. Once she understood the secret told her as if it was all an illusion, she quickly gets rid of him.

The portrayal of Tehilla as a whore is typical of a secular, sabra story-teller waging a war to the bitter end against his Jewish mother, Zion and Jerusalem, which he considers a foreign city (Oz, 1979; Weiss, 1974). In a series of articles, Israeli critics wrote about their battle with Tehilla, like Adi Zemah (1990) who claims that Tehilla committed adultery. One of the outstanding articles is "The Righteous Woman's Insanity" by Amos Oz who writes that later in life Tehilla outgrew her innocent faith, thanks to the storyteller. In my opinion, Tehilla's death should be interpreted as "interment until the advent of the Redeemer." The reason for Tehilla's disappearance is authors like Oz and Yehoshua. With authors of that sort, she knows that the Messiah will not come in this generation. Bialik's *Scroll of Fire*, indeed all of his poetry, received similar treatment, just as today they are trying to transform Alterman into a post-Zionist (Ziva Shamir's reaction to "The Worm" by Dan Merion). Tehilla quickly departs from the labyrinth of Zionism and post-Zionism, which is destroying the renascent Jerusalem. Tehilla hides herself until the Redeemer will appear, and in her words "the Redeemer will come, and may God grant that he come quickly . . . "

References

Agnon, Shmuel-Yosef (1943) *Complete Works of S. Y. Agnon*. Tel Aviv: Schocken.

Almog, Oz (1997) *A Portrait of the Native Israeli*. Tel Aviv: Am Oved.

Bartov, Hanoch (1984) *In the Midst of Writing a Novel*. Tel Aviv: Am Oved.

Ben-Dov, Nitza (Ed.) (1997) *The Opposite Direction*. Tel Aviv: Hakibbutz Hameuchad.

Berkowitz, Eliezer (1987) *Faith after the Holocaust*. Jerusalem: Yad Vashem.

—— (1988) *A Friend in Need*. Jerusalem: Yad Vashem.

Berlowitz, Yaffa (1996) *Inventing a People, Inventing a Country*. Tel Aviv: Hakibbutz Hameuchad.

Fish, Harel A. (1994) *Remembered Future*. Jerusalem: Bialik Institute.

Fukuyama, Francis (1991) *The End of History and the Last Man*. New York: The Free Press.

Golan, Avirama (1992) Masada is not our story. *Ha'aretz* newspaper, May 6, 1992, p. 4.

Gurewitz, David (1997) *Post-Modernism, Culture and Literature at the End of the Twenties*. Tel Aviv: Dvir.

Greatz, Nurit (1995) *A Captive in Her Dream: Political culture in Israel*. Tel Aviv: Am Oved.

Huntington, Samuel (1996) *The Clash of Civilizations and the Remaking of World Order*. New York: Touchstone.

Inbari, Asaf (1996), Gradual death. *Newspaper Seventy Seven* 134, pp. 27–34.

Kaniuk, Yoram (1981) *The Last Jew*. Tel Aviv: Hakibbutz Hameuchad.

Karton-Blum, Ruth (2002) *The Sources of My Poetry*. Tel Aviv: Yediot Acharonot.

Kurzweil, Baruch (1961) *Hebrew Literature Today: Continuation or revolution?* Tel Aviv: Schocken.

La'or, Dan (1995) *Did Agnon Write about the Holocaust? New perspectives*. Tel Aviv: Sifriat Poalim.

La'or, Yitzhak (1993) *A Feast for Kings*. Tel Aviv: Hakibbutz Hameuchad.

Morgenstern, Arie (2002) Diaspora Jewry and the yearning for Zion. *Azure* 12, pp. 51–100.

Oz, Amos (1971) *Unto Death*. Tel Aviv: Sifriat Poalim.

—— (1973) *Touch the Water, Touch the Wind*. Tel Aviv: Am Oved.

—— (1976) *Land of the Jackals*. Tel Aviv: Am Oved.

—— (1979) *In the Strong Azure Light*. Tel Aviv: Sifriat Poalim.

—— (1991) *The Third Situation*. Tel Aviv: Am Oved.

—— (1993) *The Heaven's Silence: Agnon wonders about God*. Tel Aviv: Keter.

—— (1995) *Panther in the Basement*. Tel Aviv: Keter.

—— (2002) *A Story about Love and Darkness*. Tel Aviv: Keter.

Rabinowitz, Yeshayahu (1967) *Hebrew Literary Story-telling in Search of a Hero*. Tel Aviv: Masada.

Sadan-Lowenstein, Nili (1991) *Hebrew Literature of the Twenties in Erez-Yisrael*. Tel Aviv: Sifriat Poalim.

Sagiv, Asaf (2001) The evil empire: Adi Ofir and the ethics of despair. *Azure* 11, pp. 146–63.

—— (2002) George Steiner's Jewish Problem. *Azure* 12, pp. 133–57.

Sartre, Jean-Paul (1946) *L'être et le Neant*. Paris: Gallimard (*Being and*

Nothingness. New York: Philisophical Library, 1956) (French and English).

Scholem, Gershom (1975) *Explications and Implications* (reprinted from *Ha'aretz*, September 14, 1966). Tel Aviv: Am Oved, pp. 96–113.

Shalev, Mordechai (2001) A year after the Rosh Hashannah war, and sixty years after the publication of the book of poetry (Simhat Aniyim) by Natan Alterman. *Ha'aretz*, September 17.

—— (2002) The culture of suicide and incest. *Ha'aretz*, July 5.

Shapira, Anita (1996) *Sword of the Dove*. Tel Aviv: Am Oved.

—— (1997) *New Jews, Old Jews*. Tel Aviv: Am Oved.

Shapira, Avraham (Ed.) (1967) *Soldiers' Discussions*. Tel Aviv: Hakibbutz Hameuchad.

—— (Ed.) (1969) *Just Between Us Youngsters*. Tel Aviv: Hakibbutz Hameuchad.

Sharan, Shlomo (1995) Jewish anti-Semitism in Israel. *Nativ* 46, pp. 43–9.

Shmas, Anton (1985) The Guilt of the Left. *Politika* 4, pp. 8–13.

Weiss, Hillel (1974) "Tehilla's death interpreted as interment until the advent of the savior." In *Interpretation of Five Stories by Agnon*. Tel Aviv: Akkad, pp. 75–93.

—— (1975) *Portrait of a Warrior*. Ramat Gan: Bar-Ilan University.

—— (2000) Where are you, Jewish People? *Nativ*, pp. 75–6.

Yahav, Dan (1994) Archeology helps to shatter myths. *Davar*, July 8, 1994, p. 21.

Yaniv, Tali (2001) *Searching Beneath the Mask – Modern and post-modern trends in contemporary Israeli literature*. Doctoral Dissertation. Bar-Ilan University.

Yehoshua, A. B. (1980) *In Favor of Normality*. Tel Aviv: Schocken.

—— (1987) *Molcho*. Tel Aviv: Keter.

—— (1990) *Mr. Mani*. Tel Aviv: Hakibbutz Hameuchad.

—— (1997) *Journey to the End of the Millennium*. Tel Aviv: Hakibbutz Hameuchad.

—— (1998) An interview with Anat Koren. *Toar*, November, pp. 24–6.

—— (2001) *The Liberating Bride*. Tel Aviv: Hakibbutz Hameuchad.

Ye'or, Bat (2002) *Islam and Dhimmitude*. Teaneck, NJ: Farleigh Dickenson University Press. (English).

Yizhar, S. (1948) *The Tale of Hirbet Hi'za: Four stories*. Tel Aviv: Sifriat Poalim.

—— (1992) *Advance Payment*. Tel Aviv: Zmora-Bitan.

Zemah, Adi (1990) *A Simple Reading*. Jerusalem: The Bialik Institute.

12

Pluralism, the Post-Zionists, and Israel as the Jewish Nation

SHLOMO SHARAN

The primary concern of Zionism at this juncture in history is to strengthen and cultivate Israel as the Jewish nation, politically, demographically, culturally and in terms of its historical-religious identity (Schweid, 1996). That goal does not entail uniformity of political, cultural or Jewish religious persuasion, by any means. Nor could such a notion prevail among the Jewish People today in all its peculiar diversity. But Israel as the Jewish–Zionist nation cannot accommodate the drift toward relinquishing its territorial and historical integrity in order to accede to a postmodern pluralism. That kind of pluralism means a multi-national, multi-religious (i.e. many religions) multi-cultural conception of a nation that has abandoned its Jewish identity (if it indeed could). Jewry must staunchly and decisively resist that trend.

What Does Cultural Pluralism Mean?

Social ideology current in academia almost automatically confers near inviolability on the notion of pluralism as applied to the beliefs or cultural patterns of individuals or groups within a given society. Pluralism is also one of the watchwords of the PZs' ideology in Israel. But what does pluralism mean, and to whom?

Frequently forgotten is the important meaning of pluralism as a positive national-political policy, an essential component of relationships *between nations* or other entities that expresses mutual recognition and respect. On that level, it exerts a force supporting international or inter-group cooperation. PZ writers demand that Israel adopt a pluralistic attitude toward the Arabs, while the Arabs – as nations or groups – do not display pluralistic attitudes, i.e. mutual recognition and acceptance, toward Israel in any manner whatsoever, with the still questionable exception so far of Jordan.

Applied to the level of a single nation or group regarding its internal life, pluralism can become a disintegrating force, depending on the specific parameters of pluralism under discussion. In this discussion the reference is first and foremost to political pluralism in the sense of the political equality of different ethnic groups within a nation. Pluralism in the PZs' vocabulary also refers to a radical individualism to the effect that Jewish ethnic identity in the postmodern world has changed its spots and it is now exclusively a matter of personal choice and decision rather than largely a product of historical and social factors. The latter claim rests on replacing social reality with abstract ethical theory that emphasizes the importance of free will for mankind's moral behavior, or with a wish-fulfilling fantasy that people can escape or discard their Jewish identity at will. Those notions fly in the face of history so blatantly that they do not warrant consideration in this context.

Social cohesiveness entails a certain degree of cultural unity. Pluralism often promotes internal atomization and sub-group insulation. By all accounts, the Jewish population in Israel has displayed an unusual degree of cultural pluralism since the late 1950s. Indeed, in terms of *varieties of Jewish life*, Israel is a pluralistic nation par excellence. The pluralistic nature of Israeli society is a natural concomitant of its growth in population as a country formed by Jewish immigrants from a large number of countries. The Jews who came here brought with them a vast variety of cultures, from Eastern and Western Europe, from many of the Muslim countries of the Middle East, from South and Central Africa, from North, Central and South America, and even from some countries of the Far East. They also brought a similarly wide variety of views, opinions and degrees of awareness about themselves as Jews.

One extreme of this wide continuum of Jewish identity, more common in the '30s and '40s of the twentieth century than today, was the notion that the Zionist enterprise provided an opportunity that was unavailable to Jews elsewhere, to live as Jews without the need for religious affiliation or observance, or, for that matter, without any sense of belonging to the historical tradition of the Jewish People. These people wanted to live as Jewish individuals without any aspect of their existence predetermined by historical–social factors beyond their immediate control and conscious-ness – to be Jews without Judaism, even Zionists without Jewish history.

For these Jews, Zionist Palestine/Israel was, ironically enough, a way out of Judaism and what had been known in history as the Jewish People. That current persists in pockets of Israeli society to this day. During the course of the years it has assumed many shapes and forms. One of these was the so-called Young Hebrews or Canaanites, a group of rebellious intellectuals during Israel's early years (Simon, 1953). In the final analysis, most of the Canaanites remained Zionists along with their call for integration into the non-Jewish Middle East.

Another strong cultural current among the Jewish immigrants to Palestine/Israel, less extreme than the Canaanites, was their desire to establish a completely secular Hebraic culture. They continued the tradition of the Hebrew-oriented Jewish Enlightenment that developed in Europe during the nineteenth century and participated in the modernization and revitalization of the Hebrew language. This view of Israel culture, not at all invented by the Canaanites, decided the nature of Israeli culture to no small degree. Israel's public institutions, social services, school system, communications media, literature, and so forth, all conducted in modern Hebrew, are almost totally secularized except for the observance of the ceremonies ordinarily associated with the "Civil Religion" accepted by the population at large (Liebman and Don-Yehiya, 1983).

For other Jews, their religious heritage – of differing intensities and degrees of devotion - was paramount in their lives. There exists a very wide range of religious devotion in Israel, especially evident among Western or Ashkenazi Jews compared to Middle Eastern or Sephardic Jewish traditions. Also, the Western schools of Reform and Conservative Judaism were not transplanted to the soil of Israel until relatively recently. The East European and Middle Eastern Jews who formed the major portion of Israel Jewry did not experience these revisionist schools of religious life that developed primarily in Western Europe and the United States and who, to this day, constitute a relatively small group in Israel. Moreover, the leadership of the Reform and Conservative movements was opposed to Zionism for decades prior to the advent of Nazism, with some notable exceptions. That, too, has changed to a great extent.

Recent decades have also witnessed the growing Zionization of the ultra-Orthodox wing of Jewry who take an increasingly active role in Israel's political and public life **(see chapter 9)**. The sheer number of ultra-Orthodox Jews in Israel has increased dramatically by virtue of their high birthrate, as well as in the wake of increased immigration. In future decades, the ultra-Orthodox wing will certainly change in many ways and will participate more widely in Israel's public and economic life.

The foregoing comments mention two extreme points in the range of Jewish cultural–religious attitudes in Israel, and two positions that are more moderate. Viewed in this manner these attitudes or cultural–religious orientations reflect the distinct pluralism of Israel society. There are, of course, many more forms of Jewish cultural orientation in Israel in addition to the few mentioned here.

In Israel, Jews from all of the great variety of origins and persuasions intermingle and affect each other, which is distinctly less true for the Jews in the Diaspora. The categories of Jewish cultural-religious orientation mentioned above do not imply that these groups are static and permanent. Israel is certainly a society in flux, and the direction of this dynamic process is not always predictable. Nor does the numerical composition of different subgroups necessarily point to the direction of change. Demography is only one variable affecting Israel's cultural–political –social development.

The Post-Zionists' Pluralism

The phenomenon of cultural pluralism in Israel among Jewish groups is not the ideology advocated by some PZ writers. They focus on the political status of the Muslim population in Israel and in Judea and Samaria, as a collectivity, including their culture and religion. PZs want Israel to grant political and cultural power to the Arabs who live under its jurisdiction. Recall that Christians and Christianity are not prominent in the social–political fabric of Israel due to the miniscule number of Christians who reside in Israel. In some measure, the small number of Christians in present-day Israel stems from persistent Muslim persecution of Jews and Christians in Palestine over the past few centuries that led many Christians to leave the region. Many Christians now living in Israel are Arabs or Arabized Christians.

Jews and Arabs in Israel co-exist, co-operate and function constructively in several walks of life, such as commercial and professional activities. For example, Muslim physicians abound in Israel's hospitals, though Jewish physicians are not to be found in hospitals located in exclusively Arab populations such as Gaza, Judea, and Samaria. But, the rapprochement existing in these limited arenas of social–cultural life are initiated or maintained by Jews as a natural feature of a democratic society, without being post-Zionist. Muslim society (except in Turkey) does not tolerate equal participation of Jews and Arabs in the occupational elites, or at any level for that matter, unless the Jews acknowledge the superiority and dominance of Islam (Ye'or, 2002). Pluralism is not part of the vocabulary of Islam or of Muslim society anywhere, in or outside of Israel. Indeed, it is renounced by the Koran and runs counter to Islamic principles that divides the world into *dar el-Islam* and *dar el-harb*. Muslims in the nations dominated by Islam are "those who reside in Islam" (dar el-Islam). Non-Muslims and non-Islamic nations are all *dar el-harb,* i.e. people who reside in parts of the world that must be subjugated and converted to Islam by "the sword" when the opportunity arises (Huntington, 1996; Ye'or, 2002). Islam displays tolerance toward non-Islamic nations on a temporary basis only for political expediency.

Muslims and all non-Jewish citizens in Israel have always possessed complete civil liberties, as well as a separate, strictly Muslim school system, newspapers, municipal Arab government, and so forth as they themselves wish – the adopted system is *not* due to segregation. What must not be overlooked is that the goal of Islam is to regain all territory that was ruled by Islamic power at any time in the past, as well as to expand its rule over non-Muslim nations. Israel falls under the category of "lost" territory that Muslims are required by Islam to reconquer.

On the Jewish side, PZs in Israel want to extend Muslim rights to the arena of ethnic politics that would give Arabs as a group equal influence in the governance of Israel. They wish to invoke a model of democracy found in the large multinational nations of Australia, Canada and the United States, and not the model of ethnic democracy typical of most nations in Western and Eastern Europe. The present political system in Israel always included ethnic-Arab political parties. That arrangement produces legislative and governmental anomalies that would not be tolerated in most democratic nations. A parallel situation in other countries would mean, for example, that Finns would give equal political rule to Russian immigrants in Finland, Swedes to Somalians in Sweden, Danes to the Germans in Denmark, Germans to the Turks or other Muslim groups in Germany, Czechs to the Slovaks in the Czech Republic and so forth. In pre-World War II Poland, Jews once had a political party. Apart from that, no country where Jews resided, even in their millions, contemplated allowing Jews to have an ethnic political representation in the legislative bodies. Political arrangements of that kind in the ethnic-national democracies would spell their early death. None of the democratic ethnic-nation states are inclined to commit suicide. Similarly, collective political equality for the Arabs in Israel's government would mean the end of Israel as a Jewish nation. No guessing is needed about the future of Israel if its government would be shared with the Arabs: The behavior of the Arab members of the Knesset is more than adequate testimony as to how dangerous a trap that is for Israel Jewry.

After a short history of only 54 years, the State of Israel and the Jewish People are forced to direct attention and resources to an ever-wider internal struggle against the post-Zionist Jews who are a distinct but vocal minority in the Jewish population at large, and who seek to undo Jewish national self- determination in Israel achieved at such a high price. And all the while there is Israel's need for constant vigilance regarding the external threats from various Arab groups and nations, and from Arabs residing within Israel's borders since its inauguration (Israeli, 2002). The European organizations and nation states have willing and ready allies in Israel in the post-Zionists. Indeed, during the past few years the European Union has brazenly paid the monthly salary, or made substantial contributions to fund the activities, of Jewish politicians in Israel who identify with the European anti-Zionist political position. The Arabs oppose Israel's existence, and the EU nations are willing to sacrifice Israel to maintain their status, politically and economically, with the Arab nations.

The opposition to Jewish nationhood in Israel certainly includes people whose views may derive in part from an ideology of transnationalism or global citizenship, and even from neo-Marxist ideas **(see chapters 4, 6 and 7)**. Yet, many of Zionism's antagonists, especially Europeans, do not necessarily have a stake in ideas connected to the remaking of the world's political order. They can be devoted to particularistic nationalisms completely disinterested in the notion, current in some academic or political circles in the West, that the nation-state be disbanded altogether (**see chapter 7**; Hazony, 2002). Those who subscribe to that view would naturally belong to the post-Zionist camp, but the opponents of Israel, particularly in the EU nations, are not limited to supporters of the transnationalist idea.

Of central concern here is the conscious identification of Jews in Israel with the Arabo-centered and Europe-oriented opposition to Israel as *the* Jewish state. The PZ ideology expresses an Arabo-centered view and advocates the transformation of Israel's national identity from a Jewish nation to "a multi-cultural . . . nation of all its citizens" that would replace its present Jewish national identity. The distinct impression is that PZs are either unaware of, or indifferent to: (1) the ultimate goal of the Islamic world to return the territory of Israel to its sovereignty; and (2) the vast anti-Semitic activities of the Arab Palestinians in Europe, the United States, and, of course, in the many committees and commissions of the United Nations, along with its direct terrorist activities against Israeli Jews. Are the Jewish PZs consciously contributing to the dissemination of virulent anti-Jewish hatred in the world through the agency of the Arabs, Palestinians or otherwise? Could it be that they really don't care that the hatred they fuel is genocidal in depth and scope as Arabs at all levels and from all quarters, with a few notable exceptions, affirm repeatedly and unhesitatingly?

The PZ ideology that adopts the Arab "narrative" and treats Zionism as a collection of myths is far more extreme than anything Ahad Ha'am conceived of when he wrote so incisively about Jewish self-abnegation (*hitbatlut*) in his famous essay (1893) *Imitation and Assimilation* (Ahad Ha'am, 1949, 86–9). Unfortunately, the phenomenon that Ahad Ha'am wrote about over a hundred years ago has continued to accompany the Jewish People. As the generations since the Emancipation march on, Jewish assimilation becomes more profound and incurs into many more realms of life and thought than was observed in the past. Few Jews who believed in the national-historical rejuvenation of Jewry as a collectivity could have anticipated that their descendants, just one or two generations later, would succumb to such a deep and encompassing rejection of their own people as we are witnessing in the post-Zionist ideology.

Jewry's Alleged Moral Culpability

A cornerstone of the PZs claims against Zionism and Israel is what is presented as a moral argument that are said to be the "reasons" for their position. They argue that, since Jews have extensive experience as victims, we enjoined to be singularly sensitive to the displacement and suffering of others. The post-Zionist and Arab view is that Israel "caused" the Arab refugee problem during the 1948 war, and displaced large numbers of Arabs from their homes. Their argument is that Israel bears moral responsibility for the fate of the Arab refugees that constitute a large part of the Palestinian Arabs now located in Judea, Samaria and Gaza, as well as in Lebanon, Jordan and other neighboring countries, where they remain in refugee camps. The PZs wish to redress this moral blight not only by supporting the establishment of an new Arab nation on the soil of Judea, Samaria and Gaza, but also by de-Judaizing and de-Zionizing Israel and transforming it into a bi-national state governed by Arabs and Jews (Segev, 2001; reviewed by Halkin, 2002).

In pre-state Israel and even afterward for some time, the pro-communist left-wing Zionist group called Hashomer Hatsair (The Young Guard) advocated the very same idea of the bi-national state. In 1953 David Ben-Gurion roundly and publicly denounced them (Yariv, 1953) for their communist-Soviet leanings that he clearly perceived as an act of treason. The spiritual offspring of Hashomer Hatsair, educated in its kibbutzim and youth groups, continue to carry its ideological banner today. Not a few of the historians and authors of belle lettres in Hebrew who are among the more articulate spokesmen of the PZ ideology spent their childhood and youth in the schools of Hashomer Hatsair. Nevertheless, the lineage pf post-Zionist ideology is primarily anti-Jewish and anti-Zionist, not communist.

Another dimension to the moral claim made by PZs is their perception of Israel's current conflict with the Arab Palestinians as an act of "occupation." Even Zionist supporters of the Left decry the "occupation" of Judea and Samaria as the root of all evil in Israel's relations with the Arab Palestinians (Gorni, 2002).

The validity or non-validity of these notions of Israel's "guilt" have been argued and debated at great length in the media, in numerous books and articles, and in the political arena. Whatever position is taken on these issues, they are not the "reasons" for the positions taken by the PZ writers and organizations. They are the consequences or symptoms, not the causes, of post-Zionism. Admittedly, the causes or reasons for social-political phenomena are not easily established with certainty. But even a cursory glimpse of Jewish history over the past century reveals unequivocally that anti-Zionism emerged long before any of the wars that Israel as a nation fought against the Arabs. Historically and legally there is no foundation whatsoever for the assertions of short-sighted dissidents that Israel's policies of "occupation," anywhere in the entire territory called Palestine before 1948, had any causal effect on the emergence of anti-Zionist thinking, including the post-Zionists.

Why the Emergence of Post-Zionist Ideology?

The natural question to be asked here is, why? *Why* have Jews in the Jewish state turned against Zionism and why do they want to destroy the Jewish identity of Israel? How did such a state of affairs come about? And so quickly in the history of the country!

It is not really reasonable to expect an answer to that question at this time. Perhaps some day someone will have the knowledge needed to provide a reply. What can be suggested here are some hypotheses that have gained currency among observers of the Israel social-political scene. It goes without saying that the ideas expressed here are not based on information about any specific person. We relate to a social-political phenomenon, not to individuals. Readers who seek information about the background and outlook of several outstanding PZ writers and activists in Israel are referred to other publications (Lord, 2000; Shiloah, 1991) in addition to the chapters in this book.

Some Hypotheses about the Reasons for Post-Zionist Ideology

Consequences of persecution

One "explanation" of the post-Zionist phenomenon is the long-term pathogenic effects of the unspeakable persecution of the Jews for most of their 1,800 years in Exile (*Galut*) in Christian and Muslim countries. Whatever justice there is in the objection that Jewry presents itself too often in the role of victim (or what one scholar liked to call "the lachrymose history of the Jews"), the blood-curdling affliction of the Jews for close to two millennia is a monumental fact of our history. To diminish the significance of that fact is far more destructive than to recall it. PZ historians and writers who advise Israel's educational system to downplay the Holocaust in the relevant school programs, intentionally or inadvertently promote a mixture of national amnesia and callousness to Jewish suffering; it arouses serious questions about their motives. The only rationale for this misguided advice is that the PZs believe studying about Jewry's extraordinary but often-horrendous past as a People would damage young people's mental health. The consequences of this egregious error on the part of the PZs is to foster apathy and alienation that are far worse than any pain or bewilderment temporarily experienced by students in an educational environment.

The twentieth century probably was the most horrifying of the past eighteen centuries in terms of anti-Semitism, but by far not unprecedented from the point of view of the planned and systematic infliction of suffering on the Jews. No other nation in the world was ever accused of killing God, or singled out by two of the major religions in the world (Christianity and Islam) for relentless condemnation and frequent persecution over so many centuries (1,600 years in the case of Christianity, 1,400 years – and still in progress – in the case of Islam).

The Nazi genocidal attack on the Jews was also unparalleled. The Nazis imprinted on history the lesson that it is not merely "difficult" to be a Jew, as the Yiddish saying goes, but downright frightening. The Jews are – and I speak as a Jew who is genuinely horrified by the current situation – an endangered species **(see chapter 9)**. Isn't it the better side of prudence to reduce to a minimum those obvious features of Jewish existence that express Jewry's particularity, such as its history, religion, national identity, its flag, national anthem, and perhaps-one of these days – even its three to four millennium-old language reborn and revitalized during the past two-and-a-half centuries? The Jews of Berlin were recently (summer, 2002) warned not to appear in public wearing clothes that easily identify them as Jews. Shouldn't Israel recoil from confronting challenges to our national security, from the terrible need to fight and kill our enemies who want to occupy our land and murder our citizens in the street? Shouldn't Israel relinquish the fundamental requirements of national integrity that involve our embroilment in armed conflict with the Arabs or whoever else seeks our destruction? Isn't Israel's military operation against Arabs the outgrowth of a misled desire for revenge, instead of the result of carefully considered policy? Even if we were to ignore the transnational "wave of the future" and not disband in favor of world citizenship, it is believed by PZs that Jewish nationality itself subjects us to unfathomable hostility. In effect, that is what Nazism proved, they say, and we Jews should heed the "lessons" of history. The world can hardly tolerate Jewish national independence, and we must beware of not provoking violent retaliation against Jewish chutzpah (Dershowitz, 1988). The Jews play a major role, perhaps a determining one, in arousing anti-Semitism. Assimilation of Jews as individuals and as a nation is the preferred solution, not assertion of our national independence. That is the message of Israel's PZ and Leftist groups, a message that has not changed in essence over the past two hundred years.

Jewish assimilation

Another "explanation" invoked here is that PZ ideology actually emerged with the advent of Zionism itself over a hundred years ago. The only feature really new about PZ notions today is that there is a Jewish independent nation against which they can direct their animosity, whereas before 1948 the object of anti-Zionist opposition was a loosely organized entity called the Zionist Organization.

The opposition to Zionism within Jewry over the past century derived first and foremost from Jews' assimilation into non-Jewish society and culture, accompanied by a near-total lack of knowledge of, or attachment to, Jewish historical tradition and culture. From the middle of the eighteenth century, Jews in Western Europe, and about a half-century later Jews in Eastern Europe, became deeply immersed in their non-Jewish environment to the extent that Jewish national re-awakening constituted an objectionable anomaly or a threat to their social–cultural–national assimilation (Kaufmann, 1932).

With few exceptions (Kaufmann, 1932, 1936), hardly anyone anticipated the inevitability and scope of Jewry's assimilation in the Diaspora. In recent years intermarriage between Jews and non-Jews in the United States has risen to over 53 percent from 6 or 7 percent after World War II. By all accounts, intermarriage will increase and gradually decimate the

Jewish population in Europe as well as in North and South America who remain outside of self-insulated ghettoes. Jewry in other countries will soon follow, unless their present path of assimilation is blocked by a huge tide of anti-Semitism, the harbingers of which might be visible now. As is well known, even such events ultimately will not eliminate, or even moderate, Jewish assimilation because it is the near-inevitable consequence of modernism and of the modern nation-state ever since the end of the eighteenth century.

European Jewry played out that entire drama just before and between the two world wars prior to the emergence of Nazism. The unfolding of Jewish life in the United States today is a recapitulation of the same scenario. The actors and location have changed (the new ones barely aware, if at all, of historical precedent), but the process remains the same. Most Jews and all decent people believe that it is unlikely – or unthinkable – that American Jewry will meet its "end" in any manner resembling the fate of European Jewry. That does not negate the fact that European Jewry was well on its way to massive and far-reaching assimilation until the rise of Nazism, and that the course of pre-Holocaust Jewish history in nineteenth- and early twentieth-century Europe provides a historical precedent for basing a prediction about the future of American Jewry.

There can be little doubt that assimilation, in all its varied manifestations, constitutes the single most potent threat to Jewish life everywhere in the modern world, including its effects on the Jews of Israel. Assimilated Jews were a natural reservoir of opponents to Zionism, since their primary goal was the fullest possible acceptance by the non-Jewish environment. The Jewish People as a historical–ethnic nation, and its entire cultural–religious tradition, ceased to be of interest or concern to them. Indeed, Jewry's stubborn survival as a collectivity was distasteful to many Jews and non-Jews, for one reason or another, such as: the need of many Jews to parade their allegiance to the country in which they live to prove their patriotism, hatred of Jews due to their damnation by the Catholic, Orthodox, Anglican etc. churches as deicidal, and numerous other "reasons," bizarre or otherwise. Some Jews even became deeply ashamed of being Jewish and tried to deny their identity in a variety of ways, even if it meant harming other Jews (as occurred so horribly during the Communist Revolution in Russia), intermarriage and, in extreme cases, conversion to Christianity (in Germany prior to World War I, for example) or suicide.

What is surprising to some Jews today is the extent to which not a few native Israelis (whose number may exceed 25 percent of the Jewish population), born and educated in a Jewish society, are profoundly assimilated and have very limited knowledge of, or sense of identification with, the

Jewish People and the nation of Israel. Their education, family life, cultural interests and total indifference to Jewish religious tradition, partake of Western modernist materialist-technological culture, although in many non-Western countries, adoption of modernism did not necessarily replace local culture and national identity (Huntington, 1996).

A glaring manifestation of Jewish assimilation among the intelligentsia is the sad fact that Israel's literary creations, social and public life, largely ignore the vast historical–cultural heritage of the Jewish People. Israeli literature, for adults and children, theatre, certainly the few motion pictures produced here, and many other dimensions of cultural life, hardly make reference to the vast expanse of Jewish life and letters – of all kinds– dating from the past 1,600 years. Students in school learn precious little about their heritage from all of those centuries, and what they do learn is quickly engulfed by the mass of popular western trivia that pervade the media, music and the movies. No Western nation lived through such a long and complex history. Jewry's continuous and extraordinary literary–cultural productivity during all of its 3,000 years of history is legion compared to that of any other nation, even to those of relatively shorter history – without detracting one iota from the monumental cultural products of many nations.

From a cultural point of view, many Israelis today, and academics foremost among them, seem to be living examples of the long-discarded theory of the mind as a *tabula rasa*: One of the oldest nations is beginning to suffer from a short memory. That is one of the truly tragic consequences of assimilation. It proclaims out loud the decay of Jewry's collective identity that concerned Jews must hear and take to heart **(chapters 10 and 11)**.

The concentration of academics in the post-Zionist camp is not altogether as strange a phenomenon as it might seem. Academics frequently emerge from a background of extensive Jewish assimilation into the non-Jewish world even if they live in Israel **(chapter 3)**. Academics and artists often receive their higher education outside of Israel, and are intensely concerned with being accepted in artistic or academic circles around the world. They are also focused on subjects that, with a few exceptions, are of an international character and bear no essential relation to Jewish historical–national culture. Their birth and early education in Israel provides them with the same shallow roots in Jewish historical culture as it does for most of the citizens. But, since they occupy relatively prestigious social status in Israel, their opinions and judgments are given special hearing in the media, although their expertise may have little or nothing to do with Jewish culture, religion or political life.

Academics serve as cultural spokesmen because they teach and write a great deal. Their views occupy a significant portion of the books and articles published by Israeli Jews in and outside of Israel. Those publications create the impression that the opinions of university instructors and researchers, a majority of who belong to Left-wing political parties, dominate the ideological–cultural scene in the country (**chapter 3**). Publication, by definition, provides authors with a relatively wide audience. The authors of the chapters in this book attribute no small degree of influence on Israel society to the post-Zionists, far beyond their actual numbers.

Occasionally this influence may have some effect on election results, but the outcome of national elections is subject to so many social–historical factors that there can be no one-to-one correspondence between the prevailing political orientations of academics and the outcome of elections. Nevertheless, the assessment of the authors gathered in this volume, who are themselves veteran academics, is that the persistent and strident criticism of Zionism and Israel by post-Zionist writers from a variety of disciplines threatens to undermine the future status and strength of Israel as a Jewish nation.

But there is more to the assimilation of Jews in Israel than can be related to the Leftists academics, their background, goals or attitudes. Their assimilationist positions and values do not account for the post- or anti-Zionist ideas and notions of non-academic, native-born Jews in Israel. Obviously, a negativistic approach to Zionism cannot be attributed to being brought up in a non-Jewish environment outside Israel, although clearly the assimilated background of many Jews who came to Israel in the previous generation, and lately as well, cannot be ignored. Their culture, views, behavioral patterns, values and so forth certainly exerted an enormous effect on their children and grandchildren. Israel Jewry cannot easily shrug off the deep social–historical–cultural assimilation of a not negligible portion of its citizens. No matter how much of an effort was, or could be, made by Israel's system of public education, it is doubtful if it could counteract the impact of the students' family life, interaction with like-minded peers, and the cultural milieu that prevails in public institutions. Add to that the fact that the educational system cannot really be "accused" of having made such an effort. Surely it is our sacred duty to try to educate Israel's youth as Jews, but factors such as threats to security and huge immigration demanded the nation's attention during its still-short history. Apparently they have sidetracked Israel from dealing effectively with the challenges to its historical–cultural–religious identity.

Finally, an important factor affecting Jewry's assimilation within Israel is its need to be accepted as a nation by other nations, in the face of a great deal of animosity on the part of quite a few nations, in addition to the Arab countries. Many Jews born in Israel appear to believe that they must behave and believe as do citizens of other countries if Israel as a nation is to be accepted by, i.e. assimilate into, the "family of nations" as they conceive it to be. Again, attitudes of this kind certainly are consistent with a transnational political agenda, as Fonte **(chapter 7)** argued. But there is also the enormous appeal of the United States as the Western world's dominant economic power and leading democracy that sets the value agenda for young secular Israelis with weak roots in their own history and traditions. How does a national education system teach national –cultural–religious particularistic orientations when the country as an entity appears to value the imitation of the United States as a social–cultural model, and not only as a political one (Schweid, 1996)? Indeed, after an initial hiatus of some years prior to and immediately following the establishment of Israel, it has been caught in the same powerful process of assimilation that overcame Diaspora Jewry since the late eighteenth century. The assimilative orientation into the non-Jewish world that tens of thousands of Jews who came to Israel brought with them has enveloped a large portion of the population.

Assimilation and Jewish national sovereignty

One of the more profound and often ignored consequences of Jewish assimilation is that some Jews today actually consider the exercise of sovereignty by Jews in Israel as reprehensible. Jews must observe a code of ethics practiced nowhere else in the world that certain elites consider to be absolutely beyond all moral reproach. Those "ethics", unremarkably, are unacceptable to all other nations **(see chapter 6)**. Many Jews in our day, in and outside of Israel, have internalized the basic existential condition of Jewry in the Disapora, a condition that is the very essence of *Galut*, of Exile itself, namely permanent lack of political power and control of the territory in which they live. Jews in the *Galut* were prevented from ruling any territory by their minority status and lack of power. That monumental fact is Zionism's point of departure (Ben-Gurion, 1959/1944). But beyond that, after hundreds of years in the Exile, the Jewish People actually relinquished any aspiration to become rulers of territory anywhere in the world except for the Land of Israel. The decisive prevalence of that view is amply demonstrated by the fact that Jews did not colonize territory anywhere with an aim to proclaiming it their homeland even when that territory was relatively unoccupied and open to conquest and control (Kaufmann, 1932). Eventually, after a thousand years of not having a country, Jewry's hope for recovering its lost homeland was completely etherialized and relegated to the realm of Divine intervention. Earthly beings were forbidden to contemplate any action directed at hastening the time when that prayed-for day would arrive. At

Napoleon's convocation of a "Sanhedrin" in 1805, he was given satisfactory assurances that the Jews had no serious interest in ever returning to Palestine to restore their soverignty there, and that whatever Jews prayed for was exlusively related to an other-worldy domain. Jewish devotion to prophetic and rabbinic morality was, for Jews and gentiles alike, a "safe and harmless" occupation that did not impinge on the real world of national power and hence did not threaten either group. That domain of religious values could easily substitute for earlier dreams of national restoration, propelled by either messianic or human intervention.

Jewry's condition of Exile as a minority everywhere implies that Jews are always part of a non-Jewish political entity. As noted, the Jews eventually adopted the view, contrary to Jewish religious tradition up to the end of the tenth century at least, that Jews should not wield political power! In the nineteenth century and afterwards, some Jews developed the doctrine that poltical sovereignty contradicts their historic role in the Diaspora as a "spiritual" entity, a nomadic church group, whose essence consists of disseminating the moral message of the Biblical prophets. That view underwent many transformations over the past two hundred years, from the assertion of Reform Jewry in the nineteenth and early twentieth century of the Jewish "mission" to spread morality, to the utopianism expressed, particularly in Germany, by scholars, rabbis and thinkers such as Moritz Gudeman, Franz Rosenzweig, Martin Buber and their colleagues. Sovereignty as a national entity collides with any utopian vision of morality. It inevitably entails the use of some forms of coercion required by the process of governance, as is explicitly provided for in all constitutions or basic laws of Western democratic nations.

In Israel today, post-Zionists' opposition to Jewry's governance of Israel has assumed the guise of political criticism claiming alleged "excesses" by the Israel government in its treatment of Arabs. These so-called excesses, frequently based on gross distortions (Halkin, 2002; Zangen, 2002), include what other nations view as accepted military actions that must be taken by any government that makes an effort to defend its population from dangerous criminals and enemies who threaten them. That is certainly true in the case of Israel whose enemies have repeatedly declared their intention and unswerving devotion to the goal of killing Jews in, and outside of, Israel. Clearly, the post-Zionists cannot acquiesce to the existence of a normal Jewish government.

By contrast, Zionism stands for the affirmation of Jewish sovereignty in its own land where, eventually, it was hoped, we would witness the emergence of "the new Jew." That phrase has been woefully misinterpreted and bandied about in a grotesque way. The expression "a new Jew" as one who will grow out of the Zionist experience meant, first and foremost, the Jew who values and supports Jewry's national sovereignty in its historic homeland, whatever may be his/her convictions in other domains of religion and culture. The concept of "the new Jew" did not imply being a radical secularist or a devoted Marxist who opposes Jewish national independence, contrary to what some groups preached. The contemporary rejection of Jewish sovereignty by post-anti-Zionists is a regressive notion suggesting that Jews return to the "status-quo-ante," before sovereignty was reclaimed by the Zionist enterprise and the nation of Israel. As such, the post-Zionist agenda is not, and cannot provide, a map for Jewish existence into the future. By definition, it is an arid, nihilistic position. As yet, the damage it will cause before it withers cannot be foreseen.

The psychology of identification with the aggressor

Another approach to explaining PZs' antagonism toward their country and People is psychological. That view stresses the Freuds' (Sigmund and his daughter Anna) notion of "identification with the aggressor" as a mechanism for defending oneself against the deeply distressing realization that people actually hate you and that you are not likely to change their opinion, whatever you might do **(chapter 8)** (Dor-Shav, 1997). By means of this mental mechanism, people perceive their oppressors' behavior as justified. The *victims* must be doing something terribly wrong to deserve the suffering imposed on them. A few Israelis, most notably academics, support the Arab Palestinians against Israel, including the suicide bombers, as a morally defensible mode of resistance to what they and the Arabs consider to be Israeli oppression of the Arabs in Judea, Samaria and Gaza.

The anti-Israel ideologists and activists in Israel rationalize the death and suffering of their own people, wrought by the Arab "uprisings" as they are misleadingly called, or by Arab resistance for the past 80 years to Jewish control of Palestine/Israel. Ultimately, say these Jewish and non-Jewish critics of Israel, the Arabs' war against the Jews and Israel will bring about an acceptance of the Arabs' justified demands. Israel must abandon the use of force against the Arabs and negotiate a peace settlement that takes their claims as a point of departure, instead of the "Zionist narrative" of Jewry's return to its mythical homeland.

"Identification with the aggressor" makes it possible for the post-Zionists to preach Israel's disarmament in the face of attack by its enemies, or, at the very least, to stop fighting the Arabs precisely because Israel possesses a powerful army! There are probably some US citizens who argue that their country should not attack the al-Qaeda terrorists because their military might is much weaker than the power of the US Army, but few if any permit themselves to utter such notions in public lest they be justly ridiculed.

Arab pressure

The Arab nations have maintained many forms of warfare against Israel and the Jews for the past eight decades, political, military, economic, religious and psychological. (The nature of the discussion here leads me to disregard Islam's war against the Jews for the past fourteen centuries.) That war has gained in vehemence and ruthlessness during the past three decades in particular. It has been argued, for example, that, given such relentless pressure, gradual acceptance by some Jews of the Arab perspective and claims is predictable and perhaps inevitable.

Arab pressure on Israel and on Jews has been sustained to the point where it has already entered the history books, even those written by authors who make a point of noting that they do not attribute much significance to Israel or to the Jews in terms of world events (Huntington, 1996). The flames of European anti-Zionism and anti-Semitism have been fanned by the Arabs and by those Christian clergy and churches who adopted the views of Islam and the Arab Palestinians hostile to Israel and the Jews (Israeli, 2002; Ye'or, 2002). In recent decades, Arab and Muslim political views have received a decided increase in support from many nations and groups who are pillars of Western society, or at least they were for a long time. Given the enormous weight of the Arab nations in the UN General Assembly that stems directly from the sheer number of Arab and Muslim nations who are members of the United Nations, plus the added weight of the EU countries whose strategic and economic interests appear to dictate their support of the Arab nations, the pro-Arab stance of the UN and its leadership is to be expected. This course of development not only coincides with Europe's interests in the Arab countries, it is also a direct continuation of its own history of anti-Semitism for hundreds of years.

A reminder of Arab political power and influence in the world political arena appeared in Kofi Anan's announcement on TV, broadcast worldwide (August 2002), that denounced Israel's alleged massacre of civilians during its battle with PLO and Hamas gunmen in Jenin, Samaria (April 2002). The "whole world can't be wrong" in its condemnation of Israel, said Mr. Anan. Not so strangely, the Nobel laureate for "peace" did not publicly retract his hastily concocted denunciation of Israel, even after the publication of the UN report to the effect that the Arab claim of a massacre was groundless. Remarkably, "the whole world" that Kofi Anan invoked *was* wrong because truth had nothing to do with that accusation in the first place.

Given that "Israel bashing" of this kind, and irresponsible inflammatory statements by UN and EU politicians and functionaries, have become an international pastime that serves the demands and pressure exerted by the Arab nations, what can be expected from dissidents within Israel, including sociologists, historians, novelists, and others? To accuse Israel of horrid crimes is, it seems, to be on the side of the (UN's and EU's) angels. At least, so says one view of the post-anti-Zionist position.

Each one of the "explanations" mentioned above of the emergence of the PZ ideology in Israel can suffice to produce what psychologists and scholars of Jewish history and society call Jewish self-hatred (Eidelberg, 1994; Gilman, 1986; Kaufmann, 1936, 1952; Stav, 1998) **(see chapter 9)**. The "reasons" mentioned here function together to affect contemporary Jewry in Israel and elsewhere in the world. They portray a powerful array of external and internal forces aligned against Jewry that can account for no small portion of the phenomenon of PZ ideology. Jewry's or Israeli's reactions to these forces might serve to support survival under different circumstances, such as trying to avoid conflict with various groups or nations, or to make far-reaching compromises with Arab entities of one kind or another, are often so overladen with assimilationist intentions and goals that they become destructive of Jewry's best interests.

What needs no further proof is the singularly negative nature of Jewish anti-Zionism and anti-Israelism. This degree of negativism and destructiveness is without parallel in any of the anti-nationalist groups that have emerged in other nations. Nowhere on earth does a large portion of a nation's intelligentsia and their followers publicly and proudly oppose and denounce the existence of their own country and People, and advocate that its People hand over its national territory and power to some other group, whoever they may be. That is the unique, unparalleled and unprecedented message of post-Zionism that only the unique, unparalleled and anomalous history of the Jewish People can possibly explain.

Zionism Fosters Jewish Unity

The preceding discussion might create the impression that Zionism is a center of contention among Jews. PZ ideology would have us believe not only that Zionism has created dissension within the Jewish people, but also that, for all intents and purposes, it is almost dead and buried. Quite the opposite is true. Despite the dissension focused on Zionism by PZ and

European anti-Semites and regimes, it is fair to observe that Zionism is the most important unifying force to operate in Jewish life over the past century. Alongside the manifestations of post-anti-Zionism within the Jewish People, other Jewish groups of ideological or religious orientations once hostile to Zionism have accepted Zionism and its embodiment in Israel as the central organizing principle of Jewish collective existence. It certainly has come to be viewed by what might be a majority of Jews as the outstanding vehicle for Jewish survival into the future. Indeed, Zionism has fostered an almost unprecedented realignment of Jewish affiliation wherever Jews reside, along with the phenomenon of Jews who remain stridently critical of, or indifferent to, Israel.

No one contends that Zionism was or is free of failures and shortcomings. Many Zionists agree that some important features of Zionist thought and activity in the Jewish state must be corrected or fundamentally changed **(chapters 4 and 6)**. There is near consensus that Zionism must re-examine its negativistic critique of the role of religious tradition and of Jewry's history in the Exile (*Galut*) during the 1800 years between the destruction of the second Temple and the re-establishment of Jewish national independence in Israel. That recognition does not affirm an acceptance of Jewish life in the *Galut* (Schweid, 1983, 1996). Continued and deepened assimilation heads the list of severe challenges to Jewish life in the Diaspora, but it is not the only item on that list. Nor does the need for rethinking Zionist principles acknowledge that Jewish life outside of the Jewish nation of Israel can be equally creative and constructive in terms of Jewry's future compared to the return of Jewry to its national homeland and independence, as Zionism has always taught. A scholar who will remain unnamed here has often said "Jewish life/identity in the Diaspora is a hobby for the Jews. Only in Israel is it a full-time occupation."

Notwithstanding the insistence on Jewish national independence as a *sine qua non* for Jewish survival, historically and culturally, Israel's *cultural* task has hardly been undertaken as yet. Jewry in Israel has known several truly great writers and scholars of Judaic–Hebrew letters, who lived and worked during a good part of the twentieth century. They made monumental contributions to Jewish–Hebraic–Zionist culture. Political and cultural Zionism always complemented each other and were not at loggerheads as was commonly thought (Roth, 1949). The majority of the extraordinary writers, poets and scholars of the first seventy years of the twentieth century were devoted to political Zionism despite the extreme Leftists in Palestine/Israel (Dotan, 1996; Lord, 2000; Shiloah, 1991), as well as concentrating on Jewry's cultural rejuvenation. Still, Zionism's cultural goals have certainly not been realized or dealt with seriously on the public level, whatever measures were taken by various organizations or individuals. The education of Israel's youth in terms of maintaining a minimum of Jewish and Zionist historical consciousness demands fundamental rethinking (Schweid, 1983, 1997), as well as extensive programmatic implementation. There is no sign that a major undertaking of this nature is imminent or planned. Israel has not had great educators to ensure the transmission of Jewish historical culture. In the education of its youth as Jews, Israel today is singularly paralyzed, hanging in a limbo that appears to require no less than a miraculous deliverance.

Yet, the unifying influence of Zionism must not be underestimated. Since the end of the eighteenth century, Jewry's long process of cultural assimilation and ideological–religious fragmentation was aided by Jewry's wide geographical dispersion, forming a minority in a large number of independent nations across Europe and the Middle East. As Jewish religious Orthodoxy declined during the nineteenth and for most of the twentieth centuries, many Jews regrouped in a wide range of organizations and/or religious subgroups. Zionism introduced one of the only political–social forces that encompassed broad sections of world Jewry and attracted the commitment of Jews from all walks of life, ideology and religious persuasion. This observation remains valid despite the existence of anti-Zionist groups within Jewry ever since the inception of Zionism itself **(see chapter 1)**. Yet, however much Leftist, post-Zionist academics, writers and ideologues publish their views, and despite the massive support they receive from the media in Israel **(see chapter 5)**, the majority of the Jewish population in Israel still ignores or does not consciously identify with those views.

Jewish life in Israel today has managed to continue its process of demographic-social-economic growth and development, despite its enormous cultural pluralism. The unifying power of external threats alone cannot account for Israel's existence and surprising, sometimes amazing, social cohesion. Only the basic fact of Jewry's historic identity as an ethnic–national–religious–cultural entity, whose political existence was transformed by Zionism from a dispersed People in exile to an independent nation-state, provides the structural scaffolding for Israel's social survival. It is this independent Jewish nation that insists on maintaining its Law of Return that offers immediate citizenship to Jews from all over the world. The Ingathering of the Exiles, the genuine welcoming "home" to Israel of Jews from everywhere and anywhere, will continue to characterize the permanent Zionist foundation of Israel. We predict that, eventually, once the immigrant population has adjusted to its new home, Israel's Zionist past will generate a growing movement among Jews "to return to ourselves" **(chapter 6)**.

References

Ahad Ha'am (1949) *The Collected Works of Ahad Ha'am*. Tel Aviv: Dvir and Hotsaah Ivrit (Hebrew).

Ben-Gurion, David (1994/1959) The imperatives of the Jewish revolution. In A. Hertzberg (ed.), *The Zionist Idea*. New York: Doubleday and Herzl Press, pp. 606–19.

Dershowitz, Alan (1988) Israel: The Jew among the nations. In A. Kellerman, K.

Siehr and T. Einhorn (eds.), *Israel Among the Nations: International and comparative law perspectives on Israel's 50th anniversary*. The Hague: Kluwer Law International, pp. 129–36. Reprinted in *Nativ* 15 (2002) pp. 30–4 (Hebrew).

Dothan, Shmuel (1996) *Reds in Palestine*. Kfar Sava: Shavna Ha-sofer (Hebrew).

Dor-Shav, Netta Cohen (1997) "The peace process:" Pathological aspects. *Nativ* 10, 1–2, pp. 296–8 (Hebrew).

Eidelberg, Paul (1994) *Demophrenia: Israel and the malaise of democracy*. Lafayette, LA: Prescott Press.

Gilman, Sander (1985) *Jewish Self-Hatred*. Baltimore, MA: The Johns Hopkins University Press.

Gorni, Yosef (2002) Left and leftism, nationalism and chauvanism, *Nativ* 15, pp. 85–91.

Halkin, Hillel (2002) Not so fast. *The New Republic* 227, pp. 38–41.

Hazony, Yoram (2002) On the national state : Part 1: Empire and anarchy. *Azure* 12, pp. 27–70.

Huntington, Samuel (1996) *The Clash of Civilizations and the Remaking of World Order*. New York: Simon and Schuster: A Touchstone Book.

Israeli, Raphael (2002) *Arabs in Israel: Friend or Foe*. Jerusalem: Eliyahu Gabbai (Hebrew).

Kaufmann, Yehezkel (1932) *Exile and Alienation*. Tel Aviv: Dvir (Hebrew).

—— (1936) *In the Throes of Time*. Tel Aviv: Dvir (Hebrew).

Liebman, Charles and Don Yehiya, Eliezer (1983) *Civil Religion in Israel*. Berkeley: University of California Press.

Lord, Amnon (1998) *The Israeli Left: From socialism to nihilism*. Tel Aviv: Tammuz (Hebrew).

Roth, Cecil (1949) Introduction. *The Collected Works of Ahad Ha'am*. Tel Aviv: Dvir and Hotsaah Ivrit (Hebrew).

Schweid, Eliezer (1983) *Between Judaism and Zionism: Essays*. Jerusalem: The World Zionist Organization (Hebrew).

Schweid, Eliezer (1996) *Zionism in a Post-Modernistic Era*. Jerusalem: Hasifriah Hazionit – The World Zionist Organization (Hebrew).

Segev, Tom (2001) *Elvis in Jerusalem: The Americanization of Israel*. New York: Metropolitan Books.

Shiloah, Zvi (1991) *Leftism in Israel*. Beit-El: Yaron Golan (Hebrew).

Simon, Ernst (1952) Are we still Jews? *Annual Almanac of Ha'aretz*. Tel Aviv, pp. 97–129 (Hebrew).

Stav, Arieh (1998) *The Israeli Death Wish*. Tel Aviv: Modan (Hebrew).

Yariv, S. S. (1953) (Pen-name for David Ben-Gurion) *On the Communism and*

Zionism of Hashomer Hatsair. Tel Aviv: The Israel Labor Party (Mapai) (Hebrew).

Ye'or, Bat (2002) *Islam and Dhimmitude: Where civilizations collide.* Teaneck, NJ: Farliegh Dickinson University Press.

Zangen, David (2002) Jenin: Seven monstrous lies. *Ma'ariv*, November 8.

The Contributors

The Editor
Shlomo Sharan is Professor Emeritus of Educational Psychology, School of Education, Tel-Aviv University and a member of the board, Ariel Center for Policy Research.

The Contributors
Edward Alexander is Professor of English at the University of Washington in Seattle, Washington, USA, and he served in the past as Professor of English at Tel Aviv University.

Hanan Alexander is Associate Professor, Philosophy of Education, and Head, Center for Jewish Education, School of Education, Haifa University.

David Bukay is Senior Lecturer, Department of Political Science, Haifa University.

Norman Doidge is a practicing psychiatrist and psychoanalyst in Toronto. He teaches at the University of Toronto, Ontario, Canada and at Columbia University, New York.

Raya Epstein received her doctorate in political philosophy at the University of Moscow, and settled in Israel in 1990. She taught at Bar-Ilan University and at several colleges in Israel.

John Fonte is a senior fellow at the Hudson Institute in Washington, D.C., where he also heads the Center for American Common Culture.

Yoav Gelber is Professor and Head, School of History, Haifa University.

Yosef Oren is a free-lance literary critic in Israel, and has published many articles and books Hebrew Literature.

Arieh Stav is editor-in-chief of *Nativ*, a bi-monthly journal of politics and culture in Israel, and is director of the Ariel Center for Policy Research.

Hillel Weiss is Professor of Hebrew Literature, Bar-Ilan University, Israel.

Name Index

Abramovitz, Amnon, 174
Abu-Mazzen, 99, 105
Achilles, 50
Adams, Jerry, 101
Adorno, Theodore, 72
Agamemnon, 50
Agnon, Shmuel Yosef, 37, 222, 224
Ahad Ha'am, 233
Aharonson, Shlomo, 125–6
Aleinikoff, Alexander, 141, 143, 148
Allah, Abu, 99
Alexander, Edward, 9
Alexander, Hanan, 78, 83
Almog, Oz, 26, 30–7
Aloni, Shulamit, 61, 67–8, 103–4, 164
Alterman, Natan, 37
Amir, Eli, 200
Amishai, M., 47–9
Annan, Kofi, 147, 243
Apple Michael, 73
Appelfeld, Aharon, 67
Arafat, Yasser, 61, 63, 87, 89, 93–6,
    99–108, 110, 111, 155–62
King Arthur, 50
A'sfur, Hasan, 105
Assad, Bashar, 103, 112
Avnery, Uri, 164
Avineri, Shlomo, 117, 133–4
Ayalon, Ami, 95

Baer, Yitschak, 37
Bach, Robert, 148
Banks, James, 141
Barak, Aharon, 63
Barak, Ehud, 57, 63, 71, 94, 156
Bartov, Hanoch, 200, 212
Berlowitz, Yaffa, 209
Ben-Yair, Michael, 113
Becker, Yakov, 32
Be'er, Haim, 164
Beilin, Yossie, 104
Begin, Menachem, 59, 65–6, 156

Ben-Dov, Nitza, 221
Ben-Horin, Yitzhak, 109
Ben-Gurion, David, 32, 42, 44, 65–6, 68,
    122, 233, 240
Bentham, Jeremy, 56
Benvenisti, Meron, 58–61
Ben-Yehuda, Baruch, 54
Ben-Yehuda, 26, 54
Ben-Zion, Shimon, 54
Berger, Peter, 118
Berkowitz, Eliezer, 208
Bethell, Tom, 142
Bin-Laden, Osama, 101, 104, 109, 159–60
Broides, Avraham, 54
Bialik, Chaim Nachman, 54
Brunhilde, 50
Buber, Martin, 65–6, 68
Buddha, 50
Bulgakov, Sergei, 129–33
Bukay, David, 93
Butler, David, 90
Bush, George W., 103, 155–7

Cassandra, 9, 50
Cassirer, Ernst, 27, 28, 40, 42
Casey, Lee, 146–9
Ceaser, James, 140
Chamberlain, Neville, 103, 157
Chazan, Naomi, 95
Chomsky, Noam, 66
Clinton, William J., 63
Clutterbuck, Richard, 99
Cohen, M., 71
Collingwood, R. G., 39–40
Crelinsten, Ronald, 91

Dahla, Mohammed, 99
Dayan, Yael, 95
Decter, Midge, 58
Derrida, Jacques, 210
Dinur, Ben-Zion, 54
Don Yehiya, Eliezer, 229

Dor-Shav, Netta, 242
Dotan, Shmuel, 20, 245
Eban, Abba, 173
Eidelberg, Paul, 244
Eldar, Akiva, 104
Engels, Friedrich, 73
Erekat, Saeb, 99
Evron, Boaz, 67

Fabian, Z'ev, 164
Fackenheim, Emil, 53
Fish, Harel, 220
Fonte, John, 6, 240
Freud, Anna, 158, 160, 242
Freud, Sigmund, 242
Friedman, Thomas, 60–1
Fukuyama, Francis, 52–3, 138–9, 152, 213

Gallimore, Timothy, 109
Galtung, Johan, 91
Garzon, Baltazar, 150
Germain, Lord George, 7
Gazit, Shlomo, 174
Gefen, Aviv, 183
Gerber, George, 90
Geyer, Georgie, 148
Giddens, Anthony, 144
Ginzburg, Yitzhak, 164–5
Gil, Avi, 112
Gilead, Amos, 98, 112
Gilman, Sander, 183–4, 244
Giroux, Henri, 73
Glele, Maurice, 147
Golan, Avrima, 211
Goldsmith, Jack, 146
Goodman, Anthony, 136
Gorni, Yosef, 234
Greatz, Nurit, 209
Greenberg, Uri Zvi, 37, 54
Gross, Eyal, 96
Grossman, David, 60–1, 63–4, 68, 161
Gramsci, Antonio, 139
Gross, Eyal, 96
Grossman, Reuven, 54
Gur Ze'ev, Ilan, 72, 73, 74

Haddad, Saad, 108
Haider, Jorg, 67
Halkin, Hillel, 233, 241
Hardt, Michael, 144
Hayek, Fredrich, 117
Hazan, Naomi, 95, 177, 178
Hazaz, Chaim, 37, 188
Hazony, Yoram, 63–9, 142
Hearst, Patricia, 160

Hector, 50
Henkin, Louis, 147–8
Henderson, Wade, 136
Hercules, 50
Herman, Eduard, 90
Herzberg, Arthur, 76
Herzl, Theodore, 3, 41–2, 64, 172, 195, 204
Hoge, Jerome, 90
Horkeimer, Max, 72
Homer, 50
Hoy, David, 73
Huntington, Samuel, 5, 11, 152, 206, 231, 238, 243
Hussein, King, 103
Hussein, Saddam, 110, 155–7, 159, 160

Iley, Karen, 137–8
Inbari, Asaf, 207
Iphigenia, 50
Isaacs, Eric, 11
Isaacs, Rael, 11
Israeli, Raphael, 232, 243

Jibril, Ahmed, 99, 106
Johnston, Philip, 141
Jung, Karl, 217

Kaufmann, Yehezkel, 36–7, 41–2, 51, 54, 172, 236, 240, 244
Karsh, Ephraim, 53, 88
Kasher, Asa, 64, 67
Katzanelson, Berl, 58, 60, 66
Kerber, Linda, 143
Kimmerling, Baruch, 62, 67
Kirkpatrick, Jeanne, 150
Klausner, Alexander, 216
Klausner, Yosef, 216, 223
Klusmeyer, D., 143
Koppel, Ted, 90
Kollek, Teddy, 59
Kurzweil, Baruch, 205, 212

Lamdan, Yitschak, 35–7, 54
Lancelot, 50
Laocoön, 9
Lapid, Tommy, 177
Laurenz, Peter, 101
Leibowitz, Yeshayahu, 59–60, 67
Lewis, Anthony, 58–61
Lewis, Bernard, 106
Liebman, Charles, 229

London, Yaron, 106
Lord, Amnon, 47, 53, 245

Lustick, Ian, 61
Luxembourg, Rosa, 133

Macdonald, Dwight, 56
Magnes, Judah, 66
Mahmid, Hashim, 106
Mannheim, Karl, 117
Maran, Rita, 148
Marcus, Yoel, 104
Margalit, Avishai, 68–9, 70
Margalit, Dan, 113
Meiron, Dan, 224
Marx, Karl, 29, 71ff, 72, 75–6, 78, 118,
    120–2, 124, 133, 171
Mazen, Abu, 99, 105
Mathews, Jessica, 143
McCarthy, Thomas, 73
McLaren, Peter, 73
McLuhan, Marshal, 208
Mcquail, 90
Meged, Aharon, 62, 69, 199
Meir, Golda, 66, 207
Meisels, Moshe, 47–9
    see also Amishai, M.
Merlin (the Magician), 50
Mill, John Stuart, 56–7, 65, 69
Mofaz, Shaul, 103
Montgomery, Louise, 109
Morgenstern, Arie, 208, 211
Morris, Benny, 62, 67, 71, 87,
    126
Moses, 213

Nacos, Brigitte, 90
Nasser, Gammal abed-El, 89
Naveh, Eyal, 71
Ndiaye, Bacre, 147
Netanyahu, Benjamin, 58–9, 63
Nasrallah, Hassan, 106
Negri, Toni, 144
Norris, Christopher, 80
Nussbaum, Martha, 144

Oçalan, Abdullah, 97
Ohana, David, 39
Oren, Yosef, 189
Orwell, George, 57, 64, 69
Oz, Amos, 57, 59–61, 64, 68, 175, 193,
    207, 218–224

Paletz, David, 90
Palme, Olaf, 160
Pappe, Ilan, 62, 67, 87
Peres, Shimon, 24, 57, 62–6, 68, 106, 112,
    142, 161, 183

Peri, Yaacov, 95
Plato, 75
Popper, Karl, 75
Powell, Colin, 155, 157
Priam (King of Troy), 50
Pundak, Ron, 102, 104
Rabin, Yitzhak, 24, 57, 60–2, 156
Rabkin, Jeremy, 146
Radek, Karl, 133
Rajoub, Jibril, 99
Ratosh, Yonatan, 205
Raz, Mussy, 95
Reagan, Ronald, 156
Richard III, 157–8, 160–1
Rieger, Eliezer, 54
Rivkin, David, 146, 149
Robinson, Mary, 136
Roth, Cecil, 245
Rousseau, Jean-Jacques, 117, 133–4
Ruge, Mari, 91

Sagiv, Asaf, 204, 207
Said, Edward, 66, 73
Samet, Gidon, 68
Sarid, Yossi, 61, 110, 111
Savir, Uri, 65
Schleier, Martin, 101
Schmid, Alex, 90
Scholem, Gershom, 57, 222
Schuck, Peter, 148
Schultz, William, 146
Schweid, Eliezer, 49, 62, 115–16, 123,
    227, 240, 245–6
Segev, Tom, 34
Shabbetai Zvi, 46, 107, 218
Sha'ath, Nabil, 99
Shakespeare, William, 157, 161–2
Sh'adeh, Salah, 96
Shalev, Meir, 190, 196, 200
Shalev, Mordechai, 216, 222
Shamir, Moshe, 199
Shamir, Ziva, 224
Shapira, Anita, 212
Shapira, Avraham, 208
Sharan, Shlomo, 124, 208
Sharon, Ariel, 94, 103, 104, 111
Shekhaki, Fathui, 97
Shenhar, Yitschak, 37
Shiloah, Zvi, 20, 25, 234, 245
Shlonsky, Avraham, 54
Shmueli, Ephraim, 33, 54
Siegel, Harvey, 80
Siegfried, 50
Silberstein, Laurence, 74
Simon, Ernst, 229

Smilansky, Yizhar, 34
  see also Yizhar, S.
Sorel, Georges, 28
Sowell, Thomas, 140
Spiro, Peter, 148
Spring, Joel, 140
Stav, Arieh, 244
Steinman, Eliezer, 54
Sternhell, Ze'ev, 59, 71, 74, 104, 128

Talbot, Strobe, 144–5
Talmon, Yakov, 116–23, 133
Tammuz, Binyamin, 193
Taranto, James, 150
Tocqueville, Alexis de, 56
Trotsky, Leon, 56, 133
Tuchman, Barbara, 7, 10, 69
Tudor, Henry, 28–9
Tumarkin, Yigal, 59, 67, 177, 178, 179
Tzalka, Dan, 200

Vilnai, Z'ev, 54

Waltz, Kenneth, 88

Weiss, Hillel, 207, 209, 218, 224
Will, George, 108
Wisse, Ruth, 58
Wistrich, Robert, 39
Wotan, 50
Woolsey, James, 103

Yahav, Dan, 211
Yaniv, Tali, 207
Yariv, S. S., 20, 233
Yizhar, S., 189–92, 200, 209, 210
Yehoshua, A. B., 61, 67, 189, 193–6, 218–
  24
Ye'or, Bat, 7, 11, 35, 42, 76, 124–5, 131,
  231, 234
Yovel, Yakov, 67

Zemah, Adi, 224
Zertal, Irith, 67
Zerubavel, Yael, 26, 45
Zimmerman, Moshe, 67–8, 174
Zinni, Anthony, 103
Zucker, Dedi, 61
Zuckerman, Moshe, 72

Subject Index

Abraham
  as father of the Hebrew nation, 48
  impact on Jewry's collective memory,
    50–1
academics
  concentration in the post-Zionist camp,
    238
androgyny
  Jews and Arabs, 220
  Jewish religion/nation, 219
  see also Jews
Aharon Meged, 213–14
anti-Semitism
  among Israeli intellectuals, 67–8, 126
  among Jewish Bolsheviks in Russia,
    130–2
  Amos Oz on, 175, 222
  anti-Israelism, 119–20
  appearance of Israelis, 177
  as an unsolved problem of Zionism, 43
  aroused by Jews according to post-
    Zionist ideology, 236, 242
  basic characteristics of, 51–2
  can be attributed to post-Zionism, 68
  enhanced by UN equating Zionism with
    racism, 173
  Gilman's theory of, 184–5
  hatred of *Haredim*, 176
  in Muslim world, 76, 130–1
  Israeli army and, 182
  Israel's Jewish population, 173
  Marxism, 172
  Nazi assimilation, 179–80
  Nazi influence of, 130
  post-Zionsim and, 205
  ritual,185
  reawakening in Europe of, 76
  remarks as daily occurence, 165
  revealed in European–Muslim alliance,
    119
  Sergei Bulgakov on, 129–33
  Zionism's failure to terminate, 172

  see also military service; post-
    Zionism/post-Zionists; terrorism;
    Zionism/Zionists
anti-Zionism
  Martin Buber and, 65–6
  three components of Zionism, 87
  university faculty recruited by Judah
    Magnes, 66
  Ze'ev Sternhell's counsel of Arafat, 104
  see also intellectuals, Israeli
apologists, 160
Arab armies, 5–6, 31, 37
Arab narrative, 51–3, 233
  see also post-Zionism/post-Zionists
Arab-Palestinians
  freedom fighters, 128
  "right of return," 104, 105
  oppression of, 82–4
  potential allies among, 129
  supported by majority in UN, 82
  see also suicide bombers; terrorism
Arab-Palestinian leadership
  failure to rectify oppression, 75
  Israeli media on, 99
Arab-Palestinian movement
  fascist meaning/goal of, 102
Arab-Palestinian state
  advocated by post-Zionist intellectuals,
    74
  as a terrorist nation, 10
Arafat, Yasser
  accusations against the West, 158
  advance of goals through terrorism, 109
  Arab leaders' views of, 103
  arch murderer of Jews, 61
  brutality and, 162
  Colin Powell on, 155, 157
  debate over responsibility of, 102
  encouragement of, 95
  "father" of international terrorism, 102,
    104
  human shields and, 96–7, 161

humiliation by Bashar al-Assad, 112
indifference of, 102, 107
"liberation of Palestine," and, 102
Mubarak on, 112
murder of own people by, 102
Hassan Nasrallah and, 106
often revived by the West, 156
prevented from broadcasting a speech,
    112
proclaimed jihad against Jews and
    Israel, 105–6
rearmed by Yitzhak Rabin, 156
removal of, 108
Ron Pundak on, 104
rule by, 107
second chances of, 158
tactics of, 111–12
ties to Iran through Hizbullah, 106
trusted by Shulamit Aloni, 103
value system of, 107
West's attitude towards, 161
assimilation
anti-Semitism
hatred of *Haredim* and, 179
decimation of Diaspora Jewry through,
    236–7
in Israel, 237–40
and Jewish dispersion, 246
inevitability of, 237
Nazi anti-Semitism targets, 179
in pre-Nazi Europe, 237–8
reflecting post-Zionist impulses, 204
as source of anti-Zionism, 236–40
Zionism and, 64
see also anti-Semitism; Lefists in Israel;
    Haredim; post-Zionism/post-Zionists

bisexuality, 220
see also androgyny; Jewish State

Christians
acts against anti-Semitism, 129
numbers in Israel, 230
ritual of the Eucharist and, 185
collective soul
Jung's notion of, 217
cohesiveness, 43–4
conflict, American–European, 149–50
conscience
Freud on, 158
and justice, 156–7
tyrants' will and, 159
continuity
historical, 2, 39–40

deconstruction/deconstructionism, 39–40
experience and history, 40
of national symbols, 141
nihilistic nature of, 43–4
self-defense and, 210
see also post-Zionism/post-Zionists;
    transnationalism
democracy
Anglo-Saxon model of, 116–17
"deficit" and the European Union, 149
determination of, 149–50
French model of, 116–17
ethnic power-sharing, 140–1
law and international action, 159
link between political messianism and
    totalitarian, 120, 123
meaning of, 151–2
in multi-ethnic nations, 231
replaced by post-Zionists with "ideoc-
    racy," 116
struggle to eradicate Judaism under
    guise of, 125
totalitarian version of, 119
transnationalism and, 151
see also European Union; transnation-
    alism
demographic imperative, 140
dissolution of Israel, 61
discrimination
as Arab slogan, 110
American transnationalists and,
    136
draft see military service
Durban conference on racism
individual freedom in, 138, 139
NGO transnational advocacy in, 136,
    147

education
as indoctrination, 34
Jewish/Israeli, 235
proposals for, 77
universities and, 66
"end of history" notion, 138
attacks on liberal democracy and, 152
Europe, 150
European Union (EU)
American policies of, 151
financial support for post-Zionists, 8–11
financial support for terrorism against
    Israel, 9–14
opponent of Israel, 232
overruling of national parliaments by,
    149
policies promoting victim groups, 149

political correctness, 120–1
popular sovereignty, 150
post-democratic structure of, 149
and post-Zionists, 8–11
tradition of anti-Semitism, 121
transnationalist policies of, 121
see also democracy; transnationalism
exile (Galut)
  Jewry's relinquishment of sovereignty, 240–1
  loss of political power and self-determination, 240
  survival of Jewry, 49

Genesis, Book of, 47–8
governance
  American versus European models of, 152
Grossman, David, 60

Hamas
  battle of Jenin, 243
  Iranian funding of, 107
Haredim (ultra-Orthodox Jews), Haredi
  alleged source of Jewry's calamities, 178
  attire of, 181
  Leftist depictions of, 177
  hatred toward, 163ff, 177, 181
  Hesed-shel-Emet organization, 165
  as parasites, 164ff
  see also anti-Semitism; assimilation; Leftists in Israeli
Hashomer Hatsair, 233
Hebrew, as language of Israel, 4–5
Hebrew literature
  1948 war in, 190
  affect of wars on, 189
  alienation from Zionism, 188–9, 200
  attitude toward Zionism, 197
  concern with Israel's future in, 188
  as conscious process for liberation from Galut, 205
  devotion to Zionism in, 198–200
  linguistic and conceptual traditions in, 205
  justification of Palestinian cause in, 207, 214
  negation of heroes and Israel's self-defense in, 209
  rejection of anti-Zionist message, 200
  see also Zionism
history
  as collection of disparate events, 39–40
  as collection of narratives, 211
historical continuity, 193

historical moralism, and historical materialism, 48
historical record, 50
Hizbullah
  al-Aqsa uprising, 105
  Arafat's relationship with, 106
  see also Arafat, Yasser
Holocaust
  Arab persecution and, 74
  nationalist mythology, 124
  post-Zionist opinion of, 235
  and sabra-centered Zionism, 212

immigration, of Jews to the Land of Israel
  historical, 1, 4, 211
  and sabra identity, 213
incest, 222
"Ingathering of Exiles"
  as Biblical vision, 40
  mention during prayer, 40
  and Messianic vision, 44
  as high priority of Zionism, 43
  and Palestine, 41–2
  post-Zionists' views on, 38–9, 210
  transformation from myth to reality, 42
  see also post-Zionism/post-Zionists
institutional values, 140
intellectuals, Israeli
  Arab propaganda and, 61
  anti-Israelism among, 59
  anti-Jewish character of, 58, 63, 64
  and anti-Semitism, 67
  contempt for "inferior" Jews, 58–60
international law
  as distinct from the "Law of Nations," 146
  versus national constitutions/sovereignty, 146
Islam, 243
Israel, population of, 3–4
Israeli army, 5–6
Israeli literature, 212
  see also Hebrew literature

Jews
  anti-nationalists' perceptions of, 222
  and Gentiles, 221–2
  meta-historic burden of, 207
  post-Zionist view of, 208
Jewish Mother, 223
Jewish State
  as androgynous entity, 219
  challenging accepted definitions of a nation, 38
  majority of world Jewry in, 43

relationship with Israel, 127–8
return to homeland, 80
and war, 191
see also Hebrew literature

Kosovo, 110–11
Leftists, in Israel, 180
  collapse of socialism and Zionism, 173
  condemnation of Judaism by, 125,
    177–8
  condemnation of military personnel by,
    206
  globalism and, 120
  hatred for *Haredim*, 181
  Jewish–Nazi comparison, 174
  opposition to peace process, 173–4
  presentation of Palestinian view by, 161
  radical element of, 205
  utopian universalist religion and, 124–5
  see also anti-Semitism; democracy;
    particularity; transnationalism
Leftist totalitarianism, 117
  danger of, 119
  exclusive truth of, 119
  neglected by Talmon, 119, 122
  see also democracy

Macedonia, 9
Marxism
  against the Jewish People, 125
  Hitler and, 176
  Karl Popper's critique of, 75
  theory of Jews as parasites disproved,
    172
  see also power, fallacy of
media
  in Britain, 101
  exaggeration in, 97
  in France, 101
  images of fanatical Arab terrorists in, 99
  influence on political policymaking, 90
  interviews with Palestinian Authority,
    99
  interviews with terrorists, 101
  in Israel, 90–1, 101
  moral equivalency and, 98
  and Oslo Accords, 107
  portrayal of terrorist killings by, 95
  presentation of terrorists and, 99–100
  profit, 90
  propagation of post-Zionist agenda, 205
  and the public, 108
  role in democracy, 108
  stance on anti-terrorist attacks, 96–7
  as superpower, 90

suppression of alternative opinions, 91
systematic irresponsibility of, 108
terrorism and, 89, 90, 92
after Twin Towers attack, 109
US ethical code for, 108
see also Oslo Accords; terrorism
Messiah complex, 216
Messianic vision
  biblical/ prophetic, 44, 46–9
  as a message of hope, 44–5
  Marxism and, 47
Messianism,
  in the works of Yehoshua and Oz,
    219
  translation of religious life into political
    action, 221
  military service
  resistance to, 94, 95
  Jewish self-hatred and, 182
multiculturalism
  as means for changing US culture,
    140
  as preceding transnationalism, 143
  see also transnationalism
myths
  Cassirer on, 27
  of fallen, 31–2
  as form of symbolic culture, 27
  and fraud, 30
  Genesis and, 47, 53
  historical meaning of, 30, 44
  as historical phenomenon, 28
  and past, 31
  post-Zionists on, 37
  purpose of, 44–5
  of Zionism, 30–3
  see also post-Zionism/post-Zionists
mythologization, 2, 30

nationalism
  radical negation of, 209
  self-determination and, 211
  see also transnationalism
New Jew
  and national independence, 241–2
  as opposite of Jewish *luftmensch*,
    171
NGOs (non-governmental organizations)
  demands of, 138
  and liberal democracy, 138
  transnationalist claims of, 143, 145
  and US self-government, 150
  and US transnationalist ideology,
    136–7
  see also democracy; transnationalism

normalcy
    as central theme of Zionism, 218,
        219

oppression/oppressed groups
    Arab-Palestinians as, 78
    Jewry and, 84
    as justification for terrorism, 79, 81
    neo-Marxists and, 72, 75–7
oppressors
    post-Zionist ideological protection of,
        78, 81
    and tyrants, 76

Oslo Accords, 102, 107
    Arafat and, 161
    Israeli media support of, 89
    legitimization of, 63
    post-Zionist ideology of, 123
    results of, 127
    terrorism against Israel and, 107–8
    transnationalism and, 122
    Yosi Beilin on, 104
    see also Arafat, Yasser; conscience; post-
        Zionism/post-Zionists;
        transnationalism
Oslo war see Second Intifada

Palestine
    accommodation of Jews in, 41–2
    Jewish restoration to, 46
    see also "Ingathering of Exiles"
particularity
    Jewry and, 232, 235
    and political correctness, 120
    and transnationalism, 232
    and US cultural dominance, 240
patriotism, 150
Peace Now
    and Judaism, 207
    as War Forever, 10
    see also post-Zionism/post-Zionists
Peres, Shimon
    idea of the "New Middle East,"
        161
    post-Zionism, 65, 68
pluralism
    and ethnic democracy, 231
    Muslims' political status and, 230
    as part of post-Zionist ideology, 222
population see Israel, population of
post-Zionism/post-Zionists
    academia and, 204
    anti-Semitic nature of, 52, 126
    as Arab-centric view, 232

authors, 213
    as code word for Israeli anti-Semitism,
        205
    danger to Israel, 6
    David Grossman on, 161
    definition of, 2
    de-Judaizing of Israel, 62–3
    democracy and, 114
    differences from postmodernism, 34
    ethics for soldiers, 64
    fact–fiction confusion, 31
    fear Jewish control of the Land of Israel,
        206
    as form of national suicide, 208
    historical reality as myth, 31
    Horkeimer and Adorno on, 72
    hostility toward Zionism, 35
    identification with Israel's enemies, 89
    and "Ingathering of Exiles," 33, 35, 210
    and Israeli "occupation," 234
    and Israeli public, 64
    Jewish immigration to Israel and, 43
    justification of murder of Jews, 123
    legitimate entities and, 209
    neo-Marxist influence on, 71, 74, 77
    nihilistic nature of, 34, 242
    own myth of, 52
    and Palestinians' suffering, 75, 82
    as post-Judaism, 116
    and racism, 76
    as reactionary statement, 213
    recommendations of, 204
    separation of state and religion, 115
    Shimon Peres and, 62, 63, 142
    space–time historical reality, 206
    support for Palestinian claims, 104
    and transnationalism, 231
    undermining Jewish history by, 41
    and utopianism, 117
    writers as agents of Zionism in, 35,
        51–2
    Zionist claims made by, 71, 73–5, 114
    see also anti-Semitism; anti-Zionism;
        democracy; "Ingathering of Exiles";
        transnationalism
power, fallacy of, 74, 77
Promised Land, the, 49
pseudo-Zionists, 88
    comparison of Zionism and Nazism, 96
    damage to Israel by, 95–6
    defense of Arafat by, 103
    "ship of fools" notion in, 112
    Shulamit Aloni as, 103
    view of "settlers," 97
    "return to ourselves," concept, 129

Sanhedrin, 47, 241
Second Intifada, 63
secularism
    universalist utopia, 120, 123
    world church in the West, 119
    see also transnationalism
self-hatred
    Jewish form of, 7, 183–5, 242
    see also anti-Semitism; Leftists in Israel;
        post-Zionism/post-Zionists; socialist
        Zionism
Serbia, 9
socialist Zionism, 171–2
Stockholm syndrome, 160
suicide bombers
    and Israeli media, 100, 109
    see also terrorism

Tehilah
    as despicable whore, 216, 221
    Yehoshua's depiction of, 224
terrorism/terrorists
    and Arab-Palestinian state objective,
        88–9
    Arafat as, 89, 94–5
    and fanatical ideology, 98
    fatalism of, 99
    as freedom fighters, 79, 81, 98
    "identification with the aggressor,"
        notion, 160
    impotence of, 90
    Israeli Knesset support for, 95
    media's perception of, 93–4, 95–6, 98,
        100
    and the media in symbiosis, 90
    middle-class roots of, 99
    moral relativist criticism, 78–80
    operation of, 159
    post-Zionist support for, 74, 76, 79
    promotion through media, 90
    publicity, 89
    resolute action of, 105
    victims' descriptions of, 160
    see also Arab-Palestinians; media;
        oppression/oppressed groups
transnationalists/transnationalism, 139–44
    definition of democracy under, 141, 151
    denationalization of citizenship,
        147–8
    and EU stance, 150
    and globalization, 143
    law, 146
    nations, view of, 145
    nation-state, 143
    unity of peoples under, 124

in the US, 136
    and US immigration, 147–8
    versus internationalism, 144
    see also democracy; non-governmental
        organizations; Oslo Accords

United Nations
    and Arab policy towards Israel, 8–9
    General Assembly, 243
    policies aligned with EU, 120
    treaties, 147, 150
    universalist utopia, 123–4
    see also transnationalism

victim syndrome
    Israeli adjustment to, 109
    weaknesses of, 155

withdrawal
    Barbara Tuchman on, 7
    from Lebanon and *al-Aqsa* uprising,
        106
women, elderly, 223

Zion, 211
Zionism/Zionists
    absurdity of, 210
    as affirmation of Jewry's future, 49
    among youth, 212
    as colonialism, 80, 210–11
    as criminal enterprise, 34
    criticism of, 127
    definition of, 2, 87
    destructive impulses and, 218
    failure to resolve Jewry's return to
        Israel, 43
    as form of false consciousness, 77
    and French revolution, 44
    historic role of, 49
    as Jewish ethnic-nationalism and indi-
        vidualism, 84
    and Jewish history, 84
    as Jewish tradition, 212
    Leftists on, 127
    as a moral enterprise, 199–200
    as myth, 26, 30
    narrative, 74, 79, 81
    new historians' views on, 73, 80
    notion of "occupation," and, 127
    opposition to, 41
    as organizing principle of Jewish life,
        244–6
    post-Zionist ideology and, 33
    as racism, 77
    rejection of, 194, 201

Sergei Bulgakov on, 129–32
and socialism, 36, 37, 127
success of, 200, 201

and universalist utopia, 127
see also Genesis, the Book of; Hebrew
    literature; universalist utopia